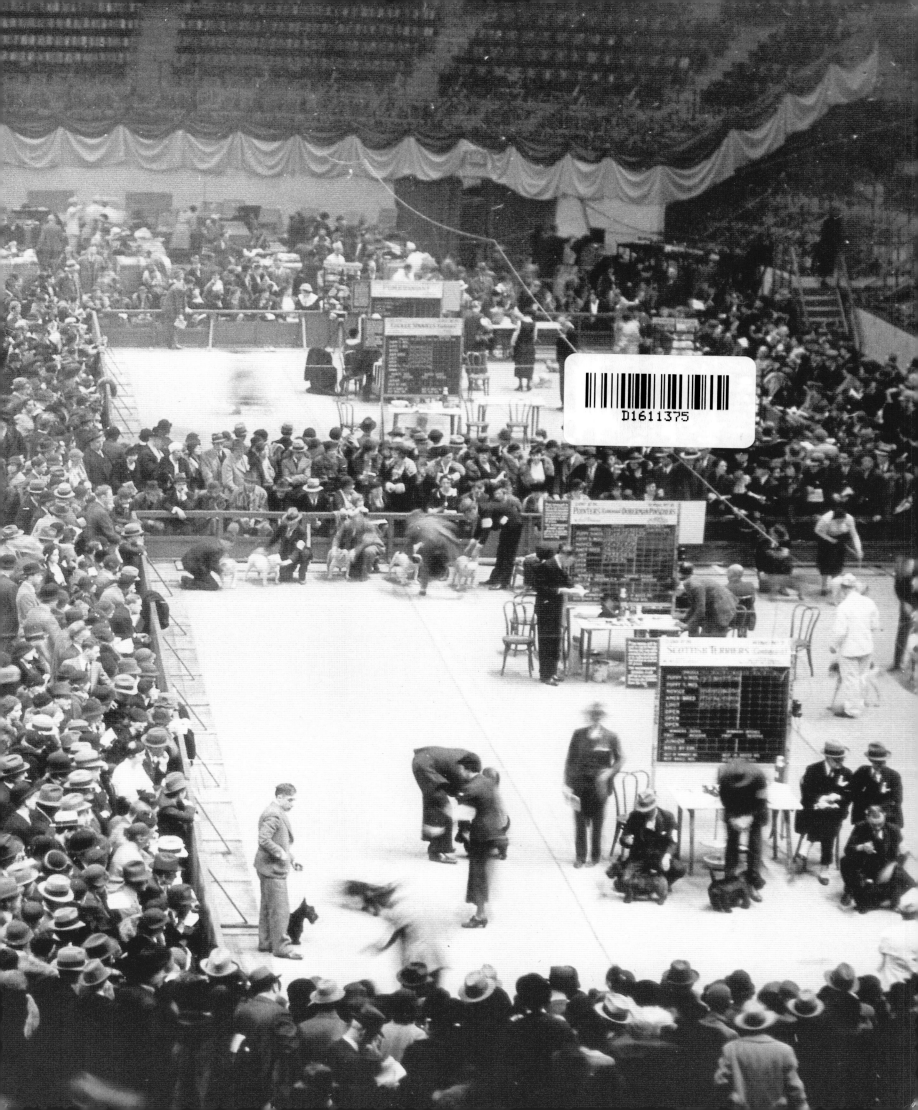

D1611375

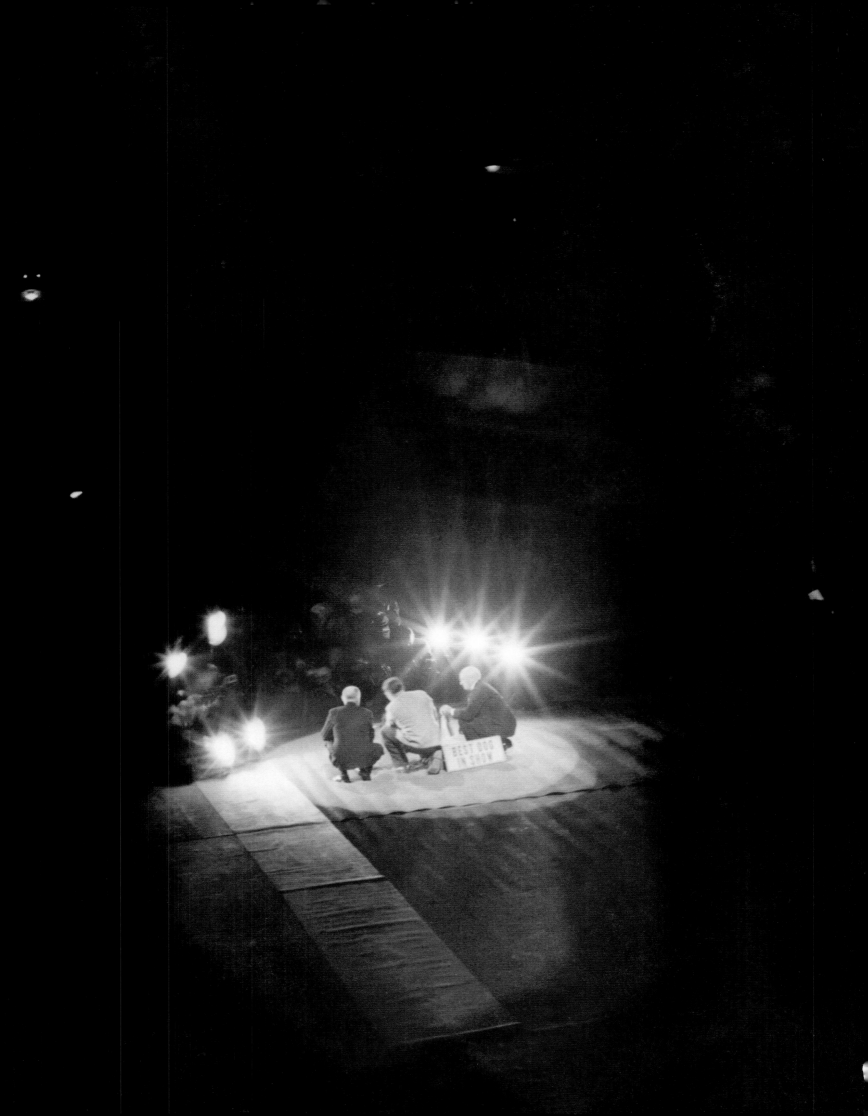

The DogShow

The DogShow

125 Years of Westminster

by William F. Stifel

THE
WESTMINSTER
KENNEL CLUB

Text Copyright © 2001 by William F. Stifel
Design Copyright © 2001 by the Westminster Kennel Club

All rights reserved. No part of this publication may be reproduced, stored in a retrieval system, or transmitted in any form or by any means electronic, mechanical, photocopying, recording or otherwise, without the prior permission of the publishers.

Published in the United States
by the Westminster Kennel Club,
149 Madison Avenue,
New York, NY, 10016

Publisher's Cataloging Information
Stifel, William F. (1922 -)
The Dog Show: 125 Years of Westminster / William F. Stifel. — 1 ed.
Includes index
1. Westminster Kennel Club—History—1877-2000. 2. Westminster Best in Show Winners—Pictures and Commentary—1907-2000.
3. Dog Shows — Exhibitors. 4. Dog Breeders. 5. Dog Owners. 6. Dog Handlers.
7. American Kennel Club—History.
Library of Congress No. 00-109798
ISBN 0-9705698-0-7

Portions of this book appeared in somewhat different form in the *AKC Gazette,* "Pointing the Way," January 1998, "Creating a Sensation," February 1999, and "Paving the Way," January 2000.

Westminster Kennel Club website address: www.westminsterkennelclub.org

Printed in Hong Kong
First Edition

Book design by Spagnola Associates

To Carolyn,
a woman of many virtues and other endearing qualities
that sweeten and adorn human life.
Without her help and her perspective, this book would
not have been written.

WESTMINSTER KENNEL CLUB
DOG SHOW 1911
FOR THE BEST BRACE OF SPORTING SPANIELS
OTHER THAN COCKER
OFFERED BY
H.K.BLOODGOOD

WON BY
CHAMPION BROOKSIDE PATIENCE
AND
CHAMPION BROOKSIDE DAWN

1911— Trophy
offered by H.K.
Bloodgood for
Best Brace of
Sporting Spaniels
other than
Cocker, won by
Ch. Brookside
Patience and Ch.
Brookside Dawn,
owned by
Brookside
Kennels, Rye,
N.Y.—*Peter R.*
Van Brunt,
Cerincione photo

Acknowledgements

The author is deeply grateful to the following: To his fellow Westminster Kennel Club members, in particular Chester F. Collier and Robert V. Lindsay, who first discussed writing this book in 1996. To Rita Lynch, WKC's Office Manager for 15 years. To Mary Zorn, who inventoried the archives at 40+ pages. To Florence Foti, who became Office Manager in 1999.

To the American Kennel Club (founded in 1884), which has given us permission to use art works, photographs and other works from its extensive collection. To AKC's Library and to Librarian Barbara Kolk and her assistants, Ann Sergi and Jeanne Sansolo. To the *AKC Gazette* (founded as the *American Kennel Gazette* in 1889) and to *Gazette* Publisher George Berger. To Geraldine Hayes, AKC Archivist/Historian.

To *The New York Times,* a major source of information about Westminster from its founding in 1877. To *The American Field* and *Forest & Stream,* the former totally field-oriented today and the latter defunct, but both of them saturated with dog show information from their founding in the mid-1870s until the early 1900s. To *Dogs in Canada.* To *Time Magazine* and *Sports Illustrated.* To photographers John L. Ashbey and Charles Tatham, plus Mary Bloom, Joe Cerincione and Eric Jacobson. To Don Bowden at AP/Wide World and to Corbis-Bettmann.

To Anne Rogers Clark and to the following though in such a list there will inevitably be omissions, for which the reader's indulgence is asked: Robert Andreas, Karen G. Armistead, David Biesel, William H. Blair, Kathryn Bonomi, Mrs. Peggy Chisholm, Alexandra MacCallum Clark, Michael Cornman, John W. Cross, III, Tom Crowe, Dorie Crowe-Mick, Kathy Darling, Annette R. Davies, Margaret Derry of the University of Guelf, Roy Frampton, Gettysburg Battlefield Guide, David L. Frei, Mrs. Sally Gallagher, Jim Grebe, Catherine S. Hansen, Henry G. Helmar, Mrs. Lawrence H. Kelly, Judith Kip, Roger Knoop, John Lander, Mrs. George Robert Leslie, Mrs. Robert V. Lindsay, Rollins Loring, Nick Lyons, Abraham Oseroff, Jill Ozechowski, Wilma Parker, Ronald D. Pemberton, Mrs. Gloria R. Reese, Kelly Rhae, Dale Rose, Arnold Roth, Franklin and Emily Satterthwaite, Lauren Schnitzer, William Secord, Mrs. Elvira Smit, Nell Stifel, Mrs. J. A. Tessel, Mrs. Patricia Craige Trotter, Lt. Cdr. John S. Williams.

To the American Kennel Club Museum of the Dog in St. Louis, Barbara Jedda, manager. To the Century Association, the Columbia University Library, the Museum of the City of New York, the National Geographic Society, the New York Genealogical and Biographical Society, the New York Historical Society, the New York Public Library, the New York Yacht Club, the Philadelphia Museum of Art, the Pierpont Morgan Library, the Westchester Library System, the Yale University Library.

To the Thayer Memorial Library, Lancaster, Mass., Sue A. Hoadley, Director. To Prof. Barbara J. Dunlap at the Morris Raphael Cohen Library at the City College of the City University of New York.

WESTMINSTER KENNEL CLUB
DOG SHOW 1903
FOR THE BEST BRACE OF
OLD ENGLISH SHEEP DOGS
OFFERED BY
S.T. PETERS
WON BY
TILLEY BRO'S
MERRY PARTY AND BOUNCING LASS

1903—Trophy offered by Samuel T. Peters for Best Brace of Old English Sheepdogs, won by Merry Party and Bouncing Lass owned by the Tilley Brothers, Shepton Mallet, England—*WKC, Cerincione photo*

Foreword

In 1877 America was a sprawling, disjointed young country with great energy and a lack of cohesion. It was the era of the entrepreneur, Rockefeller, Ford, Mellon, etc. The automobile, radio, television, the airplane had yet to arrive on the scene. No highway system or methods of communication held the country together. It was still a collection of isolated cities and towns and not the unified country we know today. It still suffered from the terrible hangover of the Civil War, which nearly split America in two. We were at the start of the Industrial Revolution and about to blossom and grow into the greatest country on earth.

There were few dog shows. The Westminster Kennel Club was formed by a group of gentlemen who cared passionately for the sport of pure-bred dogs, and this book is a tribute to these men and those who followed for the next 125 years. Their goal has been to ensure that The Westminster Kennel Club be the most positive influence in the sport.

The nation grew tremendously in the next century and a quarter. The most radical changes the world has known took place. In that era of such great change it was necessary for the Club members to keep abreast of what was happening and at the same time make sure that the Club adhered to the basic belief that they were "the guardians of the sport of the pure-bred dog" and not be subject to passing whims that would cause the sport and the Club to stray from that objective. It hasn't been easy. There have been wars, depressions, profound cultural changes, but the membership has guarded the tradition of Westminster through it all. These are the true heroes of Westminster who are often overlooked.

One such person who has given so freely of his time to ensure the continuance of this tradition is William F. (Bill) Stifel who is the author of this book. For three years Bill has worked harder than can be described to ensure the success of this book. It's all his and we the members of Westminster thank and congratulate him on this great achievement. He has proven to be one of those members who has contributed to the Club's success.

In another 125 years the club will be 250 years old. I hope the Club's members then will know the joy Westminster has brought to the sport of pure-bred dogs in the 19th, 20th and 21st centuries.

Chet Collier

WESTMINSTER KENNEL CLUB
≈1925≈
MARKWOOD MITZA
→WINNER←
BEST BULL TERRIER
IN SHOW
OWNER
MRS MAXWELL CASE

1925—Trophy offered by Westminster for Best Bull Terrier, won by Markwood Mitzi (sic), owned (at time of entry) by R.H. Elliot, Canada—*WKC, Cerincione photo*

Contents

1902—Thomas L. Manson cup for Best Cocker Spaniel, won by Chief II, owned by Brookside Kennels, Rye, N.Y.—*Peter R. Van Brunt, Cerincione photo*

Preface

Westminster 2001 will be our 125th all breed show. This book is a celebration of that anniversary.

The book is divided into two sections. Part I is history, an examination of the infrastructure, the underlying foundations on which the past, present and future of the club depend. On one of my first forays into the records at the Westminster office, I found Max Riddle's story of how the club came by its name. It was a latter-day folk tale, a good starting place. And how did a Civil War General and college president come to be Westminster's first president? Who was the Pointer Sensation? Where were the Westminster clubhouses? What were the various sites at which the shows were held?

Some aspects of Westminster have not changed at all. It is a benched show, for example, one of a small handful still held in this country. It has always been benched, which means the dogs are there for the day and that owners and breeders are with them, ready to talk to any interested persons. Benching transforms a dog show from mere competition into a noisy conference room of unrivaled value to exhibitors and spectators alike. There is no better spokesman for dogs than breeders and owners. No one can better communicate the commitment that owning a dog calls for.

Other aspects of the show have changed radically. There is now an audience of millions who watch from their homes. On television, they get a better look at the animals than most people do in the arena. When the judge opens the mouth of a Pomeranian, home viewers can count the teeth. There are also those who follow the proceedings by computer. At 8 AM on the opening day of Westminster 2000, the on-line version of the show catalog was available for viewing on the WKC website. Complete and official results of the breed competition were posted within minutes after the judging throughout the two days of the show.

Part II of the book is an album of the Best in Show dogs – pictures with commentary. Best in Show competition was first offered at Westminster in 1907. In the face of claims that it is impossible to judge a Chihuahua, say, against a Mastiff, and in spite of cautions against using such a win as proof of greatness, Best in Show at Westminster is an award that is second to none in its appeal, its magic, its attraction for the finest dogs. The winners have ranged in age from 9 months to over 8 years. Many were seasoned champions, but at least one finished his championship at the show. Some sprang from famous bloodlines, while others were plucked from total obscurity. There were imports deliberately kept under cover, who made their U.S. debut at the Garden. "Cinderella" dogs, they were dubbed.

Despite their differences, these winners all passed through the same narrow doorway into the annals of the club's history. Westminster salutes them.

October 2000

Part I

History of
the Show

The Name

Why Westminster? Where did the name come from? Max Riddle told it this way:

"Westminster gets its name from a long gone hotel in Manhattan. There, sporting gentlemen used to meet in the bar to drink and lie about their shooting accomplishments. Eventually they formed a club and bought a training area and kennel. They kept their dogs there and hired a trainer.

"They couldn't agree on the name for their new club. But finally someone suggested that they name it after their favorite bar. The idea was unanimously selected, we imagine, with the hoisting of a dozen drinking arms."

Max Riddle was an all-breed judge and one of a vanishing breed, that is, a full-time reporter who covered such things as murder trials for the *Cleveland Press* while also writing a syndicated dog column. His story on Westminster's name – which appeared in the *New York Post* in 1973 — is probably as close to the truth as

we will get. The hotel was a logical place for such men to meet. Located on Irving Place, it was quiet and elegant. A couple of the men lived nearby. It was much in vogue with English travelers. It was a favorite of Charles Dickens, who stayed there on a trip to the U.S.

A different story about the name appeared in the 1941 show catalog. It said that club derived its name from the Duke of Westminster, "from whose kennels in England many of the Association's dogs were imported." The story had a germ of truth in it. Research does not show that *any* dogs came to WKC from the Duke's kennels, but at the first show in 1877, there were two littermates entered that were offspring of a Pointer bitch named "Juno." Juno *was* from the Duke's kennels. She was not owned by WKC but one of the two littermates was, a bitch named "Whisky." Whisky was shown at that first show along with 10 of her offspring from three litters. (As always at WKC shows, dogs owned by the club were shown "not for competition.") One of those litters was by Sensation, the Pointer in the club's

logo. Whisky and Sensation were basic parts of WKC's breeding program. Her presence at the first show with 10 offspring who were "grandchildren" of a bitch from the Duke's kennels could well have led to the idea that "many" of the club's Pointers came from the Duke. But the conclusion is inescapable: Almost certainly, the club was not named for the Duke.

Then comes a further curiosity. A travel brochure of the day says the hotel "was named in honor of the Duke of Westminster whose coat-of-arms appears on its stained-glass windows, stationery and menus." There is no clue as to why the hotel should have been so named, and the building is long departed, as are the stained glass, stationery and menus. But if the club was named for the hotel and the hotel was named for the Duke, wasn't the club named for the Duke?

The Symbol

At the heart of the organization stands a Pointer named Sensation. He has been

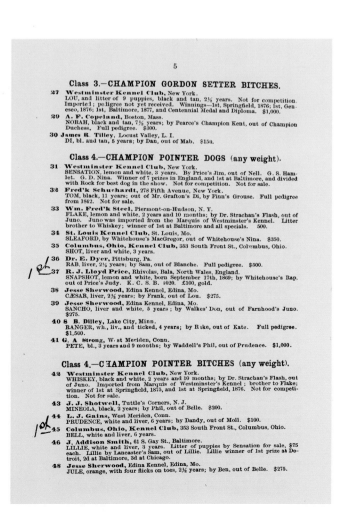

Left:
A catalog page showing the entry of Whisky and her litter-mate Flake in the 1877 show — *WKC*

BLACK AND WHITE POINTER "WHISKY."
(Owned by Westminster Kennel Club, New York City.)

Above:
Engraving of the Pointer bitch Whisky, offspring of Juno— *WKC*

WESTMINSTER HOTEL, NEW YORK.

Charles Dickens
slept here
*—photograph, nd,
Museum of the
City of New York,
Print Archive,
Irving Place*

the symbol of the club almost from the start. Bred by J. D. Humphrey in England, his name was originally Don, and that was always his call name when he was worked in the field.

In 1876, George DeForest Grant, a charter member of the club, sailed to England for the purpose of acquiring "a fine Pointer dog" and, while in Wales, picked Sensation out as the best dog he had ever seen. The lemon and white male, weighing about 70 pounds, was by R. J. Lloyd Price's Jim, out of Mr. Humphrey's Nell. Whelped in 1874, he was imported to the U.S. on November 10, 1876.

Sensation, with his distinctive profile, was reputed to have the best head of any Pointer in America, and probably in England. We are told that dog men knew the dog's head as well as lovers of the turf knew the shape of the great trotting horse Hambletonian.

Sensation began his show career in America with a first and a special prize at Baltimore in 1877 and continued the

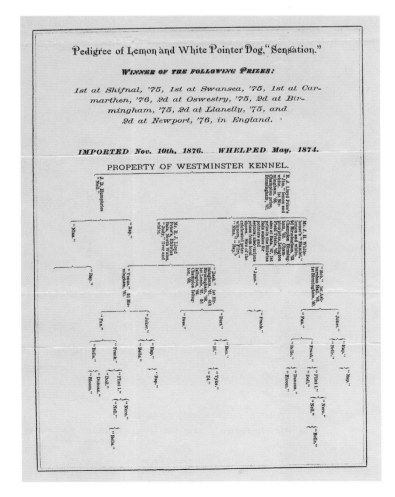

Pedigree of Lemon and White Pointer Dog, "Sensation."

*Sensation's
pedigree— WKC*

From Upper Left Clockwise: Sensation's head engraved on a Westminster medal — *WKC*

Sensation on Point, by J.M. Tracy (American, 1843-93) in the 1893 catalog. Like Wellstood, Tracy shows the dog's distinctive profile. J.M. Tracy was an active dog artist and a WKC member from 1885 unil his death in 1893 — *WKC*

Sensation on Point, by J. Wellstood — *Published by W. Wellstood and Co., steel plate engraving, 1879*

Sensation as
seen by Edwin
Forbes— *Forest
and Stream,
Dec. 28, 1880*

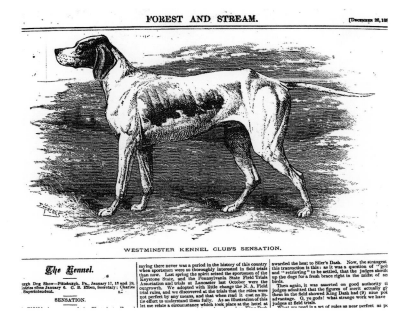

following year with firsts and special
prizes in Boston, Baltimore and St. Louis.

He also competed in the field. Most
notably, in 1880, he was entered in the
Eastern Field Trials on Robins Island.
Stephen T. Hammond, of Springfield,
Mass., trained and handled the dog for
the event. The dog's entry there was a
surprise to many, according to *Forest &
Stream*, and his excellent performance
astonished "all but a very few." There had
been a lot of talk that Sensation was only
a show dog. Sportsmen would now have a
chance to judge from a practical test
whether they were right or wrong.

When it was all over, *Forest & Stream*
concluded that Sensation could have done
better—and would have if he "had been
placed in proper hands in his early days."
But they were mightily impressed even so.
In reporting a heat in the trial in which he
was braced with a black-and-white ticked
Setter bitch, they wrote as follows:

"We shall never forget the 'Ah' that came
up from the crowd as Sensation pointed,
or how the Westminster Kennel Club
stock went booming. Naturally we
consider Sensation to have the grandest
style we have ever seen in a Pointer. His
nose is as keen as a briar, and his move-
ments graceful in the extreme."

Sensation defeated his bracemate, went
on to take third in the stake and won the
silver cup shown in our illustration for
best Pointer in trial.

"All the harm we wish those that have
spoken slightingly against the old dog,"
said the paper—Sensation was all of 6½
when this happened— "is that they had
been present and seen what we did."

Throughout his career, Sensation headed
the list of Westminster's own Pointers
that were shown, not for competition, at
Westminster. All kennel clubs in those
days owned dogs that competed at other
clubs' shows, but which were displayed,
for exhibition only, at their own events.
After his debut in 1877, Sensation came
back every year, often with a dozen or
more club-owned kennelmates, until
he retired.

During those years, Pointer entries at the
show averaged over 120, and among them
would be as many as a dozen or 15 of
Sensation's get, entered and competing.

By the time of his last Westminster in
1886, Sensation had been given to Robert
C. Cornell. A charter member of the
club, Cornell wanted to give the dog a
comfortable old age and took him into
his own home. He wrote to *The American
Field* about it, noting that the dog was
"very gray but...lively." Of the dog's work
in the field, he said, "I found his nose as
wonderfully keen as ever, and his head as
level as it always has
been. Of course, he
goes slow, and I
shall never work
him hard again."

A year and a half later, in June 1887,
Cornell wrote another letter, a portion of
which appeared in *Forest & Stream*. "I
regret to say old Don is dead," he said.
"He passed away quietly on Sunday last
simply from old age. I have been
expecting his collapse for some time, as
he had outlived the usual span of dog
life." It was a great personal loss
to Cornell.

"Never shall I forget the good old dog,"
he wrote, "and I never shall have quite
the same feeling for another. The most
satisfactory days I have ever had in the
field have been with Don."

Sensation was buried at the foot of the
flagstaff in front of the Westminster
clubhouse at Babylon, Long Island, along
with (as someone wrote on the back of
the photograph) "many other Pointers
that cost a mint of money and were the
greatest of their day." On top of the
flagstaff was a weather vane with the
figure of a Pointer—pointing always into
the wind.

Sensation has had a long career as
Westminster's logo. A likeness of his

Field trial trophy
won by Sensation,
1880 —*AKC
Museum of the Dog*

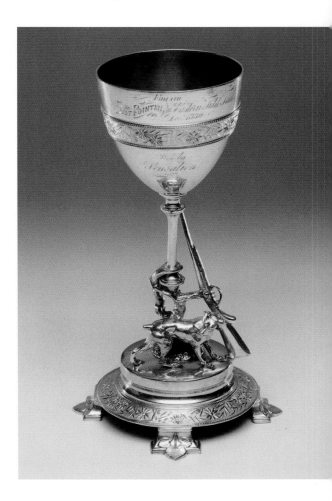

CATALOGUE
THE WESTMINSTER
KENNEL CLUB

Sixtieth Annual
DOG SHOW
Held Under American Kennel Club Rules

MADISON SQUARE GARDEN
49th and 50th Streets and 8th Ave., New York

Monday, Tuesday and Wednesday
February 10, 11 and 12 (Lincoln's Birthday)
1936

THIRD EDITION
COMPLETE AWARDS OF THE SHOW
$1.50

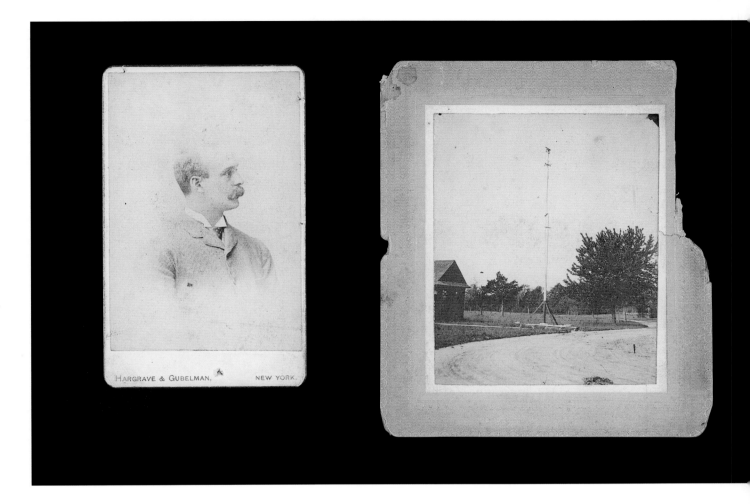

Opposite, From Upper Left Clockwise:
Sensation on Point, on the 1936 catalog cover, based on the Wellstood engraving.

Sensation engraved on a Westminster medal, 1911 — *WKC*

Quail shoot in Navesink, by J.M. Tracy. In this woodland scene, Sensation, on the right, honors the point of Croxteth— *WKC*

Right:
Robert C. Cornell— *WKC*

Far Right:
Sensation's burial place. On top of the flagstaff, a weather vane with a Pointer, pointing always into the wind

head appeared on the cover of the first catalog in 1877, before the club was incorporated, and quickly became the official insignia. It appeared on the catalogs with some regularity through 1935.

In 1936, the insignia was changed to a full figure of Sensation on point. The new image was modeled on a steel plate engraving published by W. Wellstood & Co. in 1879. Wellstood publicized the print at the show that year by offering an artist's proof of it as a prize "for the best dog, bitch, or puppy sired by Sensation."

Fifty-seven years later, when the new insignia first appeared on the catalog, the *American Field* commented at length. They took exception to what they called "the rather abrupt rise over the loin" but urged all who wanted to judge dogs, to study and remember "this interesting, yea, educational, picture of an early famous champion."

Except in 1980-82 when his head alone appeared, Sensation on point has graced every catalog since 1936. Only the style has changed. It was originally a black and white drawing. Since 1983, Sensation has appeared as an embossed silhouette in gold with a gold shadow beneath him and gold foliage behind him, all on a background of royal purple. But the dog's form—his head, body and pose—is unmistakable.

The Site

The structure was originally a railroad station. P. T. Barnum took the first step at transforming it. He leased it from Commodore Vanderbilt, who had moved his railroad operations north to 42nd Street. The real estate was the block where the New York Life Building stands today. A corner of the property abutted Madison Square Park. Barnum tore most of the building down and transformed what was left into an edifice with a 28-foot outside wall.

Inside was an arena with an oval track in it. Around the arena, which was almost as long as a football field, was a single tier of seats that were roofed over. A canvas canopy was raised over the arena in wet weather. On fair days it was lowered, and there was no other cover. This was Barnum's Hippodrome—or more properly, "Barnum's Monster Classical and Geological Hippodrome." There were chariot races there with lady drivers, acrobats, cowboys and Indians, tattooed ladies and gentlemen, prancing horses, waltzing elephants.

But Barnum disliked New York's winter weather. Within the year, he sold his lease to Patrick S. Gilmore, a showman of a different type. He was a bandmaster. He had written the song "When Johnny Comes Marching Home Again." He decorated the interior of the Hippodrome with shrubs and flowers and gravel paths and renamed it "Gilmore's Garden."

His concerts there could attract as many as 10,000 people and might incorporate church bells, anvils, cannons and hundreds of musicians. He also played host to revival meetings, temperance meetings, balls, beauty contests, flower shows, even visits of Barnum's traveling circus.

Left: Looking north on Madison Avenue. Madison Square Garden I is the low white building on the right. At near right is the home of Jennie Jerome, who became Lady Randolph Churchill, mother of Winston Churchill.
— *AKC*

in Chicago and then did the Detroit show again. By then it was felt that the success of a show depended on his running it. The *Chicago Field* said he had "ushered in, nurtured and laid the foundation of the popularity of the dog show of today."

Was the event widely publicized? As reported in *Forest & Stream* soon after the dates were announced, Lincoln received letters "from portions of England where it would scarcely be believed that news of this show could have penetrated, requesting particulars and entry blanks."

What classes were offered? In most breeds, there was a single class for both dogs and bitches, but some classes were divided by sex or age or Native versus Imported or weight or various combinations of these. In Pointers and Setters, there were also Champion classes "For Dogs or Bitches that have won First Prizes at any bench show in this country or abroad, the Centennial Bench Show at Philadelphia not included."

What dogs were eligible? Owners were urged to give sire, dam and date of birth of all entries, but these particulars were not required. Owners were also expected to submit a dog's show record, if any, for publication in the catalog. In particular, what 1st prizes and Special Prizes had the dog won and where?

What were Special Prizes? Anyone could offer a "Special," and there were virtually no restrictions on the strings that could be tied to such awards. Note Special Prize No. 15: "For the best English Setter, dog or bitch, native bred, out of a native bitch and by an imported dog." Or Special No. 5: "For the best collection of sporting dogs, of any kind, not less than 5 to be exhibited and exhibited by one person or from one Kennel."

Then, in 1877, Westminster decided to hold a dog show. Gilmore's Garden was just what they needed. The cost for three days was $1,500. The oval track was transformed into a promenade. Workmen tore down barriers and partitions that had been part of the circus that had just closed and used the lumber to construct benching, which was arranged on both sides of the promenade. They put a judging ring in the center where Gilmore's musicians had played.

Said the editors of *Forest & Stream*: "There is no place in this country so admirably adapted for the purposes of a Bench Show."

1877

To the liberal patronage of the ladies was due in no small measure the success of the show financially, for where the ladies go for amusement there will all the world go; and bench shows promise to be a more fashionable resort than the opera. —*Forest & Stream, June 7, 1877*

The First Show

Name: "First Annual New York Bench Show of Dogs, Given Under the Auspices of the Westminster Kennel Club"

Advertised Dates: "May 8-10, 1877"

Location: "Gilmore's Garden (Hippodrome), on the block bounded by Madison and 4th Avenues and 26th and 27th Streets"

Entry: 1,201 dogs

Travel: Most railroads—as reported in many newspapers—carried show entries to and from the city free of charge when accompanied by their owners. This was undoubtedly a convenience, though one cynic had it that the railroads simply found it cheaper to give dogs free transport than to assume liability for their safe passage.

Chairman: William M. Tileston, charter member of Westminster and Kennel Editor of *Forest & Stream*. Passionately fond of dogs, he was an enthusiastic breeder and exhibitor of Pointers and Setters. As a reporter, he was highly critical of the 1876 Centennial Dog Show in Philadelphia, suggesting that to eliminate dissatisfaction, they should simply put the names of the entries in a hat and "have a blind boy draw out the winners." He was a driving force in persuading his fellow Westminster members to hold their own show in New York City.

Superintendent: Charles Lincoln, an Englishman who had become "thoroughly Americanized." He superintended his first U. S. dog show in Detroit in 1875. The next year, he conducted one

What did Special Prizes consist of? Seven were silver trophies from Tiffany's. Also on the list were a double-barreled breech-loading central-fire shot gun, a fly rod, a leather sportsman's traveling trunk, a case of stuffed North American game birds, an opera glass and a pearl-handled revolver.

Were there money prizes? Yes. They were paid in gold coin, though not until the final day. In this regard, *Forest & Stream* said there was a joke "too good to keep." They said that when the premium list was prepared, gold had been quoted at 104 and that it had now reached 107 and looked as though it might go to 130. "We suggest to the club," said the paper, "to cover their shorts while they can."

What were the regular awards? Prize ribbons were blue for first, red for second, and white for third. Unplaced dogs could be marked C for Commendation, HC for High Commendation or VHC for Very High Commendation.

Who handled the dogs? Uniformed attendants took all entries into the ring. See "1878" for picture. It would be some years before owners began to feel that they themselves or someone of their own choosing might handle their dogs to better advantage.

Was the judging done in public? Yes, unlike some shows in England, judging was done, not before but after the doors were opened to the public. Further, there were no collars or labels by which the judges could know the name or ownership of any dogs brought before them.

What was the judging procedure? Whatever class a dog competed in, there was no further competition for that dog, unless a special trophy was offered and the dog was entered in the special class to compete for that trophy. In this show, for example, there would have been no "Best of Breed" in Pointers if it had not been for Special Prize No. 2: "For the Best pointer, of any weight, dog or bitch, in the show."

Who attended the show? The gate was estimated to be 6,000 to 8,000 the first day, and the class of guests was said to be of the best. "Everybody," said the *Times*, "was fashionably dressed and wore an air of good breeding."

Above: Seven Tiffany cups offered at the 1877 show. No. 4, minus its ebony base, has survived. See page 25—*Forest & Stream.*

Right: The Great Bench Show of Dogs—*Harper's Weekly,* May 26, 1877, WKC

In the benching area—*The Spirit of the Times, The American Gentlemen's Newspaper*, WKC

he could not be heard more than a foot away, "owing to the awful howling of the dogs."

Were there special attractions? After Bergh sat down, reported the *Times*, "a woman in fantastic attire amused the spectators for some time with the antics of a dozen educated, ribbon-decked poodles."

Who were the judges? Three Americans and two Englishmen:
1) John Davidson of Monroe, Mich.
2) Capt. John M. (Jack) Taylor of Bellafonte, Nottoway County, Va.
3) Dr. H. H. Twaddell, of West Philadelphia, Pa., who had judged at the 1876 Centennial Show
4) T. Frank P. Kavnagh, FRGS, of the Carlton Club, London, England
5) The Reverend J. Cumming Macdona, Cheadle Rectory, Cheshire, England.

Who was Rev. Macdona? A canine authority, one of the most celebrated breeders of English and Irish Setters in England. He arrived by ship a week before the show, accompanied by his son and Rover, a red Irish Setter. His father, G. deLandre Macdona, came later, bringing with him, among others dogs, three English Setters, three Irish Setter puppies, and two St. Bernards.

Who was Rover? Rover had never been shown before, even in England, but

The paper also noted that there were easily as many ladies as gentlemen present and that they took at least as much interest in the dogs as the men did.

Was it a success? On the first evening, the streets outside were blocked with liveried carriages. "The gentlemen who served as ticket sellers could not make change fast enough," according to the *Times*, "to suit the impatience of the throng that was continually clamoring for admittance." On the second day, there were 20,000 visitors, and on the

third, the same. This led the club to extend the show by a day. Proceeds of that day, minus expenses, were to go to the ASPCA as the nucleus of a fund to open a home for stray and disabled dogs, similar to one in London. Ten days later, club president General Webb sent the society a check for $1,295.25.

Were there distinguished guests? At 8:30 PM on the first evening, Henry Bergh, founder of the ASPCA, mounted the platform in the center of the arena and gave a eulogy on dogs. But the *Times* said

Long Island Railroad Timetable, 1877. An ad in the timetable begins: "On the 7th of May, a reception is to be given at Gilmore's Garden, under the auspices of the Westminster Kennel Club which promises to be jubilant with the music of canines... It is to this country the most important show of dogs that has ever taken place"— WKC, *Gift of John Lander*

Tiffany cup for Best Brace of Setters, 1877. The cup was offered by the New York City Association for the Protection of Game. It was won by Nip and Tuck, red and white littermates, one year and seven months old, by Pride of the Border, out of Ch. H. Raymond's Bonnet Carre. The Setters were owned by Mrs. R. A. McCurdy, NYC. Mrs. McCurdy was a forebear of the George Robert Leslie family in whose hands the trophy remained until 1999 when it was presented as a gift to Westminster by Mrs. George Robert Leslie
–*Photograph courtesy Tiffany & Co.*

General view of
the Hippodrome
on May 10,
1877 — *Corbis-*
Bettmann

"DAGMAR." "OSCAR"
QUEEN VICTORIA'S DEER-HOUNDS, VALUED AT $100,000.

D.P.FOSTER'S
"LION"

MR. JONES'S SIBERIAN BLOODHOUND "BRUNO."

McDONNA'S
"ROVER" $50,000.00

THE REV. MR. MACDONNA, WITH HIS DOG "MUNGO."

WAGNER'S
"NELLIE"

Miss B. WEBB'S
"REX"
$1000.00

JOHN MATTHEWS'S "DUKE," VALUED AT $1,000.

MR. JOHN E. T. GRAINGER'S SETTER "NELLY" AND HER PUPS,
VALUED AT $5,000.

TWO-LEGGED DOG.—PUG "REX."—THE ONLY ESQUIMAUX IN THE SHOW.

NEW YORK CITY.—THE FIRST ANNUAL BENCH SHOW OF DOGS, AT THE HIPPODROME, MAY 7TH TO 11TH, UNDER THE AUSPICES OF THE WESTMINSTER KENNEL CLUB.
SEE PAGE 203.

First Annual
Bench Show of
Dogs at the
Hippodrome
— *Corbis-Bettmann*

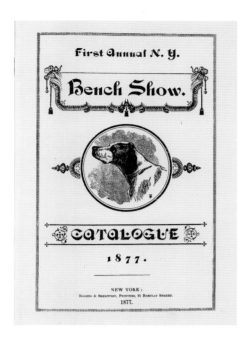

First Catalog,
72 pages, 1201
dogs— *WKC*

"Stonehenge" had selected him for illustrating a new edition of his *Dogs of the British Islands*. Stonehenge was the authority on breed standards that judges of the day were generally expected to follow. Macdona turned Rover over to Show Chairman Tileston to take care of until Macdona's return to England. While here, the dog was to be at the service of American breeders, free of charge, for any English, Irish, Scotch or American bitches that might be sent to him.

Nine years old, by Beauty out of Grouse, Rover made his first public appearance at Westminster, for exhibition only. He was widely publicized and was generally the first dog asked after by spectators. The *Times* nonetheless took the stand that at least a dozen others of the same breed were thoroughly capable of beating him.

Were there other noteworthy canines? There was a two-legged dog who was said to be "a veritable biped, and withal possessing almost human intelligence."

There were two Staghounds from the late General Custer's celebrated pack. They had been presented to him by the Grand Duke Alexis. Named Stanley and Madgie, they were shown by J. B. Miller of Newburgh, N.Y., taking 1st and 2nd in their class.

There were two Deerhounds, Oscar and Dagmar, bred by the Queen of England from the Prince Consort's famous stock. T. Medley had sent them over from London. Though Medley had put a price of 10,000 pounds ($50,000) on each, the *Times* said they "did not approach in beauty, height, length or general excellence Mr. Paul Dana's Brau," who took 1st in the Deerhound class.

Why were prices put on the entries? Selling dogs was an integral part of dog shows, and owners were urged to give a price for each entry for publication in the catalog. Prohibitory prices were allowed. The *Times* said that "fancy prices" like 10,000 pounds or $5,000 or even $1,000 simply meant that the animal was not for sale. But $100 to $250, they asserted, was "a very good price for a good dog."

Were any new or unusual breeds present? When the Fox Terrier, Tim, brought over by the Reverend Macdona's father took 1st in the puppy class, the *New York World* pointed out that the breed was "almost unknown" here. The paper added, however, that the Fox Terrier was probably the coming breed. They little dreamed that 30 years later when Westminster started offering competition for Best in Show, a Fox Terrier would win it for the first three years running, and that in the long haul, the award at Westminster would be taken by a Fox Terrier in nearly one out of every five shows.

Was there an age limit on entries? A great many females of all kinds were nursing puppies of various ages from nine days up. The *Times* called this "an interesting feature of the show."

Did Westminster members fare well? Dogs owned by the Westminster Kennel Club were shown "not for competition," while club members were allowed to show their own dogs. However, the nearest thing to top wins by a member were a 1st prize and a Special taken by member LeGrand B. Cannon's son Harry with Guy, an imported Irish Setter puppy, and a 1st prize and a Special taken by Bessie Webb, daughter of the club's president, with her Pug, Rex.

Did entries from overseas do well? R. J. Lloyd Price, of Bala, Wales, who was owner of Sensation's sire, Jim, won the champion Pointer prize with Snapshot, and Snapshot remained on this side of the ocean, having been purchased by Show Chairman Tileston. Another overseas visitor, A. A. Brown of Liverpool, won 1st with his Mastiff dog, Vandal, and 1st with his Mastiff bitch, Norma.

The Menu

On Wednesday evening, the second day of the show, Westminster member Col. Le Grand B. Cannon gave a dinner in honor of the Messrs. Macdona. Nothing more is known of the dinner except that, as reported in the *Times*, it was held at the Westminster Hotel.

Some two weeks later, on May 25, the club gave another dinner. In this case, the location of the dinner is not known, but a copy of the menu for the meal survives. It is dated. It has the WKC monogram on it as well as an engraving of Sensation's head. It was a lavish multicourse feast, and at some point during the festivities, General Webb passed his menu around the table and collected 17 very legible signatures.

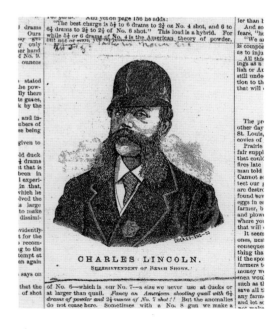

Charles Lincoln,
"Thoroughly
Americanized"
— *The Chicago Field*

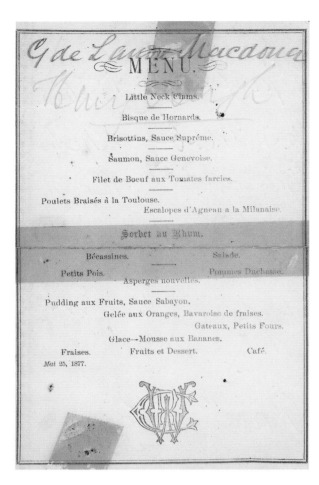

The menu with 17 signatures, 1877, Henry Bergh, F. O. DeLuze, C. Oliver Iselin, T. Frank P. Kavnagh, G. de Landre Macdona, H. Victor Macdona, J. Cumming Macdona, William F. Morgan, Charles H. Raymond, Henry N. Munn, Nicholas Rowe, Alex B. Simonds, Edmund C. Stanton, W. M. Tileston, W. S. Webb, MD, Gen. Alexander S. Webb, H. Walter Webb, — *WKC Gift of Helen Hoppin, 1946*

Among the signers were eight men who would be on the membership rolls when the club held its first official meeting the following December, plus two more who would become members at a later date. The Rev. Macdona, who judged at the first show, signed, as did both his father and son. Mr. T. Frank P. Kavnagh, the second judge from England added his signature, as did Henry Bergh, of the ASPCA, and Dr. Nicholas Rowe, editor of the *Chicago Field* (later *The American Field*). There was a mystery man —every club needs one — one Alex B. Simonds of whom nothing further is heard. Three signatures defy readability.

The menu was among the General's effects, which were eventually passed along to his granddaughter, Mrs. Helen L. Hoppin, who gave it to Westminster in 1946.

The guests presumably celebrated a successful show — and bade farewell to the Reverend Macdona and his son, who (as reported in the *Times*) sailed on the steamship *Celtic* for Liverpool the next day.

The menu is, in effect, the first written record of the Westminster Kennel Club.

The Meeting

On December 7, 1877, the Westminster members held their first meeting with formal recorded minutes. The inaugural dog show was seven months behind them. The main item of business was a vote to incorporate.

There were three primary players. One was Dr. William Seward Webb, 26, a physician at St. Luke's Hospital in New York. An active Pointer breeder and exhibitor, he had helped organize the Westminster Breeding Kennel in the summer of 1876. He owned the Pointer bitch Whisky. He had shown her at Springfield, Mass., in 1875 and 1876. In the fall of 1876, she was one of a dozen Pointers that he entered in the Centennial Show in Philadelphia. The following January, he showed her again, with one of her puppies, this time in the Maryland Poultry and Fanciers show in Baltimore. By then, he had made his

Pointers the property of the Westminster Kennel Club.

A second major player was George De Forest Grant, a banker with Grant & Co. at 33 Wall Street. He lived at 11 Gramercy Park, just a stone's throw from the Westminster Hotel. A Pointer man, he showed a male puppy out of Dr. Webb's bitch Whisky in the Centennial show and, the day after the show closed, sailed for England. This was the trip on which he acquired Sensation.

The third important player was William M. Tileston, 29, kennel editor of *Forest & Stream*. It was under his guidance that the paper opened its Kennel Register in which Grant and Dr. Webb registered their dogs. He also exhibited at the Centennial Show—a Gordon Setter and a Fox Terrier. Afterwards, he was highly critical—in print—of the event, and when the Westminster Kennel Club decided to hold a show of its own, his fellow members named him Chairman.

After deciding to incorporate, the main item of business was a vote to hold a second annual bench show the following May with Tileston as Manager. Tileston held the title for the third and fourth shows as well. But his life ended tragically six days before the fourth show opened, when a newly constructed wall at the Garden collapsed and buried him in rubble.

In addition to these three, there were other members of considerable importance. Francis O. De Luze was a wine merchant and, in 1877, the sole agent in the U.S. for Spratt's Patent of London. His ad for the dog food appeared in the 1877 catalog. Before the show closed, Westminster awarded Spratt's a silver medal for excellence in manufacture of dog food, "their biscuits having been used throughout the show."

Robert C. Cornell, 24, was a lawyer. In 1877, he was famous as the stroke of the Columbia crew that carried off the honors at the Henley Regatta in England in 1876. A graduate of Columbia Law School, he became a city Magistrate in 1895 and judge of the Court of Domestic Relations, the first of its kind in the world, when it was established in 1910. Primarily a field-dog man, he showed two black-and-tan setters in the 1877 show, one of which took a VHC. He served the club in many capacities, including that of legal counsel. A number of governors meetings were held at his residence at 29 Irving Place, near the Westminster Hotel. It was he who took Sensation into his home to give the dog a comfortable old age.

Cornell left Westminster in 1902 but turned up again as an exhibitor in the show of 1916, taking Winners dog with his Pointer Philander. The *Times* remembered the magistrate as "the old Columbia oarsman," but featured him as an exhibitor "showing for the first time." They did not recognize him as a founder of Westminster.

C. Oliver Iselin, 23, was a boatman of a different kind. According to the *Times*, he was an owner of the *Vigilant* and the *Defender*, the America's Cup winners in 1893 and 1895, and was in command of the Columbia, when it won in 1899. The paper said that "no other amateur yachtsman ever had so long or so successful a career in these famous international races."

In the first show, Iselin exhibited a Toy Terrier, which won a second-place ribbon. From a dog show point of view, he is probably best remembered for his absence in 1896. Friends wanted to exhibit the *Defender's* mascot in the show. It was a "common yellow cur," which had cost $25. A dispatch asking Iselin's permission went to Paris and finally reached him in Cairo, from whence came a cablegram directing the dog to be placed in the show with *Defender's* colors, red and black, as decoration on his bench.

Cornelius Du Bois Wagstaff became the club's first vice-president. He was owner of the Tahlulah Kennels at Babylon, New York. He was a field-dog devotee and at the first show exhibited an Irish Setter and an Irish Water Spaniel. In time, he bred Pugs. He helped Westminster acquire their property at Babylon and designed the clubhouse that would be the club's home there for two decades.

Chairman of the first meeting was Col. Le Grand B. Cannon, 62. He was something of a Civil War figure. Early in the conflict, he had led a gathering of citizens to various New York newspaper offices and demanded that the Stars and Stripes be hoisted. He raised the first black regiment, helped restore order during the draft riots in New York and wrote a history of the battle between the *Monitor* and the *Merrimack*. He remained a member only until 1880.

Recording Secretary at the first meeting was William Forbes Morgan, 36. He was a lawyer who had gone into banking. At the first show, he entered three dogs, a Mastiff, which won a second-place ribbon, a Toy Terrier (not exceeding 5 pounds) that earned a VHC, and a Maltese Lion Dog. In 1883, he retired and moved permanently to London.

A member who deserves particular notice was H. Walter Webb. He was 25, the younger brother of Dr. Webb, with whom he then shared a house on West 38th Street. He was a lawyer with an

office at 206 Broadway, where Robert Cornell's law office was located. As brother of one of the club's prime movers, Walter Webb played a major role in capturing the talents of still another major figure, the distinguished gentleman who became Westminster's first president and who held the job through the club's first 10 years. This individual was the older half-brother of Walter Webb and Dr. Webb. He was a Civil War hero, General Alexander Stewart Webb.

One of the Prime Players, Dr. William Seward Webb— *Collection New-York Historical Society, unidentified photographer, Negative number 39497*

The seven other charter members were Frederick Barnard, Robert Lenox Belknap, Huntington Denton, Dr. William Guy Richards, James Hopkins Smith, Edmund C. Stanton and Louis B. Wright.

The First President

Given the way in which he imposed West Point and Army discipline and standards of rigor on City College, I can well imagine that he was a meticulous president of the Club. — Prof. Barbara J. Dunlap, City College, 1998

General Alexander Stewart Webb was a Civil War general. He was twice wounded and five times brevetted for distinguished service. He played a crucial role in turning the tide for the Union soldiers at the Battle of Gettysburg. He received the Congressional Medal of Honor.

A striking scene: July 3, 1863, at Gettysburg, the final day. A little after 1:00 PM, the Confederates launched a cannonade the likes of which had seldom been seen. They were firing 150 guns. Shots came at the Union line at the rate of 70 or 80 a minute. It was the prelude to Pickett's Charge.

How did General Alexander Stewart Webb respond? The 28-year old warrior chose the most exposed spot he could find and stood there, leaning on his sword and smoking a cigar. In vain, his men appealed to him to take cover. But he stood like a statue, watching the enemy.

The ground attack, when it came, was spectacular. In less than five minutes, the entire enemy force was in full view: 10,000 men, marching in perfectly dressed ranks. About halfway to the Union line, they came within range of canister fire. Canisters were big tin cans filled with giant buckshot. When fired from cannons, they were like giant shotgun shells. In a storm of canister fire, the assault line staggered, but the men closed ranks and kept coming.

Some 20 yards from the low stone wall that marked the Union line where Webb and his men were stationed, there were 3,000 enemy troops. Suddenly a swarm of them rushed the wall. The men of Webb's 71st Regiment saw them coming. They knew they were outnumbered. They jumped up and ran.

Webb had just brought the 72nd Regiment up to form a second line behind the 71st. The first thing they saw was a stream of their fellow soldiers running to the rear. But they stood their ground and fired. Slowly, the Rebels retreated.

Webb then helped rally the 71st behind the 72nd. Now he urged the 72nd to go forward. But while they held their ground and fired, they would not advance. He shouted and waved his sword. He grabbed the regimental flag and tried to take it away from the color-bearer. If the General moved the colors

forward, the soldiers would have to follow. "Rally round the flag!" was not just a line from a patriotic song; it was an order heard in the heat of battle. But the color-bearer would not let go. Webb gave up and moved toward another of his regiments, the 69th. These men were settled in at the wall to the left of where the 71st had been. They needed support. As he walked toward them, a bullet grazed the inside of his thigh, but he did not stop.

At that moment, Confederate General Lewis Addison Armistead emerged from the mass of enemy soldiers. Running

General Webb at the time of Gettysburg and, to right, as college President—*Archives, City College of New York, CUNY*

forward, his hat raised high on the end of his sword, Armistead shouted, "Come on, boys, give them the cold steel," and charged over the wall. Behind him came 300 men.

Now the two generals were just a few yards apart, both on foot, both advancing. This moment, on one of the bloodiest battlefields of history, has been called the "Highwater Mark of the Confederacy." Armistead headed straight into a wall of rifle fire and quickly fell, mortally wounded, but there was a wide gap in the Union line. If enough Rebels got through, the Union line might well be broken. It was a wild melee. Men were shot at such close range their uniforms

were scorched. When they could no longer load their guns, they turned them around and swung them like clubs. They fought with bayonets and rocks. They wrestled. But if the enemy had more men, the Union troops were under better control.

While some Rebels fought on desperately, others began to see that there was no organized support for them. They started waving bits of white cloth. Cries of "Don't shoot!" were heard. By 4:00 PM, less than an hour after the charge

began, a Union countercharge was under way. Union General George Gordon Meade came along the line on horseback, amazed to find the attack already repulsed. The men cheered him. A band began to play "Hail to the Chief." A newspaperman called out, "General Meade, you're in very great danger of being president of the United States."

Born in New York City in 1835, the son of James Watson Webb and Helen Lispenard Stewart, Alexander Stewart Webb was appointed a cadet at the U. S. Military Academy at 16; he graduated in 1855. That same year, he married Anne Elizabeth Remsen. After two years in the field, he went back to the academy to teach. When the Civil War started, he returned to the field, serving at Bull Run, Yorktown, Antietam and Chancellorsville. Then came Gettysburg, after which he fought in the Battle of Bristow Station and in the Wilderness Campaign until he was severely wounded at Spotsylvania. After recovering, he became chief of staff to General Meade until the war ended.

He then went back to teaching but was not happy in a peacetime army. Finally, effective at the end of 1870, he was at his own request honorably discharged.

By then, Webb had already started a second career. In 1869, before he left the army, he was elected president of the College of the City of New York. Located at 23rd Street and Lexington Avenue, it was the first free municipal college in the nation. Webb, who was the institution's second president, had great faith in its usefulness as a people's college. For 33 years, he would maintain high academic standards, fighting against anything that would "bring contempt on the bachelor's degree." He even took on President Charles Eliot of Harvard, publicly opposing as far too

Westminster's first president, memorialized at City College in Manhattan
—*Gazette*

liberal Eliot's new "free-elective system," under which students took virtually any courses they wanted.

When he retired, enrollment had more than doubled to nearly 2,000. He had worked hard in the search for new, larger facilities, and ground was broken at the present site—at 134th Street and Convent Avenue—shortly after he stepped down.

The first printed evidence of a link between Webb and dogs appeared in 1876, during his presidency at the college. *Forest & Stream* opened its "Kennel Register," and the general's Pointer, Fritz, was among the first dogs recorded in it. But if he had dogs, he was not a dog show man, nor was he a hunter in the field or a field-trialer. He had been a soldier; he was now an educator and an administrator. He did not attend the club's first meeting in December 1877, but his two half-brothers did, and when the new organization established a nine-man board of governors, they and the general were elected to that board. In due course, the general was elected president.

An inspirational man, Webb was re-elected as president each year until 1887, when he retired because of the increasing demands of his other presidency, at City College. By then, the club had held 11 all-breed shows. The kennel population at Westminster's kennels, counting the club's own dogs and dogs boarded there for members, sometimes numbered over 200. The club entered as many as two dozen of its Pointers, "not for competition," in its own shows, and a number of these competed in the shows of other clubs. They easily held their own.

Webb died in 1911 at the age of 75. Six years later a bronze sculpture of him – a replica of his memorial at Gettysburg – was unveiled on the uptown campus of City College. It depicts Webb in full uniform, leaning on his sword, looking much as he must have looked during the cannonade at Gettysburg. All that is missing is the cigar he smoked so calmly as he awaited Pickett's Charge.

1878

May 14-18
Gilmore's Garden
1,005 Dogs
Charles Lincoln, Superintendent
William M. Tileston, Manager
Edmund C. Stanton, Chairman

We doubt if even the "Bench Show of Intellect," suggested by The World, and in which it is proposed to exhibit all classes of poets and literary people in general, would call forth more interested, aristocratic or cultured throngs than the dog show audiences.
—*Forest & Stream, May 16, 1878*

"Progress, Beauty, Refinement"

For the club's second show, formal opening ceremonies were dispensed with. Henry Bergh of the ASPCA remembered the fate of his speech of a year before when nobody more than a foot away could hear a word he said. Instead of speaking, he wrote a letter to the show managers. He closed with the words, "Go on, gentlemen, in your noble undertaking—for it means progress, beauty, refinement."

The event was a great success. Each day, the *Times* ran a new headline: DOGS HAVING THEIR DAY; DOGS STILL DELIGHTING; ALL THE PET DOGS JUDGED; ALL THE BEST DOGS KNOWN

The cover of the *Daily Graphic* (page 32) shows the crowds, which included stylish ladies. The paper's artists were not necessarily at their best in drawing dogs. *Sensation,* toward the upper left, is barely recognizable.

But note the uniformed attendants provided by the club to take dogs into the ring. Note *Fannie,* the Chinese Edible. That was the early name of what became the Chinese Crested. Owned by Fred Wood of New York City, she took 1st in the Miscellaneous Class. Fannie may have been the first of her breed ever shown in this country.

The Bull Terrier, *Lad,* in the very upper left corner, was owned by C. H. Hayes and received a Commendation. The

Pointer, *Bow,* in the lower right corner, was a 1st in Dogs, over 50 lbs. The St. Louis Kennel Club owned him. Miss Barlow's *Maida,* to the left of Bow, was the best Deerhound.

The club learned a lesson this year. The show was so popular with the public that management extended the four-day affair to five. It did not pay off. Most dogs were gone by noon the fifth day. When people learned this at the box office, they declined to buy tickets.

1879

April 8-11

Gilmore's Garden

957 Dogs

Charles Lincoln, Superintendent

William M. Tileston, Manager

George deForest Grant, Chairman

We think there are too many Bench Shows. This opinion is not alone our own, but is pretty generally expressed by the public. We believe that during the year there should be held only two great shows in the country and no more. We are satisfied that if one were held in the East, say in Boston, New York or Philadelphia...and the other in Chicago or St. Louis, two such Bench Shows would be amply sufficient.—Forest & Stream, May 23, 1878

Year of the Wellstood Print

Here we see the judges giving out prizes. The Wellstood print of Sensation can be seen just left of center in the background of this year's illustration. It was a prize "for the best dog, bitch or puppy sired by Sensation." The winner was Dutchess, a two-year old lemon and white bitch owned by George Van Wagenen of New York City. She was by Sensation out of Whisky.

This year's Premium List contained the show rules and regulations. Perhaps the most significant thing about them was the fact that they were adopted by Westminster and the Philadelphia Kennel Club together and that a Board of Appeals at the show was made up of three members of each club. It was an early step in the search for a set of rules

under which the shows all across the country might be held. There would be no national governing body until the founding of AKC in 1884.

A system of three judges instead of one was tried this year. It would take time to learn the wisdom of having each breed judged by one judge alone. The club was also pleased to have an all-American panel because of the "undoubted prejudice" on the part of exhibitors against the English judges at the first two shows. Even so, there would be two Englishmen on next year's panel.

Each dog distinguished by a placement or commendation received a "diploma"

setting forth the award, in addition to any money and other announced prizes. An example of a diploma appears in the write-up of the show of 1900.

Twice on the final day, there was a parade of all prizewinners. The *Times* called it a magnificent sight. "Dogs," they said, "never look half themselves while lying heaped up in a stall."

On Friday after the show closed, the club gave a banquet at the Brunswick Hotel for the judges and the visiting members

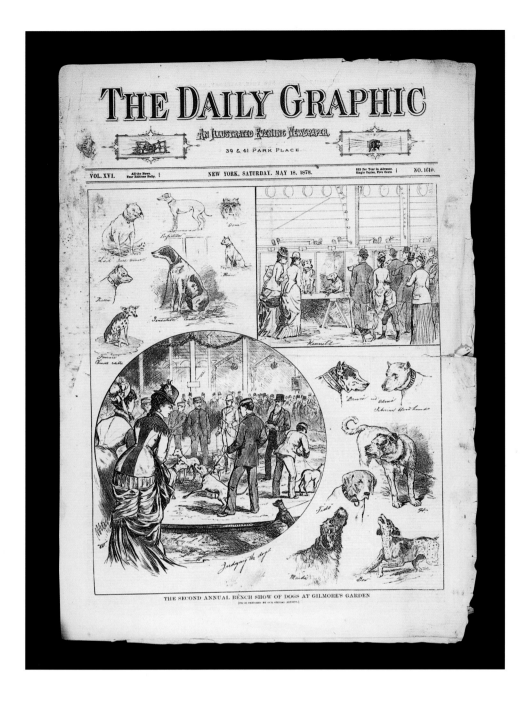

Above: *Daily Graphic,* May 18, 1878 — *WKC*

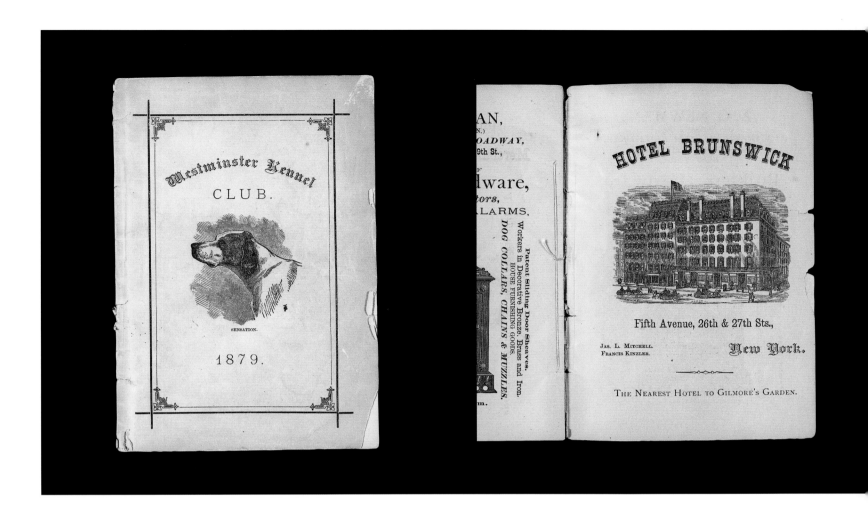

Above Left:
Wherein New York and Philadelphia joined forces — *Cover of Premium List from 1879, WKC*

Above Right:
Sixty dog men sat down to a "dainty repast" — *Hotel Brunswick ad from the 1879 premium list, WKC.*

Right:
Westminster 1879. The print of Sensation hangs to left of center on the far wall. — *"The Great Bench Show at Gilmore's Garden, The Judges awarding the Prizes" — Corbis-Bettman*

of the Baltimore, Philadelphia and Boston Kennel Clubs. About 60 men sat down to "a dainty repast" shortly after midnight. C. Du Bois Wagstaff presided at one end of the long table and William M. Tileston at the other. According to the *Times*, it was 4 AM when the "merry gathering" dispersed.

The Clubhouses

Pascack

At the time of the 1877 show, Westminster was well established in its first clubhouse. The location was Pascack, N.J. The nearest town today would be Park Ridge. The *Times* described the area as "a region filled with game and surrounded by delightful scenery." They called the clubhouse "an ancient mansion," saying it was furnished with every convenience, including a notable library of sporting and canine literature. As for kennels, they were constructed after "the most approved pattern" and were "models of order and neatness."

In the kennels was "a collection of highly-bred Pointers unrivaled on this continent." In addition to the club's dogs —a score of them with Sensation at the head—there were dogs boarded for club members, Mastiffs belonging to Robert Lenox Belknap, Sheepdogs owned by William F. Morgan, and the Setters of William Tileston who lived nearby.

Pascack was the club's home for some two years.

Babylon

In 1879, the club began a search for a permanent home with shooting grounds. In Babylon, Long Island, they quickly located 60 acres for which they signed a two-year lease at $300 a year, with an option to buy at the end of the term for $5,500. The buildings on the property were considered of little value, "the farmhouse having been built a century before." The structures were repaired, however. The barns were altered into kennels, a pigeon ground was laid out, and the house was simply but appropriately furnished.

At the end of their lease, the club purchased the property at the agreed-upon price. Two years later, they moved the farmhouse to another part of the grounds for use of the superintendent, and on its former site erected a new clubhouse. C. Du Bois Wagstaff, owner of Tahlulah kennels, who lived nearby, drew up the plans. Wagstaff, Lucius K. Wilmerding and Elliot Smith constituted the Building Committee.

The new structure cost $8,000. It overlooked a pretty body of water called Southard's Pond. The building was 40 x 60 feet in size, with a wide covered porch on three sides. There was a dining room where as many as 50 members and their guests could dine at once. There was a billiard room and a sitting room with bookcases and gun closets for the members. Upstairs there were a dozen sleeping rooms and a large veranda from which one could watch the shooting contests.

Oil paintings, etchings and old engravings ornamented the walls. Large fireplaces, with wood mantels, were in each of the lower rooms. Jacob Pentz, in *The American Field* in 1886, said that these, with huge andirons and blazing logs, gave "an exceedingly homelike appearance to all." The wine cellar was well stocked, and the food, very satisfactory. It was not unusual for parties of members to spend several consecutive days on the premises.

By the spring of 1894, the club was free of debt. To celebrate, members and guests were offered a free day of entertainment at the clubhouse. Transportation was by a special train that left Long Island City on arrival of the 9:50 boat from East 34th Street. Guests were assured that they would be back in New York by 5:30.

Westminster was still basically a Pointer club. After Sensation's retirement, Bang Bang headed the club's list of stud dogs

Right: The first clubhouse at Babylon, a farmhouse transformed— *WKC*

Left: The first clubhouse at Babylon as it looked in 1954 — *WKC, courtesy Mrs. Elvira Smit*

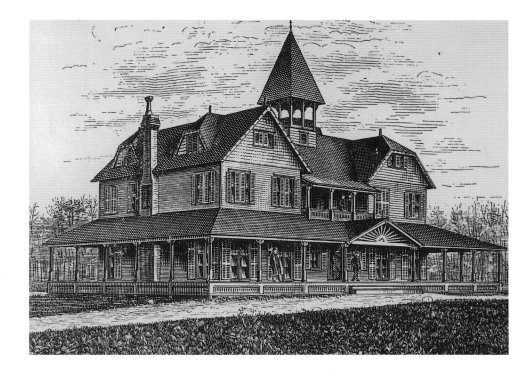

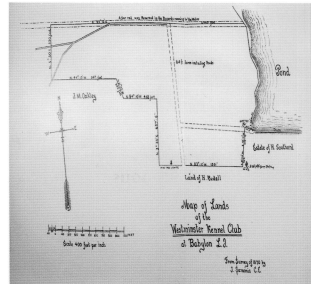

Left: The new clubhouse at Babylon; the wine cellar was well stocked
— *WKC*

Above: Southard's Pond remains a land-mark— *WKC*

from 1887 through 1889. Then came Naso of Kipping, 1890-91. WKC paid $1,700 for him. King of Kent followed, holding the premier position from 1892 to 1897. Half a century later, King of Kent would be remembered by some as "the most famous dog owned by Westminster... one of the great fountain-heads of the breed in this country." The final leader of the pack was Sanford of Druid who ruled from 1897 until Westminster got out of the business of owning and breeding dogs. Dog clubs in general were beginning to see that such work was better done by individuals than by a committee of club members.

A first step in this direction had been taken in 1892 when the club disposed of all its dogs except the stud dogs. They also made changes in the administration at the club grounds. James Mortimer had started as manager there in 1885, the same year that he had taken over as superintendent for the show. Under the revised setup at Babylon, he was no longer needed. He continued as WKC show superintendent through 1915, but almost immediately upon leaving Babylon, he moved into the world of the private kennel owner. He took the posi-tion of Manager at Hempstead Farms, at Hempstead, Long Island, owned by WKC member Thomas H. Terry.

The club had also become part of what the *New York Herald* called "a great revival" in the sport of pigeon shooting. The paper gave a typically lighthearted headline to a story about it:

HOW THE YOUNG BLOODS OF NEW YORK SATISFY THEIR THIRST FOR GORE —A DESCRIPTION OF THE CRACK SHOTS —COMING EVENTS OF IMPORTANCE.

Forest & Stream took it more seriously. They maintained that the practice was "demoralizing to man's finer sensibili-ties," "repugnant to his humanity" and "the most expensive amusement to be had with shot gun or rifle." Yet they defended it as "essential to the defense of our country through the education of our citizens to be marksmen."

However that may be, Westminster, in acquiring a permanent clubhouse "with shooting grounds," clearly meant to become part of the movement. And they

did. New members then included as many crack shots as dog people. Hardly a weekday or a Sunday went by on which some more or less important shooting match was not held somewhere in the area. Among the competing gun clubs were Riverton, Philadelphia, Cartaret, the Country Club of Westchester, the South Side Sportsman's Club, Rockaway and Meadowbrook. And of them all, according to the *New York Herald,* the grounds and equipment at Westminster were by far the best. "The Sybarites shoot at Tuxedo," said the paper, "the

Left: Sanford Druid, as seen by Muss-Arnolt — *WKC*

Hempstead Farm's SANFORD DRUID (29162).

duffers at Pelham, but the big scorers prefer the Kennel Club every time."

The ultimate test of the importance of live pigeon shooting came in 1904 when a statewide prohibition against it was enacted. The club immediately closed down Babylon and moved, lock, stock and barrel, to New Jersey, where the regulations were not so rigorous.

Right: The club-house at Babylon was sold on April 12, 1904— *WKC*

Tenafly

The site at Tenafly, N.J., was spectacular. The club had an opening-day shoot there on Washington's Birthday in 1904. There were 300 acres of land. The yearly rent was $1,200. There was a fine stone residence, which until the lease was executed, had been occupied by the owners, Kate B. Danforth and her husband, Eliot Danforth. There was a lodge, servants' quarters and spacious stables, all at the disposal of the membership. There was a huge grape arbor, a small orchard and many flowerbeds.

It was on Hudson Avenue, about two miles from Tenafly, and was reached by wagon road through an immense forest of maple, elm, oak and pine. The woods abounded with quail, partridges, pheasants, rabbits and foxes. The house was on an elevation with a beautiful view of the

surrounding country. To the east, the property opened onto the Hudson River.

The residence made an ideal clubhouse. According to the *Evening Telegram,* it had spacious halls, a library, a sitting room, 17 bedrooms, a wine cellar, a storeroom, dining rooms, a pantry and kitchen. The floors were hardwood, and the walls, richly decorated.

At best, however, it was a stopgap measure. Less than three months after the opening day, the club held its last live pigeon shoot. Like New York state, the state of New Jersey had invoked a prohibition of the practice. Westminster, hoping for a reversal of the ordinance, kept the clubhouse open until 1906, when they finally closed the doors. On December 5 of that year, the club's relics were auctioned off to the members. This

FOR SALE—Attractively situated house and grounds at Babylon, L. I. (formerly Westminster Kennel Club;) adapted for charming country residence; modern fifteen-room dwelling, open fireplaces, furnaces, &c.; bailiff's cottage, stables, sheds, kennels; 65 acres picturesque wooded, overlooking fine fresh-water lake; low price to immediate purchaser. Address JEREMIAH ROBBINS, Babylon, L. I. Tel. 22A.

included nearly 70 works of art, many books, and an elk head, a moose head, a deer head, an eagle and the first pigeon shot at Tenafly. The clubhouse furnishings, meaning furniture, china, glassware, linen, etc., were given to James Wells in recognition of his long and faithful service to the club. The lease was terminated as of January 31, 1907.

A clubhouse of its own was a luxury that Westminster would not enjoy again.

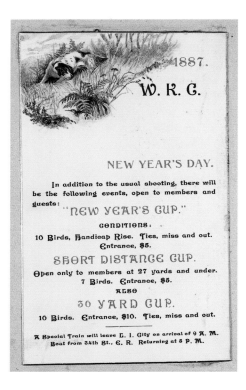

Left: Invitations to shoots at Babylon— *WKC*

Postscript

In 1934, a team of Westminster shots took part in a live pigeon shoot at the Philadelphia Gun Club in Eddington, Pa. They made it an annual affair until 1941. Two years later, in the midst of World War II, the Shooting Committee was dropped "for lack of interest."

Regarding the club's luxurious facilities at Babylon, all that remains today is the farm house that was 100 years old when Westminster acquired it and considered to be "of little value." At some point after being sold by Westminster, the "new" clubhouse burned to the ground, but the farmhouse was moved to a new foundation. In 1946, it was purchased by Mrs. Elvira Smit and her husband, who gutted the interior and reconstructed it into a residence where they lived until 1963. According to Mrs. Smit, the floor always had a "strange slant," a fault of the foundation. In addition, there were no nails in the house, just wooden pegs. Roman numerals on the floor beams suggested it might have been an early "prefabricated" house.

1880

May 11-13

Madison Square Garden I

1,121 Dogs

Charles Lincoln, Superintendent

William M. Tileston, Manager

H. Walter Webb, Chairman

He was one of the brightest, most intelligent and most gentlemanly of men. No road was too long or too rough to travel for the assistance of a friend.—Kennel Review (England), 1886

A Shameful and Terrible Accident

The show of 1880 was marked by tragedy. Manager William Tileston would never get there. An accident brought his life to an end six days before the event was to open.

That winter, 40 feet of the Madison Avenue end of Gilmore's Garden had

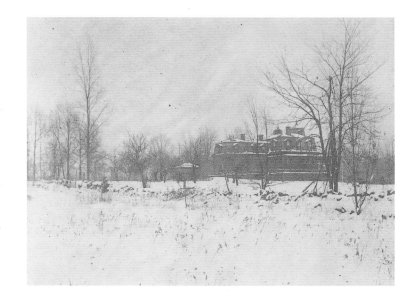

The clubhouse at Tenafly, a stopgap measure at best — *WKC*

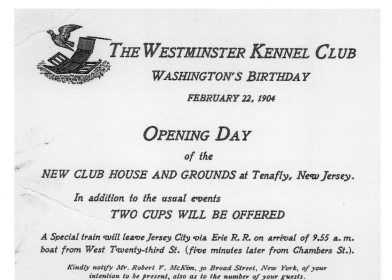

The last shoot at Tenafly took place on May 13, 1904— *WKC*

been gutted and rebuilt. In doing so, a great deal of additional space was created up over the main entrance. It was part of a plan to rehabilitate the structure, which had been rechristened Madison Square Garden—the first of four facilities to bear the name. The accident, as shown in a long series of hearings, was the result of poor design and faulty workmanship. The *Times* called it "shameful and terrible."

Tileston was in his fourth year as manager of the show, with Walter Webb as Show Chairman. On Wednesday evening, April 21, 1880, they went to the Garden on club business. A hospital benefit fair was in progress and would continue through Saturday. The dog show was to open the following Tuesday. The two men talked with the managers

of the fair and arranged to have lumber brought into the Garden the next day so that work could start on the benching as soon as the fair closed at 11 o'clock Saturday night.

(Things would not necessarily get better. A hundred years later, a common problem would be a Sunday-night hockey game, the ice for which had to be melted before the arena could be readied for an 8 o'clock opening the next morning.)

After their meeting, Tileston and Webb left the Garden to go to the Brunswick Hotel. There, they were going to discuss arrangements for their post-show dinner. They left Mrs. Tileston behind at the Garden, telling her that they would return shortly.

William M.
Tileston— *WKC*

Just outside the main entrance on Madison Avenue—above which was all the new construction—they met a policeman, who stopped them to ask about getting a friend appointed as a special detective during the dog show. They discussed the man's qualifications for several minutes, after which Tileston gave his O.K. He and Webb then moved on. But before they had taken more than three or four steps, there were two loud cracks from the building. Webb called out, "Jump, Tileston," and sprang

toward the street. He was immediately knocked down. When he managed to look around, all he could see of his friend was his arm sticking up from a pile of debris. One hundred feet of the second-story wall fronting on Madison Avenue had collapsed and showered down on top of them.

People inside the building were lucky. There had been several hundred persons in the new upstairs rooms, but falling plaster and strange grinding and cracking noises had given warning that something was amiss. They all got out of the rooms. In a stampede for the doors, there were injuries but no deaths.

Down on the street, it was a different story. Four people died, Tileston and three young women.

Webb, with a broken leg and a number of bruises, was taken to a nearby hotel and then home. Because of the accident, the show was postponed for two weeks, and when those two weeks had passed,

Webb, on crutches, his leg in a cast, was able to serve as show chairman. Tileston, however, was mortally injured. He had a compound fracture of both legs and a fracture of his right thigh, his left arm and his nose. He was taken to St. Luke's Hospital, where he died early the next morning.

William M. Tileston was born in New Rochelle, N.Y., in 1838. After college, he spent time in China and then in Los Angeles, where he bought a ranch and married. Shortly after the Civil War, he brought his family to New York where his articles on outdoor life attracted considerable attention. In 1874, he became kennel editor of *Forest & Stream*.

A breeder of Pointers and Setters, he was a founding member of a group known alternatively as the Westminster Breeding Association or Westminster Breeding Kennel. When the group decided to hold a dog show in New York as "The Westminster Kennel Club," they selected him as Chairman. For the following three years, he was named "Manager" rather than "Chairman," a change in title but not in responsibilities.

"The Tragedy at Madison Square Garden" (1880). Note the sculpture to left of door. There was one on each side of the main entrance. The *Times* said they were "hideous figures, called by courtesy 'sphynxes.'" —*Sketch by J.O. Davidson, nd, Museum of the City of New York, Theater Collection*

Tileston's years at *Forest & Stream* were briefly interrupted after the first Westminster show when he left the paper to start his own publication called *Country*. He described the new creation as a "Weekly Journal devoted to The Kennel, Shooting, Fishing, Yachting, Boating, The Road, Archery, and all Athletic pastimes and Rural Sports." Unhappily, the paper quickly folded. At the time of Westminster's third show, he was again kennel editor at *Forest & Stream*. Then shortly before the fourth show, he left the paper again, this time to form Nixon, Tileston & Co., mining brokers. He worked with them until his untimely death.

But Tileston's devotion to dogs never abated. He had entered five of his dogs in the show of 1880, not an uncommon thing for a show manager to do then. And the day after his death, the steamer *Wyoming* arrived in New York with a Fox Terrier bitch he had purchased from an English breeder. On the same day, the steamer *Italy* arrived with a Fox Terrier puppy that was a present to him from Hugh Dalziel, editor of the *London Field*.

Tileston was survived by his widow and four children, the eldest not yet 12.

The Show Goes On

After the accident, Westminster hoped against hope that the entire building would be condemned so that they could break their contract and hold the show elsewhere. They felt that exhibitors and spectators alike would be afraid to enter the Garden. However, inspectors that they themselves brought in said that, while the part of the structure where the collapse had occurred must be sealed off from the public, the rest of the building was totally safe. In accordance with show-business tradition, the show went on.

Some of the winners are pictured in *Harper's Weekly*. The engravings, made from photographs taken by Mr. Pach, were said to be "faithful and characteristic portraits of some of the most interesting specimens in the exhibition."

"Some Prize Dogs"— *Harper's Weekly*, June 5, 1880, *WKC*

The dogs, alphabetically by name, breed, owner and award, if any, are:

Charlie, Newfoundland, E. E. McCormick, NYC, 1st

Fan, Pointer, E. J. Whitehead, NYC, 1st

Flo, Japanese Spaniel, Charles E. Pratt, NYC, 1st

Glen, Deerhound, WKC member Paul Dana, NYC, 1st

Harrold, smooth St. Bernard, John P. Haines, Cranmoor Farm, Tom's River, N.J., 1st

Lyon, Siberian Bloodhound, G. F. Keller, NYC, 2nd

Patch and *Tatters*, Skye Terriers, Louis Harbiger, NYC, 1st & 2nd respectively

Prince, Greyhound, Joseph Stiner, NYC, 1st

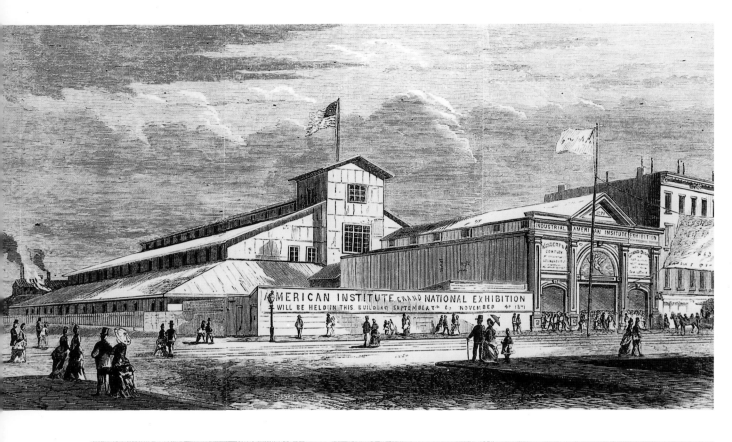

The Rink.
The American Field called it "somewhat cheerless in appearance but large, affording an abundance of room, and well ventilated." *— Engraving, Hearth and Home, Sept. 30, 1871, New York Historical Society, Negative No. 73982*

"Annual Exhibition of Dogs at the American Institute, NYC. Weighing the entries before the judges." *— Wood engraving, 1881, Corbis-Bettman*

Rory O'More, Red Irish Setter, Miss May Callender, Albany, N.Y., Special for Best Pointer or Setter in show owned by a lady

Sheila, rough St. Bernard, H. S. V. S. Thorne, NYC, 1st

Tiny, Pug, Miss Gracie Edwards, NYC, 2nd

1881

April 26-29
American Institute Fair Building
1,135 Dogs
Charles Lincoln, Superintendent
H. Walter Webb, Chairman

The owners realizing that their dogs have more confidence in their presence, generally insist on leading them into the ring themselves, and the spectacle is consequently presented of dignified gentlemen in faultless attire—graybeards some of them—patiently marching around the sawdust enclosure for perhaps an hour at a time, their countenances exhibiting the most intense anxiety and suspense.—The New York Times, April 28, 1881

The Rink

In 1881, Westminster and Madison Square Garden could not agree on rent. The club briefly considered not holding a show at all that year but then settled on what had formerly been the Empire City Skating Rink. They would stay there for two shows, 1881 and 1882.

The Rink, as it was still known, had been acquired by the American Institute for their industrial expositions. It occupied the entire block to the northeast of the intersection of 63rd Street and Third Avenue. It was far roomier than the Garden. It had an asphalt floor. There were no amphitheater seats, which took so much room at the Garden and interfered, some declared, with proper ventilation.

The club put low platforms along the two side walls and chained the larger breeds to them at intervals of 10 feet with no partitions in between. At a single glance, said the *New York World*, a spec-

tator could look down the line and see 70 dogs.

In the central part of the room were long avenues for the public and long benches on which stalls for the dogs measured four by four feet. In the center of it all was a raised platform for the superintendent and, on either side of that, a judging ring. The rings were 35 by 45 feet in size, which allowed the judging to proceed with unprecedented dispatch. A large room to the rear was used for exercising.

The most serious objection seemed to be to the location. Although both the elevated railroad and horsecars passed Institute's doors, some feared that the move from Madison Square, which was then the center of the city, to such a remote section (in the east 60s!) would cut attendance drastically. But on the evening of the opening day, the papers reported that the aisles, with nearly twice the space as at the Garden, were so crowded that moving was difficult.

During the second show there in 1882, *The American Field* reported that there was now "a capital restaurant" in the building where one could procure a well-cooked meal at short notice and for a reasonable price. It was said to be a far more suitable place for the female sex than it had been previously, "thus permitting enthusiastic owners of canine

pets to remain near their charges during the afternoon and evening without interruption."

Nonetheless, Westminster moved back to Madison Square Garden in 1883, and the show stayed there until 1890. At that point, they were forced back to the Institute for one more year. Vanderbilt had leveled the original Madison Square Garden, and Stanford White's new Garden, which was being financed largely by the American Horseshow Association, was not yet complete. In that final year at the Institute, the neighborhood no longer seemed so remote, but it was still not Madison Square. The people who lived in the area of 63rd and Third, said the *Times*, did not "make their calls or go to their theaters in carriages. They rarely put on evening dress."

"When they saw...carriage after carriage," said the paper, "brilliantly decorated with coachmen, footmen, brass buttons and crests, drive up to the dog show and deposit...ladies arrayed in priceless fineries, gentlemen in bewildering overcoats and preceded by beautiful shirt bosoms, (and) children, the cost of one of whose little frocks would support a Third-Avenue family for a month, they were dazed. They stood about the entrance for hours watching this free display, and each waiting carriage had its little crowd of ardent admirers."

Judging a Pointer—
*Frank Leslie's
Illustrated News-
paper, May 12, 1883,
New York Historical
Society, Negative
No. 73983 (Detail)*

Canine Life Save—Adventure in Babylon

The following description of an incident at the club's grounds at Babylon appeared in the *Chicago Field* of June 11, 1881:

"A remarkable piece of intelligence was displayed recently by Mr. De Luze's spaniel kennels. The superintendent (John Read) was rowing across the lake and several dogs were following him. Among the number was Mr. Elliot Smith's Skye Terrier, Wasp, who, while swimming, suddenly sank with a little cry, and did not come to the surface again. Sankey swam around the spot where the little bitch had disappeared, and dived; then came up again, and paddled about the place uttering sharp barks. After two or three more unsuccessful dives, he finally came to the surface with the bitch in his mouth. He carried her... to the shore, and laid her on the grass. Wasp was quite lifeless but after working over her several minutes the men succeeded in reviving her, and she is now as well as ever. Mr. John Read will vouch for the accuracy of this statement, as he was an eyewitness to the entire proceeding. Mr. Smith intends presenting Sankey with a lifesaver's medal, a reward the Spaniel certainly merits for this display of almost, or quite, human bravery and intelligence. (Signed) R. R. C."

1882

April 18-21
American Institute Fair Building
1,271 Dogs
Charles Lincoln, Superintendent
H. Walter Webb, Chairman

If there are still some obstinate people who persist in believing that their dogs must win on the bench, notwithstanding the testimony of dog authorities to the contrary, let us be thankful that their number is each year growing smaller.—Forest & Stream April 27, 1882

Sketches at the Dog Show

This year, we have illustrations from *Harper's Weekly*. One of the few dogs identified by the paper is the Mastiff Gurth in the lower left corner. *Forest & Stream* called him "a splendid animal." He was first in the Champion Dogs Class. In order to compete in a Champion class then, a dog had to have won first place in an open class at New York, St. Louis, Boston, Pittsburgh, London (Ontario) or Ottawa.

The paper also includes an illustration for the story of the Pug puppy Daisy, owned by William Davis of New York. The dog's bench was lined with quilted maroon-colored satin, according to the *Times*, and furnished with a mat of soft wool. But the bench was vacant. Fastened to it was a large mourning card on which was the inscription surrounded by a wide black border: "Died April 17, 1882."

1883

May 8-11
Madison Square Garden I

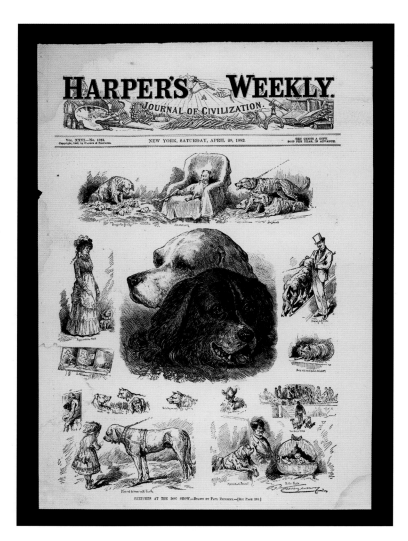

979 Dogs
Charles Lincoln, Superintendent
Robert C. Cornell, Chairman

There were Mastiffs and St. Bernards and Newfoundlands and many others there, yesterday, with incomparably more brains than half the attendants at Democratic primaries. —The New York Times, May 9, 1883

Seventh Annual Bench Show

Harper's Weekly here pictures some of the winners. As numbered in the illustration, they are, by name, breed, owner, and prize, if any:

1. *Ch. Bonivard*, St. Bernard, Rodney Benson, New York, Champion Rough-Coated Dogs, 1st. According to *Forest & Stream*, he "easily captured the medal."

2. *Turk*, Mastiff, William H. Lee, Champion Dogs, unplaced. *Forest & Stream* called him one of four "magnificent animals" in the ring.

Left: "Sketches at the Dog Show," *Harper's Weekly*, Apr 29, 1882 — *WKC*

Right: *Harper's Weekly*, May 12, 1883, — *WKC*

HARPER'S WEEKLY.

JOURNAL OF CIVILIZATION.

VOL. XXVII.—No. 1377.
Copyright, 1883, by HARPER & BROTHERS.

NEW YORK, SATURDAY, MAY 12, 1883.

TEN CENTS A COPY.
$4.00 PER YEAR, IN ADVANCE.

1. Champion "Bonivard," Rough-coated St. Bernard Dog.   2. "Turk," English Mastiff.   3. "Mike," Irish Water-Spaniel.   4. "Judy" and "Lorne," Clumber Spaniels.   5. "Romulus," Bull-Dog.   6. "Bush," English Beagle.   7. "Garry Owen," Irish Terrier.   8. Champion "George," Pug-Dog.   9. "Beauty," Blenheim Spaniel.   10. "Glencho," Red Irish Setter.

SEVENTH ANNUAL BENCH SHOW OF THE WESTMINSTER KENNEL CLUB, NEW YORK.—DRAWN BY P. FRENZENY.—[SEE PAGE 299.]

SEVENTH ANNUAL NEW YORK BENCH SHOW OF DOGS,
TO BE HELD UNDER THE AUSPICES OF THE

WESTMINSTER KENNEL CLUB,

MADISON SQUARE GARDEN, BETWEEN 26TH AND 27TH STREETS,

MAY 8th, 9th, 10th and 11th, 1883.

FORM OF ENTRY.

To the MANAGERS OF THE BENCH SHOW.
New York, 23 Park Row, Rooms 23 and 24.   P. O. Box 1727.
Gentlemen:—I enter the Dog herein named, subject to the Bench Show Rules and Regulations under which this show is held.

No. of Class.	NAME OF DOG.	COLOR.	AGE.	PEDIGREE (IF ANY).		Price.
				Name of Sire.	Name of Dam.	

Signature,
P. O. Address,

Entrance Fees must accompany all entries.   Entries close on April 23d.

Entry Form,
1883—WKC

3. *Mike*, Irish Water Spaniel

4. *Judy* and *Lorne,* Clumber Spaniels

5. *Romulus,* Bulldog, George Raper, Champion Dogs or Bitches, 1st. *The American Field* said he was "splendid."

6. *Bush*, English Beagle

7. *Garry Owen*, Irish Terrier, Robert Ives Crocker, Dogs or Bitches, 1st. *The American Field* termed him "very good."

8. *George*, Pug, Mrs. Edwin A. Pue, Champion Dogs, 1st. *The American Field* said the exhibit of Pugs at New York was always good and that this year it was better than ever. They said it was a fitting opportunity to settle "forever" the merits between George and his old antagonist Roderick. Said the paper afterwards: "It was the old story. George won."

9. *Beauty*, Blenheim Spaniel

10. *Glencho*, Red Irish Setter, William H. Pierce, Champion Dogs, unplaced. Of this dog, *Forest & Stream* said they liked him better than the winner. Glencho was, they said, "an Irish dog all over from head to tail, and a rare good one, too. He is a big dog, and not yet mature, and good as he is we shall expect to see him better next year."

Lucky Dog

Among visitors at the show this year was Samuel J. Tilden. Tilden had run for U. S. president against Rutherford B. Hayes in 1876 and, in a contested election, had lost by one electoral vote. Though Tilden acquiesced, he always maintained that he had been wrongfully deprived of victory. In any case, at Westminster, Tilden saw Duke, a Pug puppy who had received a High Commendation from the judge. As the *Times* put it, "the sage of Gramercy Park patted the native of Long Island on the head and the native of Long Island lay down and went to sleep." Recognizing "an unlimited capacity for sitting on sheepskin rugs and making himself useless, Tilden began negotiations with the dog's owner, Mrs. A. R. Randolph." The price was not revealed, but the paper called Duke "the luckiest little dog in the United States."

1884 — Spring

May 6-9
Madison Square Garden I
1,114 Dogs
Charles Lincoln, Superintendent
Robert C. Cornell, Chairman

That kind of vigorous objection to the judges known as "kicking" is an element in dog shows that is not necessary, and one that should be discouraged.—American Field, May 16, 1884

The All-Breed Show

This was a two-show year, the only one in the club's history. The regular all-breed event in the spring was followed by a non-sporting breed show in the fall. A page of pictures from *Harper's Weekly* shows some details of the earlier event. Blackboards like the one in the center sketch were introduced into the judging rings at Westminster in 1879 "so that all could see just what was going on."

The picture at the bottom shows the "ring" that the club erected down the center of the building. It was 276 by 24 feet in size, running virtually the full length of the structure. In this ring, which could be divided up as needed, the judging was done, and here the dogs were exercised morning and evening. Since it was fenced with slats close enough together to prevent small dogs from passing between them, dogs could be turned loose and permitted to gallop about.

The ring was also used, as the *Times* put it, for "speeding and testing Greyhounds." But *Forest & Stream* reported that the Greyhound racing was not a decided success, except for the winner, "whose name we were unfortunately unable to obtain."

The illustration also includes a dozen entrants, 10 of them first-prize winners. Numerically, by name, breed, owner and prize, if any, they are:

1. *Cardinal,* Foxhound, Essex County Hunt, Orange, N.J., Dogs or Bitches, 1st. *Forest & Stream* called the first three placements all good, with Cardinal "a little the best in back and loin."

2. *Irish Chief,* Irish Water Spaniel, Archibald Rogers, Hyde Park, N.Y., Dogs or Bitches, 1st. *The American Field* said he had a fair head and topknot but was "very light in color."

3. *Nemours,* Basset Hound, W. R. Chamberlain, NYC, 1st

Right: *Harper's Weekly*, February 1884—AKC

Below Left: The "first annual" was also the last — WKC

Below Right: Judges list for the forgotten show — WKC

SCENES AT THE BENCH SHOW, MADISON SQUARE GARDEN.—DRAWN BY A. BERGHAUS.—[SEE PAGE 313.]

WESTMINSTER KENNEL CLUB.
❄First Annual Show❄
OF
NON-SPORTING DOGS,
AND
Deerhounds, Greyhounds & Fox Terriers.

CATALOGUE.

OCTOBER 21ST, 22D, 23D, AND 24TH, 1884.

CHARLES LINCOLN, Superintendent.

NEW YORK:
ROGERS & SHERWOOD, 21 AND 23 BARCLAY STREET.
1884.

Entered according to Act of Congress, by the WESTMINSTER KENNEL CLUB, in the office of the Librarian of Congress at Washington.

LIST OF JUDGES.
—
For Mastiffs, St. Bernards, Fox Terriers, Sheep Dogs, Bull Dogs, and Bull Terriers.

JAMES MORTIMER, ESQ.,
NEW YORK CITY.

For Newfoundlands, Black and Tan Terriers, Hard Haired Scotch Terriers, Rough Haired Terriers, Dandie Dinmont Terriers, Irish Terriers, Bedlington Terriers, Skye Terriers, Yorkshire Terriers, Toy Terriers, King Charles Spaniels, Blenheim Spaniels, Japanese Spaniels, Pugs, Maltese Terriers, Italian Greyhounds and Dalmatians.

J. F. KIRK, ESQ.,
TORONTO, ONT.

For Greyhounds, Deerhounds, Italian Greyhounds, and miscellaneous classes.

JOS. R. PEIRSON, ESQ.,
BUCKINGHAM, PA.

For Poodles (all classes).

JOHN G. HECKSHER, ESQ.,
NEW YORK CITY.

4. *Jack,* Irish Setter, Hiram & William Harris, NYC, Dogs, 1st.

5. *Gretchen,* Dachshund, W. R. Vogelsang, NYC, 1st. *Forest & Stream* called her "more of the terrier type than the hound."

6. *Foreman,* English Setter, C. F. Crawford, Pawtucket, R.I., Champion Dogs, 1st. *The American Field* didn't like his head but called him "a splendid dog back of his neck."

7. *Meteor,* Pointer, J. W. Munson, St. Louis, Mo., Champion Dogs, over 55 lbs., 1st

8. *Ursula,* St. Bernard, H. C. Pedder, Orange, N.J., Champion Rough-Coated Bitches, unplaced

9. *Bruce,* Deerhound, Archibald Rogers, Hyde Park, N.Y., Dogs, 1st.

10. *Begonia,* Greyhound, H. W. Huntington, Brooklyn, N.Y., Bitches, VHC. Second place was withheld in the class. *The American Field* said they could not understand how a judge could commend her so highly and still withhold second place.

11. *Black Tournie,* Cocker Spaniel, Winchester Johnson, Boston, Mass., Field or Cocker Spaniel Puppies (any color), 1st. *The American Field* called her "a beautiful little puppy."

12. *Dan,* Mastiff, Harry Hill, NYC, Dogs, 1st. *The American Field* said he was "high on his legs, has a poor head, is light in bone and weak in hind quarters." *The American Field* said he "lacks Mastiff characteristics."

1884 — Fall

October 21-24
Madison Square Garden I
590 Dogs
Charles Lincoln, Superintendent
Robert C. Cornell, Chairman

The exhibition of those more religious and respectable members of the canine race, known as "non-sporting dogs" will be opened at 9 o'clock this morning.—The New York Times, October 21, 1884

The Forgotten Show

Big news this year was Westminster's decision to hold a non-sporting breed show. It would take place in the fall after the usual spring all-breed event.

When entries closed, they had nearly 600 dogs, twice what they had expected. Entries came from almost every state in the Union—and there were then 38. There were foreign breeds such as Leonbergs, Berghunds, Great Danes, Mexican Hairless and Chinese Cresteds.

Above: After more than a century, Marko's prize "came home." — *WKC*

Opposite Page: "The Non-Sporting Dog Show" (1884) from *Harper's Weekly* —Collection of The New York Historical Society, Negative No. 73984

There were two Esquimaux sled dogs from Greenland, brought from the Arctic by Surgeon Ames of the Greeley relief expedition. The *Times* said it was the largest collection of non-sporting animals ever brought together.

At 3 and 8 PM on the last day, the prizewinners were paraded around the Garden, and each was "dilated upon by a strong-lunged man from a raised platform." He was in effect the club's first Roger Caras, today's "Voice of Westminster."

But if *Forest & Stream* congratulated the breeders on the improvement brought about in nearly all breeds, *The American Field* said the enthusiasm "so characteristic of the Spring show" was lacking. It was a small version of the all-breed event and barely made expenses. The "first Annual" show of non-sporting dogs was also the last.

The show quickly dropped from sight. In Westminster's own records, it appeared in the 1886 yearbook but not thereafter. It was not until 1997 that the "forgotten" show returned to conscious consideration. On the opening day that year, dog judge Karen H. Armistead came to the chief steward's office and presented Westminster with a sterling silver bell she had received as a gift some years before. Engraving on it read: "Westminster/First Prize/Marko/Oct. 1884"

Marko was one of four Leonbergs entered. His owner was Anita Evans of New Rochelle, N.Y. Through Mrs. Armistead's generosity, Marko's trophy came home—after 113 years.

But perhaps more momentous than Marko's win was a meeting that took place at the Garden on the second night. A preliminary gathering to organize a national dog association had been held in Philadelphia a month earlier. A committee had been appointed to draft bylaws. Then on the second night of the forgotten show—October 22, 1884—a permanent organization was brought into being by the election officers. The president was Major James M. Taylor of Lexington, Ky. The Vice-Presidents were Elliot Smith of New York and Samuel Coulson of Montreal. The Secretary was E. S. Porter of New Haven, and the

Treasurer, G. N. Appold of Baltimore. As the *Times* reported, "The association will be known as the American Kennel Club."

Among the Winners

Here *Harper's Weekly* presents some winners in the Forgotten Show. Alphabetically by name, breed, owner, and award, if any, they are:

Bonhomme, Poodle, E. Berry Wall, NYC, Black Dogs, HC

Boz, Bulldog, R. & W. Livingston, NYC, Champion Bulldogs, any weight, Dogs, 1st

Duke of Leeds & Bonivard, St. Bernards, E. R. Hearn, Hermitage Kennels, Passaic, N.J. In Champion Rough-Coated Dogs, Duke of Leeds, a special for Best Rough-Coated St. Bernard. Bonivard was shown not for competition.

Frank, Sheepdog, Millbrook Kennels, NYC, Rough-Coated Dogs, unplaced

Grand Duke, Bull Terrier, R. & W. Livingston, NYC, Champion, 25 lbs. and over, Special for Best Bull Terrier

Jumbo & Ponto, Mastiffs, Samuel F. Sniffen, NYC, unplaced

Me Too, Mexican Hairless, Mrs. Hubert Foote, NYC, 1st. The *Times* noted that Me Too occupied "one of the most elegantly furnished of the dog boudoirs."

Royalist, St. Bernard, Millbrook Kennels, NYC, Smooth-Coated Dogs, 3rd. *The American Field* said he was a large dog of great bone, but faulty in head and "his hocks are too close together."

Stella, St. Bernard, Rodney Benson, NYC, Rough-Coated Bitches, 2nd. According to *American Field*, she was a good bodied bitch, standing on good legs and feet, with fair coat. They called her "rather snipey in muzzle."

Tweed II, Sheepdog, Thomas H. Terry, NYC, Rough-Coated Dogs, unplaced

DUKE OF LEEDS.   BONIVARD.   JUMBO.   PONTO.

"ME TOO."   BONHOMME.   BOZ.

GRAND DUKE.

ROYALIST.   FRANK.

STELLA.

TWEED II.   SCOTCH COLLIE.   DEER-HOUNDS.

THE NON-SPORTING DOG SHOW.—[SEE PAGE 741.]

1885

April 28-May 1
Madison Square Garden I
960 Dogs
James Mortimer, Superintendent
Francis R. Hitchcock, Chairman

Francis R. Hitchcock

Francis R. Hitchcock, 26, became Chairman in 1885 and again for the shows of 1887-89. He would be the club's delegate to AKC in 1888-89. A WKC governor for over 40 years, he would serve as vice-president from 1909 until 1926.

A Columbia graduate, Hitchcock studied law but never took it up as a profession. A devotee of the turf, he was elected to the Jockey Club in 1895 and shortly succeeded another WKC member, J. O. Donner, as Steward of the Jockey Club, a post he held until his death in 1926. When New York's antibetting laws were enacted, he transferred his turf allegiance to France and, from then on, divided his time between America and Europe. He bred thoroughbreds in France, and his colors were often seen at the racetracks near Paris. He was at sea on his way to France when he died.

Hitchcock joined Westminster in 1880. He exhibited a number of breeds, especially Pointers, sometimes entering as many as a dozen at the Garden. One of his most notable dogs was Tammany, a liver and white ticked Pointer, with a record of wins both in the field and on the bench. Tammany, whelped August 24, 1883, by Tory out of Moonstone, was bred by fellow club member George De Forest Grant.

1886

May 4-7
Madison Square Garden I
1,039 Dogs
James Mortimer, Superintendent
H. Walter Webb, Chairman

Sensation looked remarkably well considering his years.—American Field, May 18, 1886

Some Pointers and Setters

This year, *Harper's Weekly* pictures seven dogs. From left to right, top to bottom, they are:

Paul Gladstone was an English Setter owned by the Memphis and Avent Kennels of Memphis, Tenn. He did not compete at Westminster this year, but he was a traveler; he had won a dozen times in the field and on the bench, taking prizes at St. Louis in 1884 and in 1885 at the World's Exposition in New Orleans and at Philadelphia.

Roderigo was another English Setter. He and Paul Gladstone were kennel-mates. This year in a class of 28, he was unplaced but had won the all-age stakes at the Eastern Field Trials at High Point, N.C. There were those, according to *Harper's Weekly*, who called him "the fastest dog in the world."

Nora was a Black-and-Tan Setter owned by H. Clay Glover, veterinarian and proprietor of "Glover's Imperial Dog

Harper's Weekly, May 8, 1886 — WKC

Remedies" in New York. Nora had won a 1st at Philadelphia in 1885 but was unplaced here.

Elcho Junior was a Red Irish Setter, owned by Dr. William Jarvis, Claremont, N.H. The dog had a long record of bench show wins. This year, with three competing in the Champion Dog Class, he "deservedly won first," *The American Field* said. He also took a special for Best Setter in Show, scoring ninety and one-half out of a possible ninety-five.

The score was based on the scale of points in the book of standards by Stonehenge. As the paper explained, a perfect score should have added up to 100, but "owing to a typographical error in Stonehenge, which gives only 5 for nose, which should be 10, it did not do so."

Tammany was a white and liver-ticked Pointer, bred by Westminster and owned by F. R. Hitchcock, last year's Show Chairman. Tammany took a 1st this year, his first blue ribbon, and *Harper's Weekly* called him "a very promising young dog" for both bench and field.

Graphic, a liver-and-white Pointer, was a famous English champion and a recent import. He was owned by the Graphic Kennels of Jersey City. His field and bench-show record both here and in England covered over half a page in the catalog; it included not just Graphic's own wins but those of dogs he had sired. *Harper's Weekly* said he deserved special mention, although in the Champion Dog Class this year, the American champion Robert le Diable, bred and owned by the St. Louis Kennel Club, defeated him.

Bang Bang was shown here not for competition. He was the second Pointer purchased in England for Westminster by George DeForest Grant, who had acquired Sensation for the club in 1876. Bang Bang had made his first appearance at Westminster in 1883. After Sensation's retirement this year, Bang Bang headed the club's list of Pointers at the shows of 1887-89.

"The Eleventh Annual Bench Show," *Frank Leslie's*, May 14, 1887—*Collection of the New York Historical, Society, Negative No. 73985*

MAY 14, 1887.]   FRANK LESLIE'S ILLUSTRATED NEWSPAPER.   209

CHAMPION FOX TERRIER "LUCIFER," OWNED BY AUGUST BELMONT, JR.

"APOLLO," SMOOTH-COATED ST. BERNARD.

GENERAL VIEW OF THE SHOW.

THE COLLIE "DUBLIN SCOT," CHESTNUT HILL KENNELS, PHILADELPHIA.

CHAMPION ENGLISH SETTER "ROYAL ALBERT," BLACKSTONE KENNELS, W. TALLMAN.

NEW YORK CITY.—THE ELEVENTH ANNUAL BENCH SHOW OF THE WESTMINSTER KENNEL CLUB, AT MADISON SQUARE GARDEN, MAY 3D–6TH.
FROM SKETCHES BY A STAFF ARTIST.—SEE PAGE 2.5.

1887

May 3-6
Madison Square Garden I
979 Dogs
James Mortimer, Superintendent
Francis R. Hitchcock, Chairman

James Mortimer and a Conflict of Interest

As seen in *Frank Leslie's Illustrated Newspaper,* the club continued to set the show up around a long, narrow ring that was almost the length of the arena. Also visible is the new benching provided by Spratt's Patent. For solid wooden dividers, they substituted galvanized wire partitions.

Of the four dogs pictured, *Apollo,* the smooth St. Bernard shown at the upper right, was at the center of real controversy. Owned by W. W. Tucker of New York City, he took 1st in the Champion Dog Class. Calling the win "expected," *Forest & Stream* said, "Apollo's houndy head does not improve with age, and heavy work in the stud has weakened his loin and quarters. He does not transmit his hound qualities and is still a valuable stud dog, but we fail to understand how a judge of the breed could place him first in the company he met on this occasion." There was nothing wrong with this. Like everyone else at ringside, *Forest & Stream* was entitled to its own opinion.

However, the paper then went on to complain most unhappily about James Mortimer, who had judged the breed. In 1884 when he first officiated at the Garden, he got good marks. He was also highly praised in 1885 and 1886 for his work as superintendent of the show, a job he took on after the sudden death of Charles Lincoln. However, it was a different story this year when he was both superintendent and judge. "It was conceded," said the paper, "that the classes should have been better judged than on any previous occasion, seeing that the judge received the entries and had the dogs' records before him, as well as the opinions of competent authority. We hope the judge's memory failed him or that he got badly mixed, as we would be sorry to think such awards were made after careful consideration." Mortimer did not judge at Westminster again.

There was nothing comparable regarding the other three dogs whose pictures we see. *Lucifer* was a Fox Terrier owned by August Belmont, Jr., who would become AKC president the following year. In the Champion Dog Class, Lucifer took 2nd to Fred Hoey's Valet. *The American Field* allowed that Valet was "very well shown" but maintained that Lucifer was of "a distinctly different type and a better type than Valet."

The paper was not unhappy with *Dublin Scot,* the Collie owned by Chestnut Hill Kennels in Philadelphia. He "easily won" the open class, they said. "He is a large dog with a grand body and good bone; his head is just a trifle domed, but he is very good below the eye, stands on capital legs and feet; good brush; top-coat not quite as hard as it might be; a big dog full of quality and character."

About *Royal Albert,* the English Setter, the paper was downright pleased. Owned by Blackstone Kennels of W. Tallman, New York City, he won the Champion Dog Class. There was an overall breed entry of

102, of which *The American Field* said the quality was "exceptionally high."

1888

February 21-24
Madison Square Garden I
1,201 Dogs
James Mortimer, Superintendent
Francis R. Hitchcock, Chairman

Most unintentionally she has become somewhat a public character in connection with dogs.—F. C. Pierce, Whitney Genealogy, 1895

ANNA H. WHITNEY.

Anna H. Whitney

The first woman to judge a dog show in the United States was Anna Whitney of Lancaster, Mass. The year was 1888, and the show, Westminster. When she finished her assignment of 117 St. Bernards, she was presented with a handsome bouquet of flowers. In reporting the event, *The American Field* noted that in selecting her, the club had "made a new departure" and said that she "must be congratulated on the very able manner in which she handled the classes."

Whitney was, according to the paper, "the cynosure of the eyes of the enormous crowds that stood around the ring while she, the first lady who had ever

entered a judging ring in this country, was going through her by no means easy task."

After her first assignment, Whitney judged at Westminster every year for seven years, and then came back, off and on, through the balance of her judging career. However, after that first assignment, 13 years would pass, and she would judge some 30 times, before a second woman would judge dogs in the U.S.

Whitney became an extremely popular judge. *The American Field* spoke of her "well-known ability." When she finished her fifth assignment at Westminster, *Forest & Stream* noted that she "got to work on time and, in her usual quiet and confident way, brought either joy or misery to the expectant ones."

Engraving
—WKC

Born in Cambridge, Mass., in 1844, Anna Henshaw Whitney was the daughter of Asa Hammond Whitney and Laura L. Henshaw. She graduated from the Lasell Seminary in Auburndale, Mass., at 16. Within the year she started teaching and, around 1864, moved to Lancaster, Mass., where she taught for many years at Lancaster Academy, which later became the public high school.

She served on the Board of Library Trustees in Lancaster, and on the School Committee—in each case being noted as the only female presence—and as treasurer of the First Parish Church. It was said that she had considerable artistic talent and that her literary judgment was "of the highest character." She taught drawing and painting in a Lancaster studio she operated with a friend. In 1889, she quit her post at the high school and took up farming on a small, unremunerative scale.

Always fond of nature and of animals—especially dogs—she had at various times Greyhounds, Newfoundlands, Mexican Hairless, King Charles Spaniels and mixed breeds. Then in 1875, Leroy Z. Collins, principal of the school where she taught, imported some St. Bernards. She had owned two Saints before, of doubtful pedigree. Collins, who bred and exhibited

Anna H.
Whitney in the
benching area,
Madison Square
Garden (1897)
—*Museum of the
City of New York,
The Byron
Collection,
93.1.1.17714*

the breed, offered her the first choice of the first litter. She chose a female and, with it, founded Chequasset Kennels, which became known for St. Bernards and Pugs.

In 1888, on the first day of her first Westminster assignment, Whitney met at the Hoffman House in New York with a group that organized the St. Bernard Club of America. She was one of eight who signed a letter calling for the meeting—again a lone female presence— and she was elected president. However, she held the position for just 24 hours. When the club reassembled the next day, she tendered her resignation as president, after which a vice-president, K. E. Hopf, was elected in her place, and she was elected to replace him as a vice-president. She served in that capacity through 1896.

In September 1897, the club disbanded and was dropped as an AKC member. But in December, in Grand Rapids, Mich., a new St. Bernard club of America was organized, and Whitney was elected second vice-president. She was still a vice-president in 1911, when the club held a specialty show in Grand Rapids.

In 1888, Whitney was also elected a vice-president of the new National Dog Club of America. The group's stated aim was to advance the interests of American breeders. AKC then had some 30 member clubs. As a governing body, it was seen by some as too small and exclusive. To whom could individual breeders, especially those without club affiliation, address their grievances? How could they make their voices heard? A national club composed wholly of breeders looked like the answer.

Unhappily, the organization's brief history is largely recorded in letters to the editor in various sporting newspapers, arguing whether the group intended to aid breeders by cooperating with AKC or by supplanting it. Then, at midyear, AKC president August Belmont proposed new rules to provide for associate membership in AKC. For $5 (the same dues charged by the National Dog Club), an associate member—meaning any individual man or woman—would get two free registrations and a year's subscription to the *Gazette* and Stud Book. In addition, associate members could elect AKC delegates, one for every one hundred associates. The proposal passed, and in January 1889, the first list of associate members was published, 122 in all. Whitney was part of this first group.

Then the National Dog Club, barely 10 months old, voted to disband, subject to all of its 200 or so members automatically being eligible for AKC associate membership. Almost every member who had not already done so, joined AKC. There is little doubt that AKC created associate memberships because of pressure from the National Dog Club. In any case, at the final meeting, the NDC president graciously thanked the members for their support, ending with the words, "My task is done."

Whitney maintained her associate membership in AKC through 1897. (Such membership was offered until 1923.) She was one of the first official judges listed by AKC in 1889. When AKC started licensing judges, she was among the first to be so approved, and she remained on the list until 1918, the year of her last assignment.

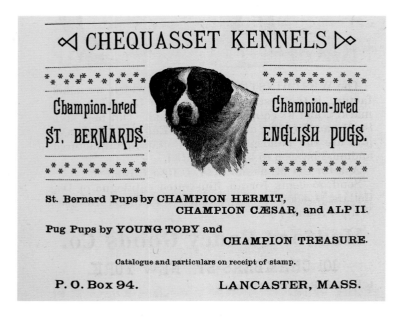

◁ CHEQUASSET KENNELS ▷

Champion-bred ST. BERNARDS.

Champion-bred ENGLISH PUGS.

St. Bernard Pups by CHAMPION HERMIT, CHAMPION CÆSAR, and ALP II.

Pug Pups by YOUNG TOBY and CHAMPION TREASURE.

Catalogue and particulars on receipt of stamp.

P. O. Box 94.   LANCASTER, MASS.

Kennnel ad, WKC Catalog, 1895—*WKC*

MISS ANNA H. WHITNEY, Judge New York Show.

Anna H. Whitney —courtesy *The American Field*

material with a black corded silk turnover collar and revers. It was worn over a shirtwaist of white stuff heavily figured with dark blue. There was a stiff collar of the same material and a long black lace tie. She wore a bonnet of black velvet, spangled with jet and with a straw-colored pompom."

In addition to Westminster, Whitney judged at the St. Louis Kennel Club, Ladies Kennel Association of America, Kansas City Kennel Club, New England Kennel Club, Eastern Dog Club, and Toy Dog Club of New England. Her last assignment was at the Ladies Kennel Association of Massachusetts in 1918, where she judged Bloodhounds, Otterhounds, Mastiffs, St. Bernards, Great Danes, Newfoundlands, Foxhounds, Old English Sheepdogs, Samoyeds, Pugs and terriers.

Whitney died in Lancaster on August 10, 1922 at age 77. In her obituary in the *Clinton Courant,* her life was remembered as "one of constant industry, with never ceasing cheerfulness." The paper said in farewell, "A brave spirit has left us."

1889

Feb 19-22
Madison Square Garden I
1,372 Dogs
James Mortimer, Superintendent
Francis R. Hitchcock, Chairman

Improvement has already begun in some of the breeds, and we hope to see it continue and extend to all breeds until it will no longer be necessary to send to England to obtain a winner.—Forest & Stream, February 28, 1889

The Thirteenth Show

It was the last year at the first Garden. It was the 13th all-breed show—and things went well.

There was disagreement about the judging. *The American Field* said the decisions "gave satisfaction generally," while *The New York Times* carried on a bit, saying that "much dissatisfaction was expressed." That aside, however, the

In 1891, Whitney wrote a history and description of the Maltese Terrier for *The American Book of the Dog.* This popular compendium on "the origin, development...training, points of judging, diseases, and kennel management of all breeds," was a forebear of *The Complete Dog Book* published by AKC 40 years later.

To those who knew her, Whitney was the consummate professional. In 1900, the *Times* described her "methodical and businesslike" judging style. "Dogs," they said, "seem to take to her as naturally as she takes to them and behaved themselves with the utmost propriety while she looked them over." Sometimes she "clucked at them with a queer little noise

made by pressing her lips together and drawing in her breath." Judge's book in hand, she eyed the dogs critically, asked a question or two of an attendant and put the dogs through their paces.

Then, her mind made up, her steward, who in 1900 was WKC member Walker Breese Smith, "would drop the monocle from his right eye and look in her book to help her find the number, and she would smile as though he had relieved her every trouble in this life."

The *Times* described even what she wore. "Her dress was of dark blue wool, the skirt of walking length, being plaited from the waist down to the hem in wide plaits. The jacket was of the same press could not have been kinder. The show managers were "deserving of great praise." The Bench Show Committee functioned "most ably." The Superintendent "covered himself with glory." Veterinarian H. Clay Glover "discharged his duties efficiently." Spratt's Patent benched and fed the show and "did it well." The judging was completed "expeditiously," and the catalog, with the awards printed in it for all but two classes, was available by 10 AM on the second day, a job that was done with "thoughtful care."

Then, not three months later, on May 13, the Board of Governors adopted a resolution that on payment of $10,000 in cash, the president, J. Otto Donner, be authorized to sell to "certain gentlemen" the goodwill of the Westminster Kennel Club as to the giving of dog shows. As part of the agreement, Westminster would not give any dog shows during the life of the organization that purchased the goodwill from them, and the group that purchased the goodwill would not use Westminster's name in connection with the shows it held.

President Donner moved ahead. On June 10, 1889, a special meeting of the governors was held at the office of Elliot Smith at 59 Wall Street. Smith, counsel for the club, had discovered a problem.

At the time of incorporation, the board had had nine members. Since then, it had twice been increased in size, first, from nine to 15 and then, from 15 to 17. The problem was that the changes had been made by majority vote of the members present at the annual meeting, rather than, as the bylaws required, by majority vote of the entire membership. In short,

1884.

Smith said, the current board of 17 governors had no legal standing. He concluded that under the circumstances, it would be "unsafe" for the board to sell the rights or for the purchasers to pay for them.

The problem was to make the 17-member board legal. What had been

"passed" by a majority of the two dozen or so members at the annual meetings, needed a majority vote of the total membership, which now stood at 114.

Donner called a special membership meeting to be held at Delmonico's at 26th Street and 5th Avenue on June 21. That meeting was adjourned for lack of a quorum. A call for a reconvened session at the Secretary's office at 44 Broadway on July 1 was quickly issued. The purpose of the meeting was explained again, and members who could not attend were urged to send in proxies. This time, they had a quorum. Between those present and the proxies that had been sent in, 62 votes were cast, all in favor of the enlarged board. Only 58 votes were needed. The problem now was that by the time all this had been accomplished, the offer to purchase the goodwill of the club in the matter of the holding of dog shows had been withdrawn.

Nowhere in the records is there any clue as to who "the gentlemen" were who made the offer to buy or why they withdrew their proposition. Nowhere in the club's minutes are these questions answered. All that is clear is that the offer was not repeated, or, if it was, that the board never again gave such an idea serious consideration.

Above: Charles Delmonico, WKC member from 1885–1901 —*WKC*

Left: Delmonico's restaurant, Fifth Avenue and 26th St. Many of the club's meetings were held here —*Collection of the New York Historical Society, ca. 1888, by an unidentified photographer, Negative No. 47501*

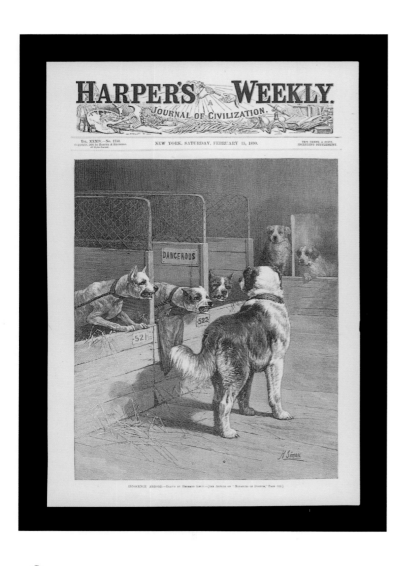

Harper's Weekly,
Feb. 15, 1890
—WKC

developed. His coat was corded, and, according to the *Times*, he had won a first prize at every American show in which he was exhibited.

Styx had had a checkered career before immigrating. In Brussels in 1885, according to The *American Kennel Register*, he had been shown unclipped, his coat matted and rusty, and was ignominiously turned out of the ring. In England, under a new owner who had done some hard work on the dog's coat, he took first in the Foreign Class, an award that was then disallowed under a rule forbidding Poodles to be shown as foreign dogs. He then took a second and three firsts in a row, at which point Sanford brought him to America.

Thomas H. Terry

Thomas H. Terry became chairman in 1890 and served for six shows. Having joined Westminster in 1883, he became a governor in 1886 and secretary and delegate to AKC in 1889. That same year, he joined the AKC board of directors. He was active in the dog world until 1895, when he stepped down from all of his elected positions.

1890

February 11-14
American Institute Fair Building
1,436 Dogs
James Mortimer, Superintendent
Thomas H. Terry, Chairman

Innocence Abroad

To go with the cover picture of this year's Westminster issue, *Harper's Weekly* wrote a fantasy. It was about a fine young St. Bernard "just in that happy period which the lady judge, Miss Whitney, so aptly termed 'neither hay nor grass.'" It was the Saint's first show, and after the visitors had all gone home, he toured the premises. Westminster was being held at the "Rink" for one last time. The old Garden had been leveled to the ground, and the new one was not yet ready.

The Saint saw hunting dogs, who scarcely noticed him, "dudes," by which

he meant Poodles, Pugs, who were cordial, Toy Spaniels, who would not rise from their comfortable beds to welcome him. He saw Bulldogs, who opened one eye and settled down again to calm repose. His last stop was in front of a trio of large, combative terriers. (The benching numbers have been changed. In real life, numbers 521 and 522 identified English Setter Puppies.) At the moment captured by the artist, the Saint had paused. But he quickly moved on. He liked none of what he had seen. He was content to be "a big, innocent, docile, ornamental St. Bernard and thanked goodness he was not as other dogs were."

Styx

Surely, one of the "dudes" that "Innocence Abroad" would have met on his tour of the Rink (see above) was Styx, a $3,000 dog that won $25 as Best Poodle in Show. Owned by William C. Sanford of Amsterdam, N.Y., Styx was seen as a beautiful specimen, large and splendidly

Thomas H. Terry,
ca. 1894—*WKC*

Styx, by F. H. Stoll (American 19th century)—AKC Art Collection

Terry owned Hempstead Farm, which consisted of 700 acres in Meadowbrook, Long Island. It was made up of 12 farms which had been combined into 3 establishments, the "Home Farm," for horses, cattle, goats, etc., the "East Farm" for poultry and game, and the "West Farm," where the kennels were located.

Terry's breeds included Pointers, Collies, Fox Terriers, Irish Terriers, Skye Terriers, Sheep Dogs, Bulldogs, Dachshunds, Retrievers, Russian Wolfhounds, Beagles and Spaniels. The farm was bounded on the north by the Hempstead Plains, some two or three thousand acres, which made a perfect exercising ground for dogs and horses alike.

In addition to breeding and showing his own dogs, Terry offered boarding, training and handling services to the general public. In 1893, James Mortimer became his kennel manager, having just left the comparable position at the Westminster Kennel Club in Babylon.

Shortly after Westminster's 1894 show, Terry's "Hempstead Farm Company"

held a livestock and dog show at Madison Square Garden. The dog portion of the event consisted of specialty shows of the St. Bernard Club of America, Collie Club of America, American Fox Terrier Club, American Spaniel Club and Bulldog Club of America.

The following year, when Terry dropped out of the dog world, Westminster acquired from him the Pointer, Sanford Druid. Bred by E. C. Norrish, Druid was whelped in April 1891 by Exon Don out of Sanford Quince. Under Hempstead Farm ownership, he established a very respectable show and field record. By 1898, he headed Westminster's list of Pointer stud dogs.

1891

February 24-27
Madison Square Garden II
1,375 Dogs
James Mortimer, Superintendent
Thomas H. Terry, Chairman

It was a summer garden, if there can be a garden without flowers, and why not? —The Easy Chair, Harper's Monthly Magazine, 1890

Madison Square Garden II

Stanford White's new Garden was ready for this year's dog show. The building was of cream-colored brick and white terracotta, in the style of the Renaissance. The main entrance was on Madison Avenue. South of the entrance, overlooking Madison Square, was a restaurant double the size of any other fashionable eating place in town. On the Madison Avenue end of the roof was a roof-garden cabaret. On the 26th Street side rose a 300-foot tower, which made Madison Square Garden the second-tallest building in the city. The tower was topped with a 13-foot bronze sculpture of Diana the Huntress by Augustus St. Gaudens. Diana stood on ball bearings, so that she always faced into the wind.

Diana was "the most enduring and controversial attraction of Stanford

Right:
Madison Square
Garden II, on a
postcard of the
day— *WKC*

Far Right: Atop
New York's
second tallest
building, Diana
by Augustus
Saint-Gaudens
(American,
born Ireland,
1848–1907),
copper sheet—
*Philadelphia
Museum of Art,
gift of New York
Life Insurance Co.*

Madison Square Garden, New York

White's Garden," wrote Joseph Durso in *Madison Square Garden,* his 1979 celebration of the Garden's centennial. He said that "her dazzling state of undress" provoked *The Philadelphia Times* to deplore "the depraved artistic taste of New York"—adding that today, the sculpture stands at the head of the grand staircase in the Philadelphia Museum of Art.

Inside the building, the amphitheater occupied two-thirds of the block between Madison and Fourth Avenues. This is where the dog shows would be held. It seated 9,000 people and would easily hold 14,000. A large stage stretched across the Fourth Avenue end.

At the opposite end, there was a wall of boxes, which the *Times*, in its report of the opening celebration, likened to "the front of a gigantic doll's house filled with little rooms draped with red curtains and containing small animated dolls in evening dress."

Along the sides of the auditorium, there were three tiers of boxes. There were windows opening onto the side streets and a sliding skylight that covered nearly half of the roof. It worked by machinery and when opened insured perfect ventilation. It was a spectacular venue, and it brought the dog show back to the right neighborhood. *The Illustrated American* said the location alone assured "pecuniary" success.

There were complaints about space. In earlier sites, there had been room to bench the entire entry on one floor. But if the old Garden and the new had essentially the same "footprint," a good portion of the new structure was set apart for a theater and the restaurant. The capacity of the main arena was not what it had been "by a very great deal." At the first show, many of the sporting dogs were relegated to the basement.

In later years, other ways were worked

out to deal with the problem, such as expanding into the theater or building temporary platforms over the arena seats. *The American Field* said that what the Garden had lost in space, it gained in comfort, as it was now free of the chilling drafts of cold air for which it had been noted. In 1900, Theodore Marples, founder of *Our Dogs,* the English dog paper, judged at the Garden and, reporting back to his constituents, said that as a dog show site, it "has not its equal in England. It is so spacious, lofty, well lighted and ventilated, and so centrally situated, and, in addition, is a handsome structure."

With the exception of 1912-14 and 1920, Westminster stayed put through 1925 for a total of 31 events. In commenting on the final show there, an editorial in the *Times* began as follows: "Diana, poised above the Garden tower, is listening for the last time to the cheerful chorus of dogs of all degrees."

Arthur Frederick Jones, a new man at the *Gazette*, phrased it in a style that was to become his hallmark:

"Rising in wordless ecstasy, the Voice of Dog has echoed for the last time throughout the labyrinthine fastness of Madison Square Garden in New York... The historic Garden is shortly to be razed and in its place there is to grow a modern office building."

Sir Bedivere

Cover dog on the dog show issue of *The Illustrated American* (see page 58) was the St. Bernard, Sir Bedivere, owned by the Wyoming Kennels of E. B. Sears, Melrose, Mass.

The paper said he cost $6,500 and was supposedly the best Saint that had ever been seen. The *Times* put the price at $25,000, adding that he had come over on the steamer with Sarah Bernhardt. In any case, there were 175 Saints entered, and Sir Bedivere was the one most spectators wanted to see.

He was as heavy as an alderman, said the *Times*, weighing 220 pounds, and he was "handsomer than the kind Tammany furnishes." He was almost 8 feet long from nose to tip of tail, and 34½ inches high. He had "a leonine head of tawny hair, large, expressive eyes, and a gentle disposition. He was accorded the honor and dignity of a double cage, artistically decorated."

Anna Whitney, who judged the breed, awarded him the blue ribbon in Open Dogs, rough-coated.

1892

February 23-26
Madison Square Garden II
1,163 Dogs
James Mortimer, Superintendent
Thomas H. Terry, Chairman

The dogs...would give away all the honors they have earned for a good scamper across Madison Square Park.—The New York Times, February. 25, 1892

Entry Fees

The news this year was the entry fee. It had stood at $2 for the first seven shows, after which it was upped to $3. Now it would be $5, which the *Times* said was in line with efforts of Superintendent Mortimer to discourage the entry of other than first-rate dogs.

The fee included a crew of attendants to feed and exercise the dogs. In the earliest days, it had also paid for handling dogs in the ring, but by now that service had been dropped.

The $5 fee would stand for over 50 years. Then in 1947, it would go to $6 and would slowly climb until it reached $50 in 2000.

In terms of the purchasing value of a dollar, what cost $1 in the 1870s cost a little over $17 in 1997 (the latest figures available from the New York Public Library at the time of writing). That increase corresponds roughly with the increase from the original entry fee of $2 in the 1870s to the $35 entry fee of 1997. In short, the entry fee kept up with but did not exceed the rate of inflation.

1893

February 21-24
Madison Square Garden II
1,319 Dogs
James Mortimer, Superintendent
Thomas H. Terry, Chairman

With the tolling of church bells and the donning of penitential vesture, Lent comes to warn society that balls must cease and that belles and beaux must turn their thoughts to other things than self. So, with becoming gravity, in Worth costumes and Paris bonnets, the ballroom beauties take their way to the Madison Square Garden, New York City, to criticize their neighbors' taste in dogs. ~The Illustrated American, March 4, 1893

Financial Giants in the Garden

There was a new exhibitor in Collies this year. It was J. Pierpont Morgan, financial titan and builder of the great Morgan Library in New York City. He appeared at the Garden with 10 dogs. He won three blue ribbons and three special prizes, including a silver cup for best Collie. It was an auspicious New York debut.

In time, Morgan became a familiar sight at the Garden, each year winning a larger number of first places and special prizes. In 1896, he brought 13 "pets" down from Cragston, his estate on the Hudson below West Point. The *Times* described a man much like exhibitors of 100 years later.

"He stood there," said the paper, "a rather impatient man of enormous affairs, much

COPYRIGHTED 1895, BY MRS. JNO. M. TRACY.

DIANA OF TO-DAY

Artist J. M. Tracy tries his hand at Diana
— WKC Show Catalog, 1895, WKC

THE ILLUSTRATED AMERICAN

SIR BEDIVERE.

Vol. VI.   FEB. 28th, 1891.   No. 54.

CONTENTS :

COPYRIGHT, 1891, BY ILLUSTRATED AMERICAN PUBLISHING CO., BIBLE HOUSE, NEW YORK, AND 142 DEARBORN STREET, CHICAGO. ENTERED AT THE POST OFFICE AS SECOND-CLASS MATTER.

more exercised over the possible action of the English judge with the red necktie and the doggy air than he usually appears when vast financial interests are being manipulated by him. He patted his champion dog, 'Sefton Hero,' on the head (and) talked to him as he would talk to a child."

Sefton Hero, who slept under Morgan's bed—and would be mentioned by name in Morgan's obituary—won first in his class that year. Overall, Morgan took seven blue ribbons and four special prizes.

Special prize ribbon, 1893 —WKC

In 1897, Morgan took first in every class. In 1898, he stayed home but the next year appeared again, winning 11 firsts in 11 classes and nine out of 12 special prizes. Spectators flocked to what was called "Collie Row" at the Garden to see his dogs.

In 1900, the financier was "bitterly disappointed." One of his old champions took a blue ribbon, but beyond that, Morgan went home with no top awards at all. For three years, he stayed away.

Then he redeemed himself. In 1904, he took eight firsts. He again had the best Collie. But this year, the paper made mention of a new element at the show. A first-time exhibitor there had taken a special Collie prize. The news came in one short sentence: "Samuel Untermyer won the cup for the best brace of American-Bred Collies." The telling word was "Untermyer." Samuel Untermyer had entered two dogs. Though Morgan did not know it yet, the Collie world would never be the same for him.

Morgan held his own that year, but Untermyer was importing good dogs from England. He was breeding good dogs at home. At each subsequent event, he upped his entry and the number of wins he took. In 1907, he appeared with 19 dogs from his Greystone Kennels. The duel for supremacy between him and Morgan promised to be a leading feature of the show that year. In the end, a headline read:

COLLIES FROM GREYSTONE KENNELS ANNIHILATE J.P. MORGAN'S ENTRIES

One of the 13 Collies that Morgan had shown was a blue merle named "Cragston Blue Prince." Blue Prince brought Morgan his only blue ribbon that year. Untermyer won 10. It was a stunning reverse. We are told that Morgan's dogs "looked ragged, out of coat." It was said that one of his $2,500 bitches, which some termed "the best Collie living," was barely looked at because of her "horrid condition." *The American Field* reported great sympathy for Morgan. He had spent "money enough" on his kennel, and it had "gone all to pieces."

"We hope to see Mr. Morgan come back into the ring again with a good, strong string," said the paper. "We do not think he will stop at one defeat."

But stop he did. He had been defeated before and come back, but this time, it was different. He would continue as a Vice-President of the Collie Club of America until he died. He became interested in Pekingese, and in 1913, Westminster's prize list included a gorgeous 24-inch silver challenge cup that Morgan offered for best Pekingese. It was to be won five times by the same

J.P.M. & Hero Oct. 96

J.P.M. & Hero

Above: The only known photographs of J. P. Morgan with Sefton Hero, who slept under his bed and was mentioned by name in his obituary—*Archives of the Pierpont Morgan Library, New York*

exhibitor for permanent possession. In the year 2000, it was still in competition, though now it was offered at shows of the Pekingese Club of America instead of at Westminster. But Morgan never showed a dog at Westminster again.

It is a familiar story in the dog world, though it is not often played with such high-flown protagonists. Who was Samuel Untermyer? What brought him into dogs and specifically into Collies? He was an attorney, 20 years Morgan's junior. He handled cases that covered almost every phase of corporate, civil, criminal and international law. He would come to be known as the first lawyer to charge a million-dollar fee.

He liked money and all that went with it. In 1900, he acquired Greystone, the former country home of Samuel J. Tilden on the Hudson above Yonkers. With its gardens and greenhouses, he made a showplace of the 171-acre estate. He also had a penthouse in Atlantic City and in time would build a luxurious summer place called "The Willows" in Palm Springs, Calif.

For all that, he was an avid legal investigator. His retention as counsel by large corporations did not prevent him from attacking what he saw as corporate abuse. In a case involving Standard Oil, he called John D. Rockefeller as witness and subjected him to two hours of "hard interrogation." In 1912, he was counsel to a committee of the House of Representatives, which was looking into the so-called "Money Trust." The Money Trust Hearings were meant to find whether the wealth of the country—and control of that wealth—were concentrated in the hands of too few people. Morgan was a prime witness. He testified for an hour one afternoon and then "held the stand for nearly five hours the following day under the questioning of Samuel Untermyer."

If Untermyer liked money, he had a horror of the means by which men like Morgan seemed to acquire it. However, to pursue Morgan through legal proceedings was one thing. To go after him by buying Collies and breeding them and taking his duel with Morgan into the show rings of Westminster was quite different. It exposed an odd mix of worshipful adulation and downright ill will.

Oddly, 1907 was a year of triumph for Morgan in the country at large. As set forth in the *Times*, he reached the pinnacle of his power in handling the panic of 1907. He was 70 years old. He had withdrawn somewhat from business matters, yet by general consent, was the man that lesser giants turned to, to save the country from financial disaster. Men like John D. Rockefeller and E. H. Harriman, not to mention the presidents of banks and trust companies, put themselves and their

resources at his disposal. The Secretary of the Treasury, who came up from Washington with Federal money to deposit where it would do the most good, sought Morgan's advice and followed it to the letter. There even came a point when President Theodore Roosevelt agreed not to object to what he would normally have considered a completely unacceptable violation of antitrust law. When the panic ended, Morgan, at least briefly, was a national hero.

And Untermyer was also a hero of sorts. While Morgan was staving off disaster in Wall Street, Untermyer was holding off a crisis at the American Kennel Club. AKC was the governing body for dogs in the United States; it was an association of dog clubs. According to *The American Field*, in 1906, in the process of incorporating the organization, AKC's leadership, under the

First Prize Ribbon, 1893 —WKC

presidency of August Belmont, had disenfranchised its member clubs. Management of AKC's affairs had been taken away from them and put into the hands of a board of 30 businessmen. It didn't matter whether they knew anything about dogs or not.

In 1907, a group of the disenfranchised dog men met at the Ashland House Hotel and made plans to sue AKC. They demanded restoration of their right to vote. The suit never came to pass, but counsel for the so-called Ashland House

Committee was none other than Samuel Untermyer. His preparations for legal action against AKC were highly visible. They played a decisive role in the negotiations. In the end, August Belmont was elected to stay on as AKC President but not before the voting power of the member clubs was totally restored.

1894

February 20-23
Madison Square Garden II
1,344 Dogs
James Mortimer, Superintendent
Thomas H. Terry, Chairman

About one hundred shows were held last year. Noted dogs like Sir Bedivere and Beaufort's Black Prince spend as much time on the road as travelling theatrical companies.—The World, February 24, 1894

Valuable and Distinguished Exhibits

Some of the dogs sketched in *The World* after this year's Garden are identified:

Sir Bedivere, a St. Bernard (center), now owned by the Argyle Kennels, Little Rock, Ark., took 1st in his class and then won three specials, including one for Best St. Bernard. *The American Field* said he was "fully able to still retain his high title as the king of his division." He was familiar and popular. However, the paper said of the entry as a whole—there were 173 Saints—that except for 25 or 30, they were "an extremely seedy lot." *The New York Times* agreed, saying that "more than half of them" should have been in the Miscellaneous class.

Ch. Victor, a Bloodhound (left, next to bottom), owned by J. L. Winchell, took 1st in the Challenge Dogs Class. *The American Field* said he won "comfortably." Earlier, *The Illustrated American* had described Victor thus: "Tawny in color; weight, one hundred pounds; height at shoulder, twenty-nine inches. His head is twelve inches long and his ears have the extraordinary spread of twenty-nine inches."

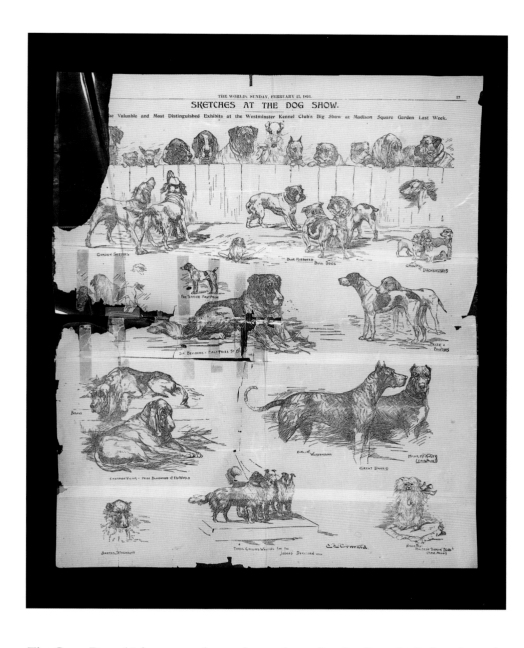

The World,
February 25,
1894—WKC

trophies, including —three times— a $100 silver cup offered by *The American Field* for best American-bred Bulldog. The last of these three wins came this year. He took second in the Open class to a recent import named King Orry, whose picture we see in the accompanying photographs from *Harper's Weekly* (see page 62). King Orry picked a fight with him later at the show, and, according to the *Times,* Handsome Dan "bit the Englishman's nose." But the defeat by an import left the way open for Dan to win as best American-bred Bulldog, which he did.

Next year, however, Dan would be totally defeated. The *Times* published the details. The usual line about Bulldogs then was that ugliness was their glory: "The more homely the brute, the more certain he was to be the center of attraction." Dan lost, thanks to two dogs even uglier than he. They were entered through the machinations of "the Athletic Advisory Committee of Harvard University, headed by Yale's particular enemy, Prof. Ames." No one else, said the paper, could have found such competition for Dan, two dogs that were so homely "it actually makes a man's face ache to look at them."

The Great Dane (right, next to bottom) *Earl of Wurtemburg* won 1st in the Open Class, Dogs. *The American Field* called him "a nice headed dog, very flat in ribs and somewhat deficient in action and temperament." *Major McKinley* of the South Bend Kennels took 1st in the Challenge Class, Dogs. The paper said he had "very much improved in hindquarters and action since last year, but gone slightly coarse in head and more throaty."

Nellie Bly owned the Maltese Terrier, *Duke.* Duke divided 1st place in the Miscellaneous class with two other dogs, Dewr, a Welsh Terrier from the Col. A. B. Hilton's Woodlawn Park Kennels, Saratoga Springs, N.Y., and Clydesdale Pride, a Clydesdale Terrier (an early name for Skyes) belonging to E. T. Slocum.

Nellie Bly was a famous American

journalist. In 1890, she had made a trip around the world in 72 days, 6 hours, and 11 minutes, racing against the record of Phineas Fogg in Jules Verne's *Around the World in Eighty Days.*

1895

February 19-22
Madison Square Garden II
1,406 Dogs
James Mortimer, Superintendent
Thomas H. Terry, Chairman

Handsome Dan

Handsome Dan, Yale's first Bulldog mascot, came to Westminster six years running, starting in 1891. He won many

Handsome Dan—
Manuscripts and
archives, Yale
University Library

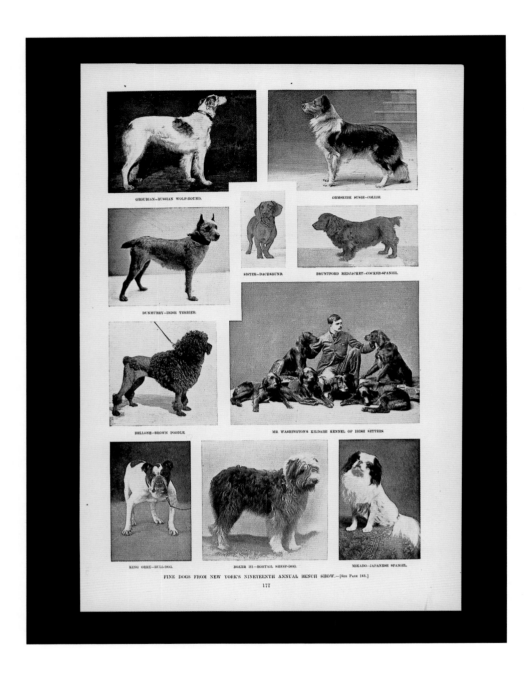

FINE DOGS FROM NEW YORK'S NINETEENTH ANNUAL BENCH SHOW.—[SEE PAGE 183.]

177

1896

Feb. 19-22
Madison Square Garden II
1,409 Dogs
James Mortimer, Superintendent
Elliot Smith, Chairman

Among fanciers of poultry years ago there was a sort of hysteria that affected the breeders known as the poultry fever. It was never so infectious, never so rabid in its workings, as the fever that infects the man who is a breeder of fine dogs. ~The New York Times, February 20, 1896

Elliot Smith

Elliot Smith was this year's Show Chairman. He served as a governor of Westminster in 1880-87 and again from 1892 until 1897. A lawyer and counsel for the club, it was he and Major James M. Taylor who issued the call for a meeting in Philadelphia in 1884 that resulted in the founding of AKC. On the original slate of officers, Taylor was president, and Smith first vice-president.

At AKC's second annual meeting, both men were re-elected, but after a stormy seven months of his second term, Taylor resigned the presidency, and Smith was elected in his place. He served out what would have been the balance of Taylor's

Handsome Dan, whelped November 6, 1887, by Caliban out of Peg, was owned by Yale student Andrew B. Graves. In 1896, Graves took him to England, where they settled permanently.

Some Winners

The dogs shown in *Harper's Weekly* that are identifiable as entries by the names given are, by name, breed, owner and award, if any:

Boxer III, Old English Sheepdog (bottom center), Woodlawn Park Kennels, Saratoga Springs, N.Y., 1st. He "has a rare good square head," said *The American Field,* "and when in full coat will take a lot of beating."

Dunmurry, Irish Terrier (second from top, left), Walter J. Comstock, Providence, R.I., 1st. "She could not be denied," said *The American Field.*

King Orry, Bulldog (bottom, left), Woodlawn Park Kennels, 1st. He was "the Englishman" who picked a fight with Handsome Dan and was bitten for his pains. See "Handsome Dan" above.

Mikado, Japanese Spaniel (bottom, right), Mrs. F. Senn, NYC, Open, 2nd

Ormskirk Susie, Collie (top, right), Woodlawn Park Kennels, 4th. "She is not flat enough in skull," commented *The American Field,* "but she is a very sweet bitch, with a charming expression and good coat."

Elliot Smith, AKC's second president
—*AKC*

term and was then re-elected, serving a full term. In 1894 at a 10th anniversary celebration of the American Kennel Club, a toast was offered to the governing body's former officers. Smith made a gracious response to the toast and, as related in the *AKC Source Book*, gave some insight into the period of his presidency. He said in part: "Everything was novel, we had no example to follow nor avoid. Everyone had a different view to be discussed."

The year after his presidency ended, Smith became delegate to AKC for the Pacific Kennel Club. He represented WKC in 1896-97 and was then delegate of the Oakland Kennel Club for a brief period.

Little is known of Smith's personal life. Records show he was a native of Brooklyn. After joining Westminster in 1880, he quickly became known as one of the club's "crack shots." In the 1880s, he entered up to a half dozen Pointers in the shows at the Garden. In 1887, Mrs. Elliot Smith showed a sable and white Collie there.

Freedom of the Press

The papers were hardly unanimous in assessing this year's 81 Bostons.

The American Field said they were "a capital exhibit...Three...were purchased...for a thousand dollars each, and there is no telling where the craze for this 'cute little dog' will end if the Boston Terrier Club continues its hard work in its interest."

Forest & Stream said they "were all in excellent condition. A number were uncropped....There was shown a great diversity of size and texture of ear. A noticeable gain in breeding to types was apparent. The judge was not over generous in the matter of prizes, and the commended cards were noticeably absent."

The New York Times saw it this way: "There was well nigh a riot among the breeders and exhibitors of Boston Terriers this year because of the decisions of the judge, Mr. W. C. Hook, and if he knows what is best for him, he will leave town on the first train.... He is from Boston and is therefore supposed to know all about the Boston

Terrier....(He) declared that the dogs... were far from...up to the...standard. The incipient riot occurred when...he had declared a number of prizes would be withheld because the animals...did not come up to his ideas as to the standard.... It was useless to point out to them that the breeding had been overdone, and that proper care to secure what are supposed to be characteristics of a type had been neglected, and that the dogs did look to be a rather commonplace lot."

The Boston Herald spoke more matter-of-factly: "The judge of Boston Terriers disappointed the owners of these dogs... by deciding that there were no dogs in the open heavy-weight dogs, open heavy-weight bitches, open light-weight dogs and open light-weight bitches that were sufficiently up to the standard to take first prize. The blue ribbon was, therefore, withheld in those classes."

Opposite page: *Harper's Weekly, February 23, 1895—WKC*

Right: The first of a series of six special catalog covers. That of 1900, except for date and background color, was identical to this one—WKC

1897

February 22-25
Madison Square Garden II
1,438 Dogs
James Mortimer, Superintendent
George deForest Grant, Chairman

Parisian Breed

This year's catalog cover was the first with a dog other than Sensation on it. In his place, we have a stylishly dressed lady with a French Bulldog in her arms. It is a gallant bow to an up-and-coming non-sporting breed.

Last year, there were just seven Frenchies, but they were all handled in the ring by fashionable ladies, including Mrs. P. Lorillard Ronalds, Jr., Mrs. P. Cooper Hewitt, Mrs. J. L. Kernochan, Mrs. J. H. Smith-Hadden, Mrs. Frederick Neilson

64

Left and Opposite:
1898, 1899 and 1902 catalog covers
— *WKC*

Far Right: *Colliers Weekly*, March 11, 1899 — *WKC*

and Mrs. Walter W. Watrous. The ringside was crowded, said the *Times*, while this decidedly unusual picture unfolded. The winner was Mrs. Neilson with Bellechose (pedigree unknown).

This year, there were 19 of the breed entered, a very respectable number. But the cover also commemorates a serious dispute. The judge was George Raper, an Englishman who favored the "rose" ear over the "bat" ear. Reaction to his decisions was so intense that before the show ended, a group of fanciers met in the Garden to form the French Bulldog Club of America. The new club's first item of business was to make the "bat" ear an absolute must. Over a century later, the club still exists, as does a disqualification in the breed standard for "other than bat ears."

Raper would do the breed again next year with a slightly smaller entry, but in 1899, with John R. Buchan of New York officiating, the entry would be 49. The breed was here to stay. In 1913, the entry would peak at an even 100.

This catalog cover was the first of a series of six on which there was a picture of a stylish lady accompanied by one or more dogs. A Frenchie appears on five of those six covers, and a Pointer just twice.

1898

February 21-24
Madison Square Garden II
1,330 Dogs
James Mortimer, Superintendent
Benjamin R. Kittredge, Chairman

Corrected and Signed

On the catalog cover seen here, note the handwriting across the upper left corner. It reads: "Corrected Copy, G. W. Gall, for Secretary." Superintendent Mortimer's official title now was "Superintendent and Secretary of the Show." Gall was Mortimer's assistant and, having marked

the awards in the catalog, signed it for him. Gall would take over as Superintendent of the show in 1916.

1899

February 21-24
Madison Square Garden II
1,530 Dogs
James Mortimer, Superintendent
Winthrop Rutherfurd, Chairman

The Twenty-Third Annual

The photographs in *Colliers Weekly* tell us more about the benching—and the bed of straw that would be essential for so many years—than they do about the dogs. Of their so-called "Prize-Winners," none won first, and only two Bull Terriers took placements. Frank F. Dole's Edgwood Flyer II, captured a 2nd and M. T. Finn's Tavern Duke, a 3rd.

J. P. Morgan's Collies, which won 11 firsts in 11 classes and 9 out of 12 Specials, are just off camera.

Dogs that are identifiable, left to right, top to bottom, are as follows:

Bull Terriers:
Edgwood Flyer II, Frank F. Dole, NYC, 2nd

Tavern Duke, M. T. Finn, 3rd

Billy Fairplay, C. Albert Stevens, Roslyn, L. I., VHC (Very High Commendation)

Royal Prince, James Parker, NYC, VHC

Rough Collies:
Don of Maple Grove, R. G. Steacy, Brookville, Ontario, Commended

Emerald of Maple Grove, R. G. Steacy, Brookville, Ontario, Unplaced

Arcturus, George Hall, Bridgeport, Conn., Unplaced

Bulldogs:
Tommy Atkins, George M. Valentine, Perth Amboy, N.J., VHC Reserve

Beauman's Pagan, W. Beales, Boston, Mass., Unplaced

Charondas, E. K. Austin, NYC, Unplaced

1900

February 20-23
Madison Square Garden II
1,516 Dogs
James Mortimer, Superintendent
Shepherd K. DeForest, Chairman

*The "almighty dollar" has played sad havoc in the ranks of English dogdom in late years.
—Theodore Marples, The American Field, March 10, 1900*

Diplomas

For several years certificates, known as "diplomas," were issued to Westminster exhibitors as an official record of either a placement or a commendation. Commendations were awarded at three levels, Commendation, High Commendation and Very High Commendation (C, HC and VHC).

On page 66 we see a 1900 diploma for King Quality owned by Edwin Fiske of Mt. Vernon, N.Y. King Quality earned a VHC.

1901

February 19-22
Madison Square Garden II
1,549 Dogs
James Mortimer, Superintendent
William Rauch, Chairman

Left: WKC prize diploma—*WKC*

Opposite: 1901 catalog cover —*WKC*

*At the Fourth Avenue end of the Garden the Bulldog Club of America had its exhibit, most artistically arranged. The title of the club, in letters formed by electric lights, shone forth resplendently and could be seen distinctly from any place in the amphitheater.
—Forest and Stream, March 2, 1901*

Twentieth Century Day

As 1999 drew to a close, there was a lot of arguing about whether the 21st century would begin on January 1, 2000, or January 1, 2001. A hundred years earlier, there was no such controversy, within the walls of the Westminster Kennel Club at least, as to when the 20th Century would start. In the visitors' book at Babylon, an unknown hand recorded the club's position very clearly. Twentieth Century Day was January 1, 1901 (see page 68).

Members who brought guests to Babylon that day were George B. Magown, Eben Wright, H. C. Mortimer, George Schley McAlpin, Walton Ferguson, Jr., and Harry K. Knapp.

William Rauch

William Rauch, 38, became Westminster's Chairman this year and served for more than a quarter of a century (see page 68 for picture). Perhaps the most visible of his accomplishments concerned the show of 1907, when he convinced his fellow Governors that a trophy should be offered for Best in Show. The club's board had held out against such an offering for nearly three decades. The award, as noted by Arthur Frederick Jones in the *Gazette* in 1965, was made for the first time in the U.S. at the Franklin Bench Show of Dogs, Franklin, Pa., in 1881. By 1906, nearly a third of the 57 all-breed shows offered the prize. Rauch held that it would be a mistake not to accede to the clear wishes of exhibitors. While initially the win was not even recorded by AKC as part of the official results, it clearly changed the nature of dog shows in the U.S. It marked the beginning of a new era for Westminster.

Born in England in 1863, Rauch came to

this country at the age of 22. A famous shot, he was essentially a gundog man rather than a dog show exhibitor. He took great pleasure shooting over Pointers and Setters and to Spaniels. He was said never to have missed the field trials held by the English Springer Spaniel Field Trial Association on Fishers Island, New York.

However, he was a devotee of all sports pertaining to dogs. He joined Westminster in 1900 and within a year was elected a governor, a position he held until his death in 1930. *Popular Dogs* said that as President of the Club from 1923 until he died, he had seen the New York show become "the best, brightest and most attractive of all canine exhibitions."

Rauch was also Westminster's delegate to AKC in 1907-25, during which time he served on the AKC Board of Directors. In a resolution adopted at the time of his death, his fellow Westminster governors said that Rauch stood for "everything that was best and highest in the advancement of dogs and dog shows."

Officially Marked Jas Mortimer Supt

WESTMINSTER KENNEL CLUB

25th ANNUAL

DOG SHOW 1901

Feb. 19-20-21-22.

MADISON SQUARE GARDEN

Aspell

1902

February 19-22
Madison Square Garden II
1,678 Dogs
James Mortimer, Superintendent
William Rauch, Chairman

Beauty's Tribute

We might call the tribute of *Leslie's Weekly* to the show an unfair come-on. For all the artistry of the cover (see opposite page), inside there is not one word about the event or about dogs.

Rabies

There was a real jar on the opening day when the officials refused to admit the Irish Terriers of Mrs. James L. Kernochan. Several weeks earlier at Hempstead, Long Island, a rabid dog had attacked her terriers. She promptly had them subjected to the Pasteur treatment, and she had a certificate from the veterinarian who treated them. He said they were in no danger of developing rabies.

The show veterinarian, however, held that the treatment had not extended over a sufficiently long period, and he barred the dogs from the show. This resulted in "a warm outburst of indignation" from Mr. Kernochan, who was a

WKC member. But there was no way to overcome the decision, and the terriers, confidently thought of as prize winners, were not shown.

1903

February 11-14
Madison Square Garden II
1,650 Dogs
James Mortimer, Superintendent
William Rauch, Chairman

The Bar Sinister

It was a Westminster story, a tale told by a dog. "The best fighting Bull Terrier of my weight in Montreal," he called himself. But he had no pedigree. Sire, dam and date of birth? Unknown.

The story called "The Bar Sinister" appeared in *Scribner's Magazine* in 1903.

The author was Richard Harding Davis, newspaperman, war correspondent, novelist and dog man. His kennel name was Crossroads.

Kid, as our hero was known, was suddenly rescued from the underworld of barrooms and dogfights. He became a stable dog on a big Long Island estate. The only proviso was that he keep away from the St. Bernards. There were 40 of them, pure-bred show dogs every one.

When word got out that "the New York show" was coming, we get his dog's eye view. "Such goings on... I never did see," he says. "The kennel men rubbed 'em and scrubbed 'em. And trims their hair and curls and combs it, and some dogs they fatted and some they starved. No one talked of nothing but the Show." It was "our kennels" against "theirs." It was this champion against that one. Should this dog go into the Open or the Limit class? Couldn't this dog beat his own dad, and couldn't his little puppy sister beat them both?

Above Left:
William Ranch Chairman for 27 shows
—*WKC*

Left: Twentieth Century Day—*Visitor's Book at Babylon, WKC*

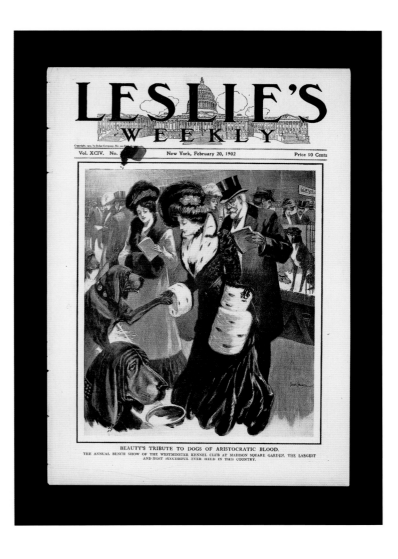

BEAUTY'S TRIBUTE TO DOGS OF ARISTOCRATIC BLOOD.
THE ANNUAL BENCH SHOW OF THE WESTMINSTER KENNEL CLUB AT MADISON SQUARE GARDEN, THE LARGEST AND MOST SUCCESSFUL EVER HELD IN THIS COUNTRY.

Left: Inside, not a word about dogs.—*Leslie's Weekly, February 20, 1902, WKC*

Far Left: Illustrations for "The Bar Sinister," 1903 —*Scribners, WKC*

"How well Kid is!" she says.—Page 319.

Nolan leans against the rails, with his head hung down. —Page 321.

For a long time he kneels in the sawdust.—Page

"I, being so far out of it," he tells us, "couldn't have felt meaner if I had been running the streets with a can tied to my tail."

Then Kid, to his astonishment, is taken to the show. His best friend, the stableman, gives him a bath and, worse, sandpapers his tail, shaves his ears and sprinkles him over with pipe clay. He is led into the judging ring. He is suddenly face to face with 33 Bull Terriers, each of them so beautiful that he wants to break his chain and run home and hide under the horse trough.

The judge is a fierce-looking man with specs on his nose and a beard. Kid tries to hide, to no avail. The judge gets a good look at him and waves him to the corner. "Take him away," he says. "Over there and keep him away." Kid's handler hangs his head as though he has been whipped.

But of course, Kid has been sent to the corner because the judge's problem is with how to place the other dogs in the class. Once he has lined them up, he calls Kid back and gives him first place. Kid is very pleased with himself.

Then he goes into the ring again, this time to compete with all of the other class winners, including the best champion. This champion catches Kid's eye. He is the handsomest Bull Terrier that Kid has ever seen, and he turns out to be his true father. And not only that. In the ring, Kid defeats his father. Kid is the better dog, says the judge.

So it is more than just the story of an underdog who is unexpectedly entered in a show and wins. In winning, he dethrones his own father who was king of the breed. He embarks on a show career. He becomes famous. He gets registered. He even finds his mother, and she moves in to share his Long Island home with him.

"And they lived happily ever after"—Davis never actually says it, but he certainly could have.

Some Winners

For 1903, *The American Field* offers a page of winners. See below left.

1. *Remlik Bonnie,* Boston Terrier, Willis Sharpe Kilmer, Binghamton, N.Y., 3rd

2. *Balmoral Prince,* Collie, Balmoral Kennels, Ottawa, Canada, 2nd

3. *Parsifal,* Dachshund, Mrs. Karl A. Keller, Wellesley, Mass., 3rd. *The American Field* said he "should have been first according to intelligent standard interpretation and accepted ideas of some of the best European judges."

4. *Oakmount Peggy,* Boston Terrier, Oakmount Kennels, 3rd

5. *Princess Alice,* Pointer, George S. Mott, Babylon, N.Y., 1st

6. *Yankee Banner,* Pointer, George S. Mott, Babylon, N.Y., 1st

7. *Prince's Boy,* Pointer, George S. Mott, Babylon, N.Y., 2nd

8. Mrs. Jack Brazier with Scottish Terriers—under her right arm, *Ch. Silverdale Queen,* Winners Bitch, and under her left arm, *Ch. The Laird,* Winners Dog

9. *Mott's Regent,* Pointer, George S. Mott, Babylon, N.Y., Field Trial Class, 3rd

10. *Alonsita Bessie,* Beagle, Alonsita Kennels, Reserve

11. *Westlake Surprise,* Pointer, R. E. Westlake, Winners Bitch

12. *Ashton Merry Scamp,* Pomeranian, Ashton Kennels, Southampton, L. I., 1st

13. *Emin Pasha,* Great Dane, with his owner, George W. Schenck, Lyons, Iowa, unplaced

14. *Darnall Kitty,* English Toy Spaniel, Nellcote Kennels, Riverdale, N.Y., Winners Bitch. *The American Field* described her as "frisking ahead of all competitors." In 1904, she would win a special at Westminster for best dog in show, any breed, exhibited by a member of the Ladies Kennel Association of America.

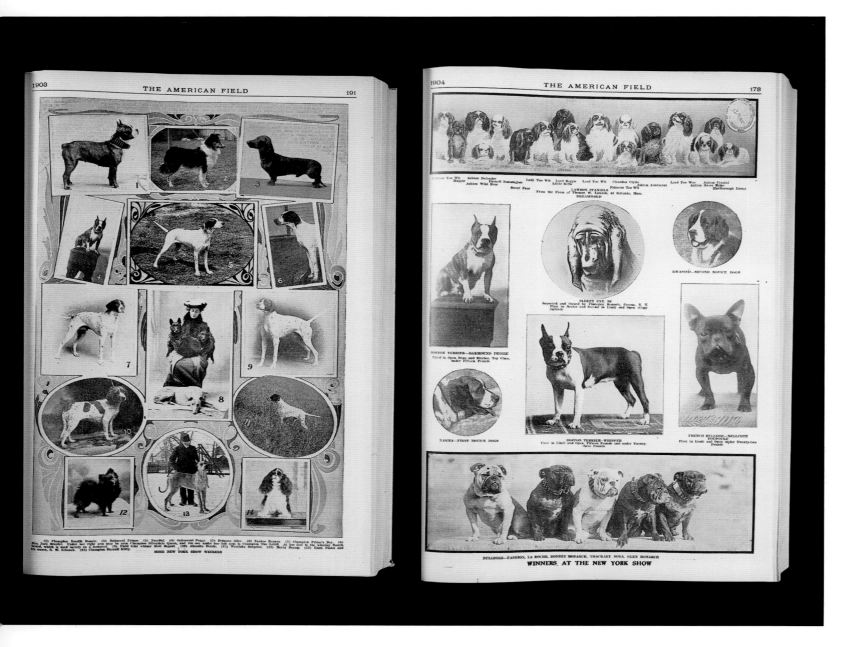

1904

February 10-13
Madison Square Garden II
1,709 Dogs
James Mortimer, Superintendent
William Rauch, Chairman

Arm Cards

A number of papers commented on an innovation this year, though other show-giving clubs had tried it. This was the wearing of arm cards bearing the catalog number of the dog each person in the ring was handling. The numbers were large and easily read from ringside. *Field and Fancy* said that because of them, people were taking much more interest than usual in the judging.

There had always been complaints from spectators if they came to a show before the judging was done and there were no catalogs available with the awards printed in them. Arm cards helped them see that the judging itself could be interesting, even exciting.

Carrying Their 200 Pounds with Ease and Pleasure

The 17 English Toy Spaniels shown on *The American Field*'s page of "winners" were owned by Dreamwold Farm of Thomas W. Lawson, Scituate, Mass. They were part of a total entry of 51. However, the flashiest winner in the breed, whose photograph appeared last year, was Darnall Kitty owned by Nellcote Kennels, Riverdale, N.Y. Kitty was best tri-color and won a special for best dog in show exhibited by a member of the Ladies Kennel Association of America. The paper called her a "peerless champion."

The five Bulldogs pictured at the bottom were also owned by Dreamwold Farm. *La Roche,* second from the left, was winner's bitch and *Thackary Soda,* second from the right, was reserve.

The French Bulldog, *Nellcote Poupoule,* won the bronze medallion, shown here, for Best Bitch in Open Classes.

The Bloodhound *Sleepy Eye* was first in Novice but second in Open Bitches.

Of the two Bostons, *Whisper* won a blue ribbon in her class, while *Oakmount Peggie,* owned by A. F. Mount, Jersey City, N.J., took third in hers.

The paper's most extensive praise was reserved for the two Saints, *Nahma* and *Kwasind.* They were littermates who won first and second respectively in Novice Dogs. Miss M. A. Roby of Ridgewood, N.J., owned them. *The American Field* called them "strikingly beautiful, massive, good all rounders, rich in color

and markings, a lesson to all exhibitors in their brilliant bloom and perfect condition, carrying their two hundred pounds with ease and pleasure."

1905

February 13-16
Madison Square Garden II
1, 752 Dogs
James Mortimer, Superintendent
William Rauch, Chairman

The Illustrated Sporting News Visits the Show

The Lincoln's Birthday holiday crowd thronged the Garden all day.

The *Illustrated Sporting News* called it the largest dog show ever held in the world.

"The previous record in the number of dogs benched," they said, "was at the last show held at the Crystal Palace in London, the dogs numbering 1,739, but this enormous show was surpassed at the Garden last week when 1,752 dogs entered the ring."

Opposite Left:
American Field,
February 21,
1903 —*courtesy*
American Field

Opposite Right:
American Field,
February 20,
1904 —*courtesy*
American Field

Above: Bronze
medallion won
by Nellcote
Poupoule for best
French Bulldog
Bitch, 1904 —
WKC, Gift of
Robert R. Marshak

Right:
The Benching
Area —*Illustrated*
Sporting News,
February 5, 1905,
WKC

THE ILLUSTRATED SPORTING NEWS.

FACING THE PHOTOGRAPHER—A KENNEL OF RIBBON-WINNING ST. BERNARDS.

The Westminster Kennel Club Show of 1905.

ful one. Never before had the oldest visitors witnessed such a sight; indeed it seemed that all fashionable and sporting Gotham and innumerable neighbors were there to see it and join in the general acclamations that greeted the representatives of the leading packs of English foxhounds on the North American continent. Round after round of applause, with now and then a holloa, met the Montreal hounds, those perfectly mannered dogs from the Dominion. It is thought that their comparative grossness went against them when compared with the higher quality

The management of the show was perfect, and the one detail that up to the present year has been omitted by the Westminster Kennel Club—that of duplicate ring numbers—was in full swing. This is a custom that it is to be hoped every show executive of this country will adopt. Both sporting and non-sporting breeds were well represented, while the very many new importations gave piquancy to the sauce of competition, and let it be added, that more than one decision of the judges was not in accordance with those made by the experts on the outside of the ring. The interna-

critical, she could have more length of coat, but it was generally conceded that she was the best looking Gordon setter bitch that has been seen here for a long time.

Much interest was taken in J. Pierpont Morgan's recently imported collies, Orms Kirk Olympian and Wishaw Clinker. The latter won, but it must be written that Olympian is a sheepdog of remarkable quality, with a somewhat better eye and expression than the winner. Mr. Pegg, the English judge of bulldogs, could not find anything to beat Ivel Doctor, the Selwonk Kennel's

Photos by Burton.

A GENERAL VIEW OF THE WESTMINSTER KENNEL CLUB SHOW.

Far Left:
The Arena—
Illustrated Sporting News, February 5, 1905, WKC

Left:
First Prize Ribbon for 1905—*WKC*

1906

February 12-15

Madison Square Garden II

1,963 Dogs

James Mortimer, Superintendent

William Rauch, Chairman

It will go down as a bad day for champions, for never were these titled dogs so rolled in the sawdust.—The American Stock Keeper, February 24, 1906

Iris

A frantic phone call from Canada one evening in 1999 informed Wilma Parker that an important piece of Cocker history was at auction on the Internet. She logged on and very quickly found herself owner of the T. L. Manson prize for best Cocker Spaniel at Westminster in 1906. The trophy, a handsome silver water pitcher, was won by parti-colored Cocker bitch, Mepal's Iris, whelped January 10, 1904, by Mepal's Shotover out of Mepal's Bella. The breeder-owner was Mepal Kennels of Hildreth K. Bloodgood, New Marlboro, Mass. A cut from *The New York Times* of 1910 shows both Iris and her sire.

Mepal Kennels was one of the most successful Cocker kennels in the country. In her lifetime, Iris won 93 prizes, more

than any other Mepal Cocker. Although Mepal Kennels never won Best in Show at Westminster, three Cockers did, in 1921, 1940-41 and 1954, and Iris was behind the latter two. She also traced back to Baby Ruth, who was behind all three top winners. Baby Ruth, a Canadian-bred purchased by Bloodgood, was the true start of his Cocker breeding. According to Francis Greer's *A Century of Spaniels,* Bloodgood's interest in the breed "reached fever pitch" when he first saw Baby Ruth at the American Spaniel Club show in 1894.

In addition to the trophy pictured here, Iris won a dozen other special prizes at the 1906 Westminster. A sampling of these will show the complexity that was the rule in the world of special prizes. Some were open to all, and some, only to

American Spaniel Club members or Spaniel Breeders' Society members. It took a concerted effort on the part of judge, steward and exhibitors alike to determine a dog's eligibility. Iris took a special for each of the following:

Best Cocker
Best Cocker other than black
Best Cocker parti-colored
Best Cocker parti-colored whelped after January 1, 1903, bred by exhibitor
Best Cocker parti-colored bitch, whelped after January 1, 1904
Best Cocker bred by exhibitor
Best Cocker bitch whelped after January 1, 1903, bred by exhibitor
The Cocker with best neck and shoulders
Best sporting Spaniel bitch

Cockers from the Mepal Kennels—*The New York Times, February 6, 1910, published by permission*

Iris was also the puppy paired with her sire who won the award for best sporting Spaniel stud dog with one or more of his get, or best Sporting Spaniel brood bitch with one or more of her produce, the get or produce to be bred by exhibitor.

1907

Women are yearly taking a more important part in the bench show world...They are breeders, owners, exhibitors, and judges, and when it comes to talking dogs, they can back the average man right off the block and will jockey for position in the ring with the best of the old-time handlers. ~The American Field, February 23, 1907

Two Landmarks

This year's premiere of the Best-in-Show award at the Garden marked the start of a new era for Westminster. The competition was offered at the insistence of Chairman William Rauch. The Fox Terrier bitch, Ch. Warren Remedy, was the winner.

The Garden itself also reached a landmark. Four months after the 1906 show, it was the site of a dramatic murder. Stanford White, the architect who had designed the Garden, was shot and killed in the cabaret on the roof of his own exquisite structure. The killer was Pittsburgh playboy Harry K. Thaw. White had seduced Thaw's wife, Evelyn Nesbit. *Vanity Fair* headlined a story about it:

Stanford White, Voluptuary and Pervert, Dies the Death of a Dog

Joseph Durso in his history of the Garden called it "a tough act to follow." He said that in the lull between Thaw's two murder trials (he was finally found innocent by reason of insanity), Warren Remedy, taking Best in Show there in 1907, was the arena's star performer.

Above Left:
Hildreth K. Bloodgood—*Field and Fancy, May 1905, AKC*

Left:
A piece of Cocker history found on the internet—*Austin/AustinImage.com*

Above Right:
Gustav Muss-Arnolt—*Courtesy American Field*

1908

Muss-Arnolt

Gustav Muss-Arnolt drew one of his distinctive pen-and-ink portraits of Warren Remedy shortly after her second triumph at Westminster. It was part of a series published in the *Gazette*. Copies could be purchased for 10 cents each.

Muss-Arnolt lived and worked in New York City and Tuckahoe, N.Y., for most of his life. Over 170 of his canine portraits and illustrations were published in the *Gazette* in the 1890s and early 1900s. While he produced many oil paintings of sporting dogs in the field, his drawings reflect a deep involvement with show dogs. He exhibited a number of Pointers at Westminster and over a period of 30 years judged there on 13 occasions, the last time in 1922 as part of a panel of three who did Best in Show.

1909

The Rutherfurds

Winthrop Rutherfurd and his brother Lewis M. got their first Fox Terrier in 1876. It had no pedigree, having allegedly been stolen in Liverpool, smuggled to the U.S., and sold to them by a seaman.

They started showing the breed at Westminster and in 1882 entered a total of 17. The next year, they used the prefix

The Rider and Driver
An Illustrated Weekly of Outdoor Sport

Vol. XXXI. No. 20

Feb. 10, 1906

J.C. Freeman

Kennel — — Number.

Price Ten Cents.

"Warren," which would become a by-word in the breed.

The brothers, having joined Westminster in 1880, were elected to the board in 1891. Lewis served for a year, but Winthrop remained a governor for 40 years. He judged at Westminster 11 times. The two brothers helped found the American Fox Terrier Club, Lewis being its first president, 1885-1886. Winthrop became president ten years later, serving through 1921 and then again from 1931 until his death in 1944. Lewis Rutherfurd died around 1900, but as the late John T. (Jack) Marvin put it in his *Fox Terrier Scrapbook,* Winthrop "continued the strong competitive spirit of the Warren kennels for many years to come."

The Warren Kennels, home of Warren Remedy, who was Best in Show in 1907, '08 and '09, were located in Allamuchy, N.J., on property that had belonged to the family for over a century. It extended across a wide fertile valley and was one of the finest game preserves in the state. The American Fox Terrier Club 1942 yearbook was dedicated to Winthrop Rutherfurd, containing encomiums of nearly 100 admirers. This included the congratulations of Westminster whose senior member he was, having joined Westminster 62 years earlier.

In 1902, Winthrop married Alice Morton, whose father was governor of New York and formerly Vice-President of the United States. They had five children. Mrs. Rutherfurd died in 1917, and in 1920, Rutherfurd married Lucy Mercer. Lucy Mercer was a friend and companion of Franklin D. Roosevelt, then Assistant Secretary of the Navy, and was with Roosevelt at the time of his death in Warm Springs, Ga., in 1945.

1910

Fire Department Dogs

For the first time, a class was offered for fire company Dalmatians. The *Times* said that many firemen and their friends were there to watch.

There was an entry of four, who were the winners of a preliminary match with an entry of over 60, which had been held before Westminster opened. Mike, owned by Dan M. Lynx of Engine Co. 8 at 165 E. 51st Street, took first. Mike was by Okey out of Bess, both sire and dam being owned by members of Engine Co. 39 in East 67th Street. Okey had been presented to Engine Co. 39 by William K. Vanderbilt, Jr., who had raised him on his Long Island farm.

As recounted by Kate Sanborn in her 1916 book *Educated Dogs of Today,* Mike was the only dog in the world to hold a street railway pass. It hung from his collar and allowed him to ride on the Third Avenue Railroad as a "deadhead." Sanborn was told positively that Mike did not use the pass to go to fires but only to go at mealtime to the homes of the various firemen.

Mike's mother, Bess, was also entered, but her son outclassed her. Shortly afterwards, after five years of leading the way on some 40 fire runs a month, Bess was sent, heartbroken, into retirement. Her fate, said Sanborn, pointed to the end of a picturesque scene of city life that featured "plunging horses" and "bounding, barking Dalmatian dogs which ran ahead to clear the traffic for the fire-fighting apparatus."

"Horses and dogs are doomed," she said. "In another five years the whole department will be motorized."

Above: Benching tag of 1911— *WKC, Gift of Mrs. Lawrence H. Kelly*

Left: Winthrop Rutherfurd— *American Fox Terrier Club Yearbook, 1942, courtesy American Fox Terrier Club*

Far Left: *The Rider and Driver* pays its respects to the show —*AKC*

1911

Just think of the size of that catalog. An ordinary catalog runs to about 64 pages or at a pinch to about 80 pages, but here... it totaled 240 pages.~The *American Field, February 21, 1911*

Benching Tags

For all the hundreds of brass benching tags manufactured in the early 1900s – Westminster issued one as ticket of admission for each dog entered in a show – only one has made its way back to the club's archives. It was found by a couple in Larchmont, N.Y., when they dug up their property to put in the foundation of the house where they subsequently lived for 18 years. The tag ended up in a box of trinkets, which members of the family could not bring themselves to part with.

In 1999, suspecting that the "KC" of WKC stood for "kennel club," they made some phone calls, finally reaching Westminster.

The 1911 catalog identifies the tag, shown in our photograph, as belonging to Bob, an Irish Setter owned by St. Val Kennels. The address of the kennels is, care of Warren Delano, 1 Broadway, NYC. Bob took second in the puppy class.

timing was ideal. People had been bidding fond farewells to Stanford White's Madison Square Garden for several years. Westminster was able to move into the new facility in 1912.

The thirteen-story structure occupied the entire block-front on the west side of Lexington Avenue between 46th and 47th Streets. Three floors were devoted to exhibitions and entertainment, while the other floors were occupied by industrial companies.

One entered from Lexington through a broad, well-lighted vestibule. There was a wide marble stairway, flanked by Doric columns. The main exhibition floor was

All three exhibition floors were needed for the dog show. There were eighteen judging rings, all told, seven on the first floor, five on the second and six on the third. There was benching on each level as well, with the smaller breeds on the higher floors. The building offered real benefits. There was a third more space for benching than at the Garden. The light was almost equal to that outside of the building, and the judging rings were all placed near the tall windows, so that the light of day would have full play on the animals shown. The interior of the building could also be kept at a uniform temperature. And it was all new.

But many exhibitors regretted leaving the Garden. What they missed most was not having all of the judging rings and most of the benching on a single level. And of course the old Garden was not immediately torn down. After three years at Grand Central Palace, Westminster moved back to the Garden for five years. Then in 1920, they moved to Grand Central Palace again, only to return to the Garden once more for five additional shows. By then—it was 1925—a new $5½ million amphitheater was under construction in the West 40s. Westminster would move there in 1926.

The new Grand Central Palace in 1923. The tracks were still open to the sky
—Corbis-Bettmann

1912

New York needs Madison Square Garden ~ and the prospect of losing it hurts and alarms. ~The New York Times, 1911

The New Grand Central Palace

The *Times* called it a "new amusement building." The New Grand Central Palace opened in the summer of 1911.

It was the first of a number of imposing structures planned by the New York Central to cover the open railroad yards north of Grand Central Terminal. The

up the flight of stairs, and one's first impression, as one reached the top where a view of the main floor opened out, was of spotless purity. Except for the floors, everything was pure white.

There was also a feeling of solidity. There were double rows of "stately pillars" to support the structure, but they were so placed – and there was so much available space – that their intrusion into the line of vision was hardly apparent.

The reporter for the *Times* likened it all to "the architectural monuments of Greece in its palmy days."

1914

Every Dog Has His Day

Under the above title, Charles Pike Sawyer complained good-naturedly in *The Evening Post Saturday Magazine* this year that every Westminster seemed to bring out "some breed of dog new to America." One newcomer he spoke of was the Boxer, which he described as "more like an English bull than anything else, with tail and ears cropped." The *Times*, before the show opened, reported that the Boxer was "said to resemble a Boston Terrier, but is somewhat larger and has both its ears and tail cropped." Two days later, having seen some Boxers—there were 11 entered— they revised their description: "Its head is typical of that of the Bull Terrier, while its body shows the lines of the Mastiff."

Of the 26 judges on the panel, 20 were American. Two came from Canada, and three, from England. The foreign judge that most interested the *Times* was Lieut.

Left: *The Evening Post Saturday Magazine,* February 21, 1914—*WKC*

Below Right: James Mortimer, 1843-1915—*WKC*

by bringing in 54 wounded soldiers. Having done his bit in the war, he was brought to the U.S. and shown at Westminster by Mr. and Mrs. L. F. Wanner of Lewanno Kennels.

"Where is the war dog?" was the question everyone asked. Having won the popular prize for heroism, Filax was decorated with three red ribbons, which he won in show competition.

Pacifists also had a representative in Max Donath's Lucie Doberman, a mild-mannered Doberman Pinscher bitch that had joined the peace pilgrims in Sweden a year earlier and traveled to this country on the Henry Ford peace ship. She won first in the Open class.

James Mortimer

The James Mortimer Memorial Trophy first went into competition this year. It was a prize for the Best American-Bred Dog or Bitch in the show. In 2000, the trophy was still in competition, no one having met the requirement that it be won five times by the same owner for permanent possession.

In 1961, in line with AKC rule amendments, the trophy's conditions were changed to read: "For dog or bitch going Best in Show, if American-bred."

The trophy memorialized a man who wore many hats. As John T. (Jack) Marvin wrote in the *Gazette* in 1975,

Baron von Forstner of Stuttgart, Germany. He had come over to judge German Shepherd Dogs, Boxers and Doberman Pinschers. Much interest would attach to his work in Shepherds, said the paper, since the breed—there was an entry of 64—had become "a big factor in American kennel circles."

A German judge would not visit Westminster again for some time. World War I would start in less than six months.

1917

Society...takes more than a passing interest in Manhattan's dog show. This, with the horse and automobile shows, are the sporty functions which New York's four hundred feel called upon to attend.—The American Field, March 3, 1917

World War I

August 1914 marked the beginning of World War I. The U.S. would enter the conflict in April 1917.

On this year's slate, according to the *Times,* there were originally three English judges, Major E. R. L. Hoskins, from Burnham, Lady Savory of Stoke Pogis, Bucks, and Frank Walker, a London businessman who was coming over on vacation. They planned to leave home after the Cruft's show, held at Islington shortly before Westminster. However, the U-boat peril prevented two of them from coming. Only Major Hoskins got through the prohibited zone.

Major Hoskins had been at the front in Flanders until about a month before. Badly wounded several times, he was finally so injured that he was given an honorable discharge and invalided out of the ranks. He judged Fox, Irish, Welsh and Sealyham Terriers and terrier variety classes.

The *Times* also noted that "in these bellicose days" a show would not be complete without the dogs of war. One German Shepherd Dog attracted special attention. Filax of Lewanno had served for more than a year in the Allied trenches. During that time he had made a record

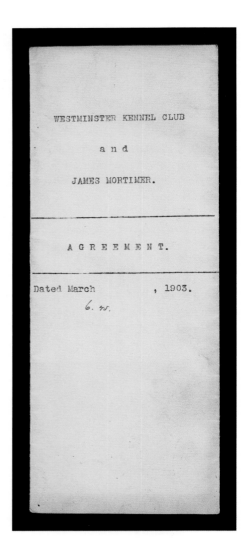

WESTMINSTER KENNEL CLUB

and

JAMES MORTIMER.

A G R E E M E N T.

Dated March   , 1903.

The contract under which Mortimer agreed to superintend the show for 5 years at $1000 and 10% of the net profits per show—*WKC*

Mortimer was prominent in the dog world "as a breeder, exhibitor, kennel manager, superintendent, handler, importer, judge and above all, as an advisor, for his knowledge was extensive and well considered." Marvin quickly added that AKC had long since curtailed such a spread in activity, but that in Mortimer's day, it was all quite proper and legal.

Born in England in 1842, Mortimer first appeared on the American dog scene at Westminster's first show where he exhibited a Bulldog named Crib. It was a brindle and white, priced at $100. Mortimer's address then was 22 Greenwich Street, New York.

In 1885, he became resident superintendent of Westminster's kennels at Babylon. Later that year, at the death of Charles Lincoln, he took over as superintendent of the club's dog show. In 1892, he left Babylon, but he stayed on as show superintendent until his death in 1915. He ran a total of 31 Westminsters. In this capacity he was widely known.

The American Field described him in the midst of the trials and vexations of a dog show as "ubiquitous, suave, and even-tempered." They noted that his gray whiskers and Westminster's logo—the head of old Sensation—had a long association together in the minds of the dog public.

1918

War and War Dogs

The profits of the show this year, in the amount of $2,500, went to the American Red Cross. The club was pleased with the entry though the number of dogs was the smallest since 1901.

Two English judges were on the panel, J. J. Holgate and W. J. Nichols. However, they were passengers on the torpedoed steamer *Livonia*. They survived but did not get to the show. The *Times* said it was the second time that the U-boat campaign had prevented judges from reaching the Garden. Only a few exhibitors withdrew their entries because of the change in judges.

A decided improvement was noticed this year in German Sheepdogs. The breed was getting much attention because of its utility. Thousands of them were being used in the war. They were valuable as sentries because of their silence and were also used extensively in Red Cross work.

The judge of the breed, the *Times* noted, was Benjamin H. Throop, now in the Army Ordnance Department. An exhibitor in the breed was Lieut. Col. Jack Clifford of the British Army, who led his own dog, Elf, into the ring. Colonel Clifford had been wounded in action in France and was in this country recuperating. Elf won 2nd in Open Bitches.

1919

The Victory Show

They called it The Victory Show. The profits in the amount of $4,000 went to the American Red Cross.

With the war over, the *Times* reported that the show had come back into its own. "There was more real enthusiasm displayed around the rings where the entries were being judged," the paper said, "than has been shown for several seasons."

To honor those who had served or were still serving in the Army, Navy, Air or auxiliary forces of the United States and allied countries, the club offered special "Service Classes," which were judged on Washington's Birthday, the last day of the show.

First prize was won by Capt. Quincy Adams Shaw McKean with his Wire Fox Terrier, Ch. Pride's Hill Tweak 'Em.

Second went to Kinnelon Kennels' Old English Sheepdog, Kinnelon Selection. Third place was won by Collie, Alstead Beldam Satisfaction, exhibited by Mrs. Lunt, a Lieutenant in the Motor Corps of the Red Cross. Lieut. Tyler Morse, with his Sealyham, Brazen Brimful, took fourth.

Irene Castle

Irene Castle was a Brussels Griffon exhibitor, and this year at the Garden, with Nofa Joseph, she won 3rd in Open dogs, and with Nofa Nomee, 1st in Open Bitches and Winners Bitch.

The widow of Vernon Castle, Irene and her husband were ballroom dancers and the toast of New York from the start of World War I until 1916 when he enlisted in the Royal Flying Corps. After earning a Croix de Guerre for bringing down two German planes, he was sent to Texas as a flight instructor. In 1918 he was killed in a midair collision with a cadet. Later, remarried, Irene Castle would run an animal shelter in the outskirts of Chicago.

1921

Poster Dogs

The poster for this year's show is the only poster to survive in the WKC archives.

The club has the artwork for a poster for the 1926 Jubilee show, but it is not known whether any posters based on this model were actually printed.

1923

February 12-14
Madison Square Garden II
1,827 Dogs
George W. Gall, Superintendent
William Rauch, Chairman

There was no competition this year for the best dog in the show. In other years this was the high spot in the exhibition, but...it must have been pretty tough on the judges. Fancy the competition narrowed down to a Bulldog

Left: Poster Dogs, 1921 —*WKC*

Left, opposite page: Irene Castle, with the Brussels Griffons she showed at the Garden in 1919—*Corbis-Bettman*

and a toy Maltese or between a Mastiff and a Chihuahua? Something like trying to decide between a lavaliere and a farm tractor, or between an angel cake and a pair of rubber boots. No common denominator, no broad meeting ground for the judgement.— "A Dutchess County Farmer," The New York Times, February 18, 1923

Close-Clipped

It was a Westminster romance, a story of love unrequited, of revenge and retribution.

The story, "Close-Clipped," appeared in the January 1924 *Gazette.* It was by Albert Payson Terhune, a writer for the *New York Evening World,* author of many novels, and breeder of Sunnybank Collies.

In this tale, a man and a woman each entered a Collie puppy at the Garden.

They were benched next to each other. She admired his dog, whose coat was even longer and heavier than her dog's coat. She felt that, except for her own entry, he was easily the best puppy there. When they were judged the next day, she knew it would be nip and tuck between them for the blue ribbon and the silver puppy bowl.

But if she liked his dog, she detested the man. He had proposed to her a half-dozen times and would not take "no" for an answer. Not that this in itself was unflattering. But the man had lost his temper after the seventh rejection. He had declared noisily that he would get back at her if it took him a lifetime.

His opportunity for revenge came that very evening. He learned that our heroine was planning to leave her Collie at the Garden for the night. He ascertained that the dog would not be on its

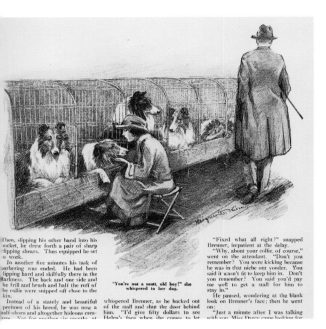

Then, slipping his other hand into his pocket, he drew forth a pair of sharp clipping shears. Thus equipped he set to work.

In another five minutes his task of barbering was ended. He had been clipping hard and skilfully there in the darkness. The back and one side and the frill and brush and half the ruff of the collie were snipped off close to the skin.

Instead of a stately and beautiful specimen of his breed, he was now a half-shorn and altogether hideous crea-

"You're not a mutt, old boy!" she whispered to her dog.

"Fixed what all right?" snapped Bremer, impatient at the delay.

"Why, about your collie, of course," went on the attendant. "Don't you remember? You were kicking because he was in that niche out yonder. You said it wasn't fit to keep him in. Don't you remember? You said you'd pay me well to get a stall for him to stay in."

He paused, wondering at the blank look on Bremer's face; then he went on:

"Just a minute after I was talking with you, Miss Darcy came looking for

A Marguerite
Kirmse
illustration for
"Close Clipped."
— *Gazette*,
Courtesy AKC

bench but instead would enjoy more secluded comfort in stall #36. Just as the show was closing down for the night, he made his way to the stall. Most of the lights had been turned out. It was very dark there. No one could possibly see him, and with his clippers, in a matter of five minutes, he butchered the dog's coat. It would be six months before the dog could go into the ring again.

Then in a surprise ending worthy of O. Henry – and too good to give away – our villain, having acted out his rage, gets his comeuppance.

1926

Jubilee

In celebration of the club's 50th show, Chairman Rauch (for whom it was the 26th show) assembled a list of prizes that were highly praised. Not the least of these was the Golden Jubilee Medallion offered for Best of Breed. The one here pictured was won by Edward V. Ireland and G. H. Ireland, Hempstead, N.Y., with their Irish Setter, Rory II.

Madison Square Garden III

The Jubilee show was held at a new site. Tex Rickard, who raised the money to build the new Garden, called it "the largest indoor amphitheater in the world." He said it seated 24,000 people, 9,000 more than Olympia in London and 10,000 more than Stanford White's Garden on Madison Square.

A bronze plaque on the wall outside read, "Dedicated to Athletics, Amusements, and the Industrial Arts." It was a box of a building on the west side of 8th Avenue between 49th and 50th Streets. Kurth Sprague in his centennial book on The National Horseshow Association, summed up the architectural impression very nicely:

"With a water tower squatting on its flat roof and not a…naked bronze nymph in sight…Garden III was nobody's dream of a pleasure dome. It was, indeed, a coliseum, but a strictly functional one."

This was home to 43 Westminsters and 43 Best in Shows. The building had opened in December 1925 with a six-day bike race, a basketball game and a hockey

game. It had already been booked for the Republican National Convention in 1928. Westminster's first show there was in 1926.

The facility was divided into two parts, a main level, which was an arena somewhat like the old Garden, and a lower level, which was a large hall for commercial exhibitions. The first dog show was

Top Right: Artwork for Jubilee Poster, 1926 — *WKC*

Above: Golden Jubilee medallion in presentation box offered for best of breed, 1926 — *WKC*

Right: Edwin Megaree records his impressions for the *Gazette*, 1926 — *Courtesy AKC*

New Madison Square Garden, New York City.

Madison Square Garden III —*postcard of the day, WKC*

staged entirely on the lower level. The benching and all eight judging rings were in the basement. Charles G. Hopton, reporting in *The American Field*, allowed that the new structure had many novel features (among other things, its arena seats were reached by escalators) but complained of crowding.

The next year – and from then on – the club rented the entire facility. Benching remained in the basement, with all judging in the arena. To help get dogs up the ramp to the rings at the right time, a telephone system was installed, connecting ring stewards with the benching area. Hopton could not have been happier. The rings were now "perfect," the light was "splendid," and the main ring, with a huge stretch of canvas on which the groups and Best in Show were judged, was a "revelation."

"Veteran railbirds of the sport," according to the *Herald Tribune*, "called it an ideal show."

Not the least of it was that the judging of groups and Best in Show could now be seen by thousands of people instead of just few a hundred. Louis W. Lewis of the *Gazette* saw real potential in this. He said

that, once publicized, the spectacle of group and Best-in-Show judging in the arena was "bound to draw a record gate."

Westminster stayed put until Madison Square Garden III closed. The final event of any kind there was the dog show of 1968, with Lakeland Terrier Ch. Stingray of Derryabah taking Best in Show. He was the last winner in the building.

1927

Mint Condition

It is the second show at Garden III but the first one to be held upstairs in the main arena (see page 82).

Two wide aisles divide the floor into four parts. Each quadrant is then divided by rope into three judging rings.

A bouquet of loudspeakers hangs from the ceiling. Spratts lights up the far wall. In the foreground is the toy breed benching.

This is the show's new home in near mint condition.

1928

Mrs. Reginald F. Mayhew

This year for the first time, a woman had a voice in deciding Best in Show at Westminster. Mrs. Reginald F. Mayhew of Forest Hills, Long Island, was part of a panel of five judges who made this decision.

Mrs. Mayhew and her English husband were breeders and exhibitors of Wire Fox Terriers and Pomeranians. They lived on Staten Island until around 1911 when they moved to Long Island. Reginald Mayhew was for 20 years the turf and kennel editor of the *New York Herald,* retiring in 1910. He was considered one of the top authorities in the U.S. on Wires. He officiated at Westminster 11 times, his final assignment there being in 1909. He died in 1920 at the age of 59.

Mrs. Mayhew judged at the Garden in 1907, 1911, 1915, and finally in 1928 when she drew the largest entry of Pomeranians ever seen at the Garden and then represented the toy breeds on the panel of five who officiated over Best in Show. No picture has been found of Mrs. Mayhew.

the show, the magazine tried to put itself inside the mind of the dog, whose life so far had consisted of "running in fields and smelling footprints in the grass." This "Prince of Basset Hounds," as the publication dubbed him, was by English and American Champion Walhampton Andrew out of Walhampton Dainty. The magazine said he was destined for shows and wondered what his reaction would be if someone told him what shows were all about.

To *Time,* the worst of it seemed to be that dog show winners were given "not a good bone, but a blue ribbon."

1929

No Quarrels across the Back Fence

Spratt's Patent started feeding the show in 1877. They began to provide benching just a few years later.

At this show, the benching was entirely new, an "innovation" that *Popular Dogs* said worked for the greater comfort and peace of mind of exhibitors, to say nothing of the greater safety of the dogs. The "enclosed cages," seen here in an ad from Spratt's, fully protected the dogs from the spectators as well as from each other.

Fighting was stopped before it began, said the magazine. The dogs, "to their possible sorrow," could have no quarrels "across the back fence."

Puppy Makes Time

Gerald M. Livingston, 54, became Westminster's president in 1937, serving for five years. Involved with dogs since childhood, he first showed at the Garden in 1916 and ran English Setters at his first field trial in Thomasville, Ga., in 1926. He joined Westminster that year and became a governor in 1927, a position he held until his death in 1950.

Born in St. Paul, he was the son of Mr. and Mrs. Crawford Livingston. He bred Pointers, English Setters, Labrador Retrievers, Dachshunds and Wirehaired Pointing Griffons. His kennel name was Kilsyth. His Walhampton Bassets from England were considered important in the breed's early development in the U.S.

In 1928, a puppy from these imports made the cover of *Time*. In reporting on

Far Left: *Time,* February 27, 1928—*Time Cover © 1928 Time Inc./ TimePix, reprinted by permission*

Left: Gerald Livingston, Westminster's tenth president —*WKC*

1930

New Telephone Number

In the matter of pigeon shooting, Westminster was a long time getting totally out of the woods. When the club was at the height of its fame as the home of crack pigeon shooters, Capt. Adam H. Bogardus was a famous—some said "infamous"—professional in the field. The sometime star of Buffalo Bill's Wild West show billed himself as "the champion wing shot of the world." In his

Right: Two catalog ads with scenes from the show, 1930 —*WKC*

Below: New Benching by Spratt's, 1929 —*AKC*

Opposite: Madison Square Garden III in near mint condition, 1927— *Edwin Levick photo, WKC*

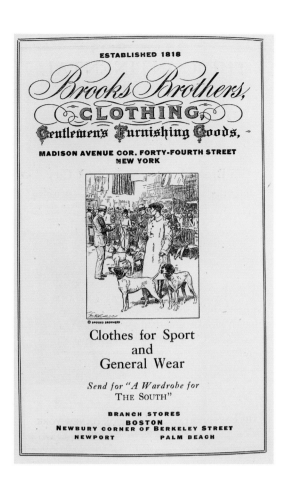

book, *Field, Cover and Trap Shooting,* he proudly related that in a match in Chicago, he won a wager of $1,000 by killing 500 pigeons in 528 minutes, loading his own gun.

This year, 25 years after Westminster had closed its clubhouse and the image of its members as pigeon shooters had all but faded from memory, the club's New York office got a new telephone number. The telephone exchange—telephone exchanges then still had names, not numbers—was Bogardus. To call Westminster, you picked up the receiver and said to a living person at the other end of the wire, "Bogardus 4889, please."

Catalog Ads

Advertising in the show catalog sometimes included illustrations of the show site. Here we see two examples from 1930, an ad for Brooks Brothers and another for Abercrombie & Fitch

1933

Despite the depression, there are almost as many entries benched as last year—The New York Times, February 14, 1933

Junior Showmanship

"Junior Showmanship Classes are among the most competitive events featured at today's dog shows, drawing spectators and exhibitors from all parts of the United States and abroad." Such were the words of Andrea D. Korzenik in AKC's 1984 *Source Book.*

Junior Showmanship was originally called Children's Handling. The first "qualifying" classes were held in 1933, beginning at Westminster and including all events where the competition was

offered during the next twelve months. The classes were open to boys and girls under 15. The judges were members of the Professional Handlers Association. The dogs had to be owned by the child or a member of the family. Awards were to be based solely on skillful handling, the points of the dog not to count. One win in these classes qualified the junior to compete for the Children's Handling Grand Challenge Trophy, first offered at Westminster in 1934.

The competition was established through the efforts of Leonard Brumby, Sr., founder and president of the Professional Handler's Association. Through it children learned professional handling skills and grooming techniques and were provided with a public forum in which sportsmanship, meaning the acceptance of wins and losses with equal grace, was a matter of high priority. Through their ranks would pass many of the dog world's ranking sportsmen and sportswomen.

Participation became immensely popular. In the early years, the entry might stand at 20 juniors, each of whom had won one class during the previous 12

84

The 1939 winner of Children's Handling, Mona Saphir and her Old English Sheepdog, Crest of the Wave, with judge James Sullivan
— *WKC, Archive Photos, Photo by Bert Morgan*

The 2000 winner of Junior Showmanship, Nicholas Urbanek and his Pointer dog Ch. Oncore's C'Wood Sportin Good, with, from left, judge Frank T. Sabella, trophy presenter Kimberlie Steele, who was last year's Junior Showmanship winner, and WKC member William M. Duryea, Jr. Duryea has managed the competition at the Garden since the 1970s and remains one of its strongst advocates.
— *Ashbey photo*

Junior Showmanship Winners, 1934-2000

1934 Betty Anne Clark, Philadelphia, Pa.

1935 Joseph Sayres, Peekskill, N.Y.

1936 Dorthea McAnulty, Atlantic City, N.J.

1937 Jerry Werber, Great Neck, N.Y.

1938 Arthur F. Mulvihill, Jr., Syracuse, N.Y.

1939 Mona Saphir, New York, N.Y.

1940 Jerry Werber, Great Neck, N.Y.

1941 Betsy Long, Hewlitt Harbor, N.Y.

1942 Betty Lee Hinks, Owings Mills, Md.

1943 Walter Wilson, Baltimore, Md.

1944 Betty Bolger, Sewickley, Pa.

1945 Evelyn Straubmueller, Bronx, N.Y.

1946 Frank Hill, Havertown, Pa.

1947 John Herr, Lancaster, Pa.

1948 George Metz, Oceanside, N.Y.

1949 Monica Rumpf, Syosset, N.Y.

1950 Hope Johnson, West Hartford, Conn.

1951 Theodore Hollander, South Hamilton, Mass.

1952 William Henry

1953 Phyllis Claire Campbell, Edgewood, R.I.

1954 George Alston, Vienna, Va.

1955 Mary Donnelly, Jersey City, N.J.

1956 Patricia Leary, Pluckemin, N.J.

1957 Pat Matson, Massapequa, N.Y.

1958 Nancy Kelly, Stamford, Conn.

1959 Bethny Hall, Greenville, R.I.

1960 Allen Kirk, Roanoke, Va.

1961 Betty Lou Ham, Holyoke, Mass.

1962 Susan Heckmann, Baltimore, Md.

1963 Lydia Ceccarini, Westbury, N.Y.

1964 Clare Hodge, Bryn Mawr, Pa.

1965 Jennifer Sheldon, Massapequa, N.Y.

1966 Laura Swyler, Commack, N.Y.

1967 David Brumbough, Perry, Ga.

1968 Cheryl Baker, Chicopee Falls, Mass.

1969 Charles Garvin, Columbus, Ohio

1970 Pat Hardy, Cincinnati, Ohio

1971 Heidi Shellenbarger, Costa Mesa, Calif.

1972 Deborah Gagny von Ahrens, Edison, N.J.

1973 Teresa Nail

1974 Leslie K. Church

1975 Virginia Westfield, Huntington, N.Y.

1976 Kathy Hritzo, Hubbard, Ohio

1977 Randy McAteer, Ocala, Fla.

1978 Sondra Peterson, San Diego, Calif.

1979 Susan M. Schneider, Lorton, Va.

1980 Laura Mazzaro, Huntington, Conn.

1981 Valerie Nunes, Newport Beach, Calif.

1982 Francesca Weisser, Olympia, Wash.

1983 Tracie A. Laliberte, Norton, Mass.

1984 Brad Buttner, Hayward, Calif.

1985 David Harper, Richmond, Tex.

1986 Wendy Rene Mattson, Newbury, Calif.

1987 Heather E. Christie, Milford, Conn.

1988 Patricia Fearing, Raleigh, N.C.

1989 Michelle Samson, Duncannon, Pa.

1990 Jessica Wiwi, Berkeley, Calif.

1991 Kara Purcell, Central Pt., Ore.

1992 Christina Marley, Meridian, Ida.

1993 Stacy J. Duncan, Woodinville, Wash.

1994 Melanie Schlenkert, Peach Tree City, Ga.

1995 Kyle Covill, San Jose, Calif.

1996 David Stout, Jacksonville, Fla.

1997 Cassandra Clark, Tustin, Calif.

1998 Angela Lloyd, Clarksburg, Md.

1999 Kimberlie Steele, Riverside, Calif.

2000 Nicholas Urbanek, Glenshaw, Pa.

months. By the show in 2000, there were 143 juniors, each of whom had a record of no less than eight wins during the previous year.

In 1949, the Grand Challenge Trophy was replaced by The Leonard Brumby, Sr., Memorial Trophy, Brumby having died in 1947. In 1951, Children's Handling was renamed Junior Showmanship. Over time, the age limit was raised from under 15 to under 18 years old. Starting in 1974, former Junior Handlers could be approved to judge the competition. Since 1977, when AKC stopped licensing professional handlers, only breed judges and Junior Showmanship judges have been eligible to officiate.

The Old Guard

At the show in 1920, a new club known as "The Old Guard of the Kennel World" was established. The organization was open to anyone who had been associated with the American kennel world as judge or exhibitor for 20 years or more. They held a luncheon or dinner at some point during Westminster for many years. They offered trophies. They gave recognition to persons who had done special service on behalf of dogs. In 1945, for example, they would joins forces with the Dog Writers Association of America and the Gaines Dog Research Center to give Freeman Lloyd, dog judge, dog writer and "Grand Old Man of American Dogdom" an award commemorating his 70 years of service to dogs.

The Old Guard was not unlike today's Dog Fanciers Club, which since the

1950s has held a luncheon after the close of Westminster to celebrate the entire extended dog show weekend and the judges, exhibitors, handlers, writers, spectators—anyone who was part of it. Neither dog club was ever interested in holding a dog show.

Bring on the Dogs

Mrs. M. Hartley Dodge judged Best in Show this year, the first woman to officiate as the sole judge of this competition at Westminster.

She would be better remembered later on as Geraldine Rockefeller Dodge. It was through her generosity that the Geraldine R. Dodge Foundation was created.

She was known as "the first lady of dogdom." She was called "the chatelaine of Giralda" or "Our Lady of Giralda." For sheer elegance, the Morris & Essex Kennel Club dog show was never equaled. It was held outdoors at her Giralda Farms estate in Madison, N.J., from 1927 to 1957—except for the war years of 1942-45. In 1939 there were 4,456 entries. Steve Cady in *AKC's World of the Pure-Bred Dog* gives details:

"Picture the wide green expanse of a polo field. Hoist 160,000 square feet of canvas for tenting...Put up six enormous tents for the six groups...Set up...a public cafeteria and a special area where 4,600

exhibitors, judges, and others officials can be served lunch by a famous caterer...Stake out 57 judging rings with a colorful umbrella over each judge's table. Hire 70...policemen to handle traffic... for a crowd of 50,000. Then stack 383 pieces of sterling silver on the trophy table—and bring on the dogs."

1935

Members of the Canadian Kennel Club were out in force this year as if to prove that the depression was actually a thing of the past in this country.—Kennel and Bench (publication of the Canadian Kennel Club), March 1935

The Scribes

The Dog Writers Association of America, patterned after the Baseball Writers Association, came into existence at the show of 1935. The first president was Milton Danziger, dog editor of the *Springfield* (Massachusetts) *Republican*. He and George Foley, show superintendent and publisher of *Popular Dogs*, arranged the initial meeting. The gathering took place at the Garden on Wednesday, Feb. 13. DWAA records give the time of birth as "approximately 4:30 PM."

Maxwell Riddle, a distinguished president of DWAA, stated the group's original mission: "To improve the quality of the writing on dogs and to get more dog writing into general newspapers and magazines."

Sixty-six years later, perhaps the most visible aspect of DWAA is its annual writing competition—which is no longer limited strictly to writing. Through it, the group celebrates excellence in both dog writing and dog photography and art, in print and non-print media. It is open to writers, editors, publishers, photographers and artists. The awards include the Maxwell Medallion for regular category winners (the awards are named for Maxwell Riddle), as well as a variety of special corporate-sponsored cash grants. The awards banquet in New York at the time of Westminster has become an institution.

DWAA also runs the Dog Writers Educational Trust, established to provide scholarships for young people "desiring a college education, who are interested in the world of dogs or who have participated in the Junior Handling classes at dog shows in the United States or Canada."

1937

Dr. Young came into the hotel early in the evening, saying he had just fed his Sealyhams for the day. We asked, "Up in the hotel room, you mean?" He said, "No, back in Chicago." It seems that he had flown down from Chicago. ...He had left Chicago at 3:45 that afternoon. At 8:30, we were visiting together in the hotel lobby in New York. —E. W. Leach, Kennel Club News, March 1937

Hounds

There were no movies or trained dog acts this year. The special attraction was the New York Hound Show. For the first and only time, it was held in conjunction with Westminster.

Opposite Left: Memento from the Old Guard, 1933—*Courtesy David B. Biesel*

Opposite Right: DWAA brochure, 1999

Opposite Center: Mrs. Geraldine Rockefeller Dodge as a young lady—*Gazette, photo of oil painting, AKC*

Left: Horn-blowing contest, 1937—*Underwood and Underwood, Corbis-Bettman*

Under the auspices of the Masters of Foxhounds Association of America and the National Beagle Club, it offered classes for seven breeds of working hounds – Beagles, English Foxhounds, American Foxhounds, Welsh Foxhounds, Crossbred Foxhounds, Basset Hounds and Harriers. It was a self-contained event, with its own judges and stewards. It included a horn-blowing contest. In the final judging for Best Pack in Show, there were 60 hounds in the ring. The hunt livery of the masters, huntsmen, and whippers-in brought generous splashes of pink and green to the arena.

W. Plunkett Stewart, master of the Cheshire English Foxhounds, carried off the Grand Champion Pack Trophy, offered by Westminster president, John G. Bates.

There had been "Hound Days" at Westminster in the past when a limited number of packs of hounds competed there. Always popular with the public, they sometimes offered true excitement. In 1913, for example, they made headlines in the *Times*. A revolt of the hounds

began just as the American Fox Hounds of the Middleburg Hunt of Virginia were led into the ring. They broke away from the master and scattered pell-mell through the spectators around the ring. "Women screamed and tried in vain to get out of the way," said the paper. It was some time before the dogs could be corralled.

However, there was no such disorder in 1937.

1938

In a great show at Westminster last May, Britons saw a coronation. At another Westminster show, held in Manhattan's Madison Square Garden, Americans last week saw another coronation of less solemnity but more suspense.—Time, February 21, 1938

Westminster As Cover Story

This year, John G. Bates, 57, did Best in Show at the Garden. *Time* gave the show nearly two pages of coverage and put Bates on the cover.

88

Bates was a member of Westminster from 1925 until his death in 1944. He served as treasurer 1927-30, vice-president 1930-35, and president 1935-37. He was Chairman 1928-34 and, during World War II, was called upon to serve again for the shows of 1943-44. Arthur Frederick Jones in the *Gazette* remarked that running dog shows was almost as much of a hobby with him as breeding dogs.

Born in New York, he graduated from Columbia, class of 1903. He was a member of the New York Stock Exchange. He was founding president of the Leash Club.

Finding Greatness

All-breed judge Howard Tyler once said, "You can't use Westminster or any other

Africa. The merits of her coat, structure, head and gait were still being debated when she returned to the Garden in 1938 as defending champion.

Under the rules of the day for all-breed shows, the best Wire and best Smooth competed for Best of Breed. The winner of that competition then competed in the terrier group. Under the guidance of Percy Roberts, Spicypiece was best Wire, and in competition for Best of Breed, she came face to face with Saddler, the best Smooth, who was handled by Leonard Brumby, Sr. The judge was Robert Sedgwick. Both dogs were superb. The general feeling was that the dog that won Best of Breed would go on to take the terrier group and Best in Show.

Above:
John G. Bates
—*WKC*

Above Right:
Time, February 21, 1938—*Time cover© 1938, Time Inc./TimePix, reprinted by permission*

Bates first showed at Westminster in 1898, winning third in a large class with a black curly standard Poodle. He took the kennel name, Blarney, in 1906. He was active in Irish Terriers until 1925, serving a term as president of the Irish Terrier Club of America. He joined the American Fox Terrier club in 1911 and started showing the breed in 1920. With a wire Fox Terrier bitch, he won Best in Show at Westminster in 1930 and 1931.

His kennels were near Morristown, N.J. He had 100 acres with barn, main kennel, winter kennel, manager's house and owner's cottage. The kennels usually housed 40 to 50 Wires and 10 Pointers and English Setters. The Setters were purely gun dogs. He handled the dogs himself, whenever possible.

single major show as a barometer for evaluating the greatness of a dog. Top dogs often get beaten in the breed at Westminster."

Ch. Nornay Saddler was one of these. Winthrop Rutherfurd once said of him: "When the Fox Terrier standard was drawn up in 1876, they closed their eyes and dreamed of Saddler."

Saddler was a smooth Fox Terrier owned by Wissaboo Kennels of James M. Austin, Old Westbury, N.Y. Saddler was first shown at Westminster in 1937, taking 3rd in Open Dogs. It was not an auspicious start, but within a year, he had begun building a record of Best in Show wins. He became well known. There were those who began calling him invincible.

In 1937, when Saddler made his less than promising Garden debut, Spicypiece of Halleston, a Wire Fox Terrier, took Best in Show there. After that win, her fame spread. Her breeding was discussed at shows in Honolulu, India, and South

Brumby's son, Leonard Brumby, Jr., remembered the decision as the most dramatic he ever saw. He never forgot the judge finally lining the two dogs up and saying to the handlers, "All right, gentlemen, drop those leashes." He wanted the dogs to stand alone.

"As it happened," said Brumby, "Saddler happened to lean a little backwards...and the bitch leaned forward which was the right kind of assertiveness for a terrier. The judge picked the bitch." She then captured the group though she did not repeat her previous year's victory by taking Best in Show.

As for Saddler, he returned to Westminster in 1939 and '40, taking breed and group both times. By then, he had established what was an all-time record for Best in Shows, with 51 to his credit. But he never took the top award at the Garden.

Below:
Ch. Nornay Saddler, 1940, by Edwin Megargee (American 1883-1958)—*AKC Collection*

Westminster As...

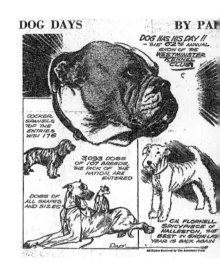

Left: Westmister as host to new breed—*Newark (N.J.) Star Eagle,* WKC

Below: Westminster in the Nampa Idaho, *Free Press* — *AP Wide World*

Above: Westmister for hotel guests —*WKC*

Right: Westmister as nostalgia—*WKC*

Below: Westminster as radio news —*WKC*

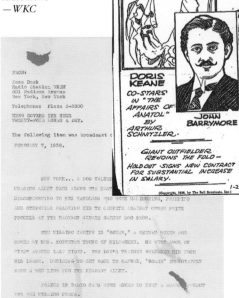

Right: Westminster for Garden regulars —*WKC*

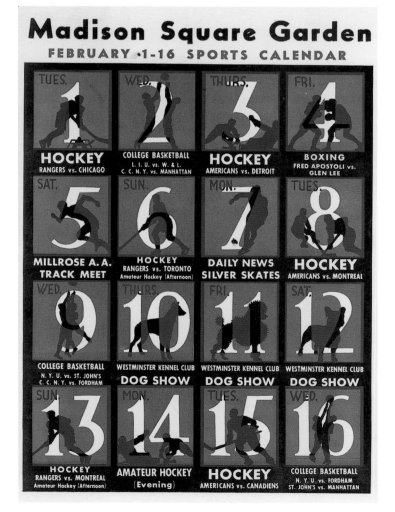

Entry Limits and Restrictions – An Overview

This year for the first time, a limit was set on the number of entries to be accepted. There had been over a thousand dogs in the first show, and on only four occasions did the number ever drop below that, in 1879, '83, '85, and '87.

In 1908, the number of dogs entered reached 2,000, though it was not until 1925 that it exceeded 2,000 and stayed there. In another 10 years, it was clear that the capacity of the Garden would soon be reached. In 1937, having gone over every inch of space available and rearranging things, they managed with a total of 3,140. The following year a limit was set at "approximately 3,000 dogs," meaning that entries closed with the mail that included the 3,000th dog.

In 1941, the show was cut from three days to two, and the club closed entries with the mail that included the 2,500th dog. This numerical limit would be unchanged until 1970. Entries were also restricted to dogs (puppies excepted) that had won a first, second or third prize at an AKC show.

In 1942, after announcing that the entry restrictions would be tightened to include only blue-ribbon winners, the club reverted to the 1941 requirement. William Kendrick, in a report for *Popular Dogs,* complained that this requirement worked a hardship on Canadians, a faithful contingent of whom made the annual pilgrimage to New York their sole appearance in American competition. He also regretted the loss of Westminster as a show where there could be such surprise and genuine enjoyment in withholding a good dog under cover for "the fated day." Arthur Frederick Jones in the *Gazette* called these dogs "Cinderella" dogs.

A year later, the qualifying-ribbon requirement was suspended because of World War II.

In 1948, a blue ribbon, won at an AKC or a Canadian Kennel Club show, was needed to qualify. The Novice class, by definition not open to dogs that had won a first place, was also dropped.

In 1950, entries for Exhibition Only were excluded.

Left:
Marie Leary wih her German Shepherd Dogs, Hugo of Cosalta and Marlo of Cosalta, best Working-Brace in 1939—
WKC, Archive Photos, photo by Bert Morgan

Below:
Team judging, always popular at ringside—*WKC*

For the shows of 1951-69, entries for Junior Showmanship Only were not permitted. Dogs in this competition had to be entered in one of the regular classes.

In 1958, 6-9 month-old puppies were excluded, and in 1960, all puppies were barred. The classes now open to non-champions were Bred-by-Exhibitor, American-Bred and Open.

In 1961, Team competition was omitted. The judging of dogs in teams of four dogs each, with each team evaluated on the basis of uniformity as well as quality, was always popular with spectators. See the picture of Dr. Calvarisi's team of Maltese, which were Best Team in Show in 1956. As reported in the *Times,* entries eventually would drop until the competition was not truly meaningful.

In 1964, by direction of AKC, the Miscellaneous Class was dropped, and a CKC win no longer qualified a dog for entry.

In 1967, it was required that an entry have won at least one championship point. To qualify in 1969, a dog had to have at least one major win on its record, a major win being a win of three or more points at a single show.

In 1970, one-day benching began, with three groups judged each day, the group order to be reversed yearly. The numerical limit was raised to 3,000.

In 1972, Brace competition, the judging of dogs in braces of two dogs each, was omitted. Like Team competition, it was popular at ringside but had been patronized less and less by exhibitors. See illustration of Marie Leary and her German Shepherd Dogs.

In 1982, the numerical limit was again lowered and entries closed with the mail bringing the 2500th dog.

In 1983, after AKC established the Herding group, making seven groups in

"They were wildly applauded," said William Kendrick. Dr. Calvarisi's Maltese, Best Team in 1956. — *Popular Dogs*

all, four were judged the first day, and three, the second, with the group order being reversed each year.

Starting in 1990, four groups were judged on the first day, and three on the second, with the group order not being reversed yearly.

In 1992, the show was restricted to champions only, the first such event ever held under AKC rules. Liz Bodner, editor of the *Gazette*, found the change well

received. "Students of the breeds," she said, "thought they had died and gone to Harvard."

The club also introduced the awarding of Certificates of Merit. The number of Awards of Merit that could be made by the judge in any breed or variety was based on the number of entries in the breed or variety.

For the show in 2000, the method of entry was modified to make sure that every breed could be represented. Invitations to "pre-enter" the show were sent to the top five dogs or bitches in each breed or variety, based on the number of dogs defeated in breed or variety competition only, at AKC shows held from January 1 through October 31, 1999. AKC's computerized records made identification of these dogs easily manageable. These special entry forms had to be returned to the Superintendent by a stated deadline, after which entries would be accepted in the normal manner, closing at 2,500, not including dogs entered for Junior Showmanship only.

1939

The little dog that walks around the jump when that's easier than jumping over, will always have the sympathy of the gallery. —Lawrence A. Horswell, Popular Dogs, March 1939

City Dog

Space and time constraints made it impossible to hold full-scale obedience trials at the Garden. However, AKC first licensed obedience competition in 1936, and in 1939, recognizing dog training as vital to survival of the urban dog, WKC held an obedience exhibition.

The event pitted men against women, in two teams of seven dogs and handlers each. More than half of the dogs taking part were bench champions. Chairman of the demonstration was Mrs. Whitehouse Walker, who, assisted by Blanche Saunders, was a main driving force in the development of obedience competition. The judge was Josef Weber, dog trainer and author from Princeton, N.J. To cap the group competition in each session, the handlers formed a large circle in the arena, then left their places to assume positions beside other dogs. Then on command, all the dogs proceeded to their respective handlers, passing each other in the center of the ring but completely ignoring each other as they did so.

According to both the *Gazette* and the *Times*, the women shaded their rivals in the afternoon with a point score of 74 to 70, but at night the men's combination prevailed, 82 to 69, to triumph by a total of 152 to 143.

On the other hand, in the official catalog in the AKC archives, it clearly states as follows: "The Women's Team and the Men's Team scored equally and were awarded equal first prizes."

1940

Canadians sent close to eighty dogs to Westminster this year. Three of these came all the way from British Columbia, and one from Manitoba. —Dogs in Canada, March 1940

World War II

"This year's Westminster, in spite of European wars, embargoes on importing dogs, general worldly unrest, a Presidential election and a blizzard, held its own in attendance, public interest and excitement to the end, to say nothing of high

MIDWINTER DOG SHOW

quality and keen competition among the dogs themselves." So wrote George N. Owen in *Popular Dogs*.

World War II was under way in no uncertain terms. In 1938, Hitler had marched into Austria and partitioned Czechoslovakia. In 1939, he had occupied Bohemia and Moravia and invaded Poland. Britain and France then gave Hitler an ultimatum. On September 3, with no satisfactory response, they declared war on Germany. More than two years would pass—and two Westminsters would be held—before the attack on Pearl Harbor of December 7, 1941, which brought the U.S. into the war.

As this year's show approached, two writers for the *Times* took note of canine stars appearing on the scene. Kingsley Childs said that people in Europe who would normally not have parted with their best dogs at any price, were now letting them go to get them out of danger. Henry R. Ilsley wrote that more outstanding dogs were being brought over than at any time since the boom days of the late twenties.

"Foreign breeders," he said, "have faced the possibility of invasion, food rationing and other war hazards and have been willing to dispose of the best in their kennels to insure their safety."

But four of the six dogs in this year's final were American-Bred.

J. Gould Remick

J. Gould Remick, 43, became Chairman in 1940 and served through the show of 1942. A Second Lieutenant in World War I, he was a Major in World War II, on active duty until 1944. He was club treasurer, 1945-50, and president, 1950-53. While AKC delegate for the Cardigan Welsh Corgi Club, he served on the AKC Board, 1945 through 1953.

During those years, he was part of an AKC committee charged with creating new executive positions to deal with the dramatic increase in dog activity after the war. This committee, among other things, established the position of AKC Field Representative and saw to the

Above:
Midwinter Show, 1939, by H.H. Stewart— *Popular Dogs*

Left:
J. Gould Remick with his Curly-Coated Retriever, Dennington Mayfly of Marvadel, Best of Breed at Westminster 1936 —*UPI/Corbis-Bettman*

hiring of Leonard Brumby, Sr., the first person to fill the position. Brumby started work in 1946, his first assignment being to attend the Florida shows in January, returning to New York in time for the Garden.

1941

A Final Bow to Peacetime

This was the last Westminster before the U.S. entered World War II. The proceeds from the event totaling $5,000 were donated to the New York Chapter of the American Red Cross.

There was a new show format. The event was cut from three days to two. The numerical limit was reduced to 2,500. The toy benching was moved from the arena to the basement where the other benching was, allowing for 16 rings instead of 12. Breed judging took a day and a half. Groups, with one large ring, started on the second afternoon, with final awards in the evening.

An obedience demonstration was a big attraction. In a mass drill, after being put through intricate maneuvers, the dogs were lined up at one end of the arena, and their handlers, at the other. The dogs

were then summoned one at a time, all remaining at attention until called.

The firemen of New York had their innings when 25 Dalmatian mascots competed in the ring. As Henry R. Ilsley of the *Times* reported, they were judged on "alertness, obedience and other characteristics of the breed that would fit them for guard dogs in the city's fire stations." The judges: Fire Commissioner John J. McElligot, Col. John Reed Kilpatrick, president of Madison Square Garden, and Westminster president, Gerald Livingston. The winner: "King" from Engine Company 311, Springfield, Queens, handled by George Donnelly.

Before the dog show opened, there was a Style Show in the Oval Room at the Ritz Carlton. "Kennel Champions Accompany Manikins Wearing Attires Matching Their Color," read the headline. Virginia Pope in the *Times* called it a "dress rehearsal" for the dog show. She said the dogs, straining at their leashes, drew the girls over the runway at such a rapid pace

Right: 1942, Dr. Samuel Milbank turns over the show proceeds to Mrs. David Chalinor, Executive Chairman of the Women's Committee of the Red Cross War Fund of Greater New York— *WKC, Brown photo*

that at times it was not possible to take in details of the costumes. But the clothes, she said, won their own blue ribbons of success.

A Dog Hero award went to Tim, a German Shepherd Dog owned by John Muncio. Tim had saved the life of 11-year-old Charles Bossman, who was buried under bricks and debris when a building collapsed. The dog led his owner to the wreckage and the lad was discovered. "Little Charley" was present on the final evening as Lowell Thomas, news commentator, announced presentation of the award.

1942

The American Red Cross

Arthur Frederick Jones of the *Gazette* observed that the crowd at Westminster always mirrored the times. This year, he

Above: Judging Best in Show, 1940 — *WKC, Brown photo*

said, the reflection was full of uniforms, American, Canadian and English.

Burris Jenkins, Jr., as we see in his cartoon from the *New York Journal American*, looked at the war and the dog show from a different angle. If we don't get busy and win the war, he said, we are doomed.

The event netted the Red Cross $5,000. There were just 158 fewer dogs than a year ago. Henry R. Ilsley in the *Times* saw the show as far more than a notable institution with an unbroken record. It was a

show of the finest canine specimens from many lands and demonstrated the intellectual powers and the trainability of fine dogs. It was part of "carrying on," he said, in line with public policy in wartime. It would also aid America's greatest war and peacetime charitable organization.

There was a display by the New England Disaster Squad, exemplified by firemen and their Dalmatians from the Boston Fire Department. They gave a thrilling demonstration of rescue work during a "blackout."

The New England Dog Training Club put on an obedience demonstration directed by Boston newspaperman Bert Turnquist. The participants were amateur trainers, each with his or her house pet. They executed an intricate military drill, a number of games, and a "Salute to Victory."

On closing night there was a Red Cross pageant. The lights were dimmed, and the 100-piece band of the New York Fire Department ushered in a large number of Red Cross nurses, defense workers, air raid wardens and firemen with their dogs. At one end of the arena, there was a large Red Cross poster, showing four members of the armed forces and a Red Cross nurse. This was spotlighted while Hilda Burke of the Metropolitan Opera sang Irving Berlin's new song "Angels of Mercy." The poster then "came to life" – when five uniformed service personnel burst forth through the paper of the poster and marched into view. The American flag was raised. One and all sang "The Star-Spangled Banner."

1943

The dog has been recognized by the War Department and the Navy Department as possessing endowments of loyalty and courage and highly developed perceptive senses which make him an ideal teammate of soldiers and sailors.—Harry I. Caesar, Popular Dogs, February 1943

Dogs for Defense

This year's Westminster was given for the benefit of Dogs for Defense.

The show's final session, which emphasized the War Dog, seemed to rouse more enthusiasm than the colorful ceremony of choosing Best in Show. It was an exhibition of dogs by servicemen in uniform. There was a marching band. Muriel Dickson, operatic soprano, sang an original composition by Arthur Roland dedicated to the "Canine Corps." It included a demonstration of straight drilling to music and also of the more serious tasks of their guard, rescue and combat work.

In *Popular Dogs*, William Kendrick, who sometimes spoke of special attractions as

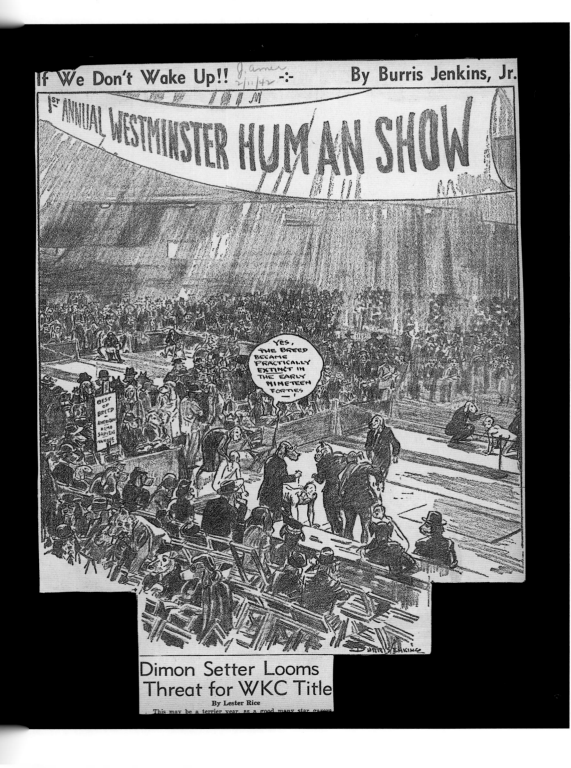

"prolonged periods of entertainment," declared the War Dog program "excellent."

There was also what Kendrick called "the most unique Parade of Champions in history." Only Champions with one or more Best in Shows to their credit were eligible. The entry fee was $5 for every Best in Show a dog had won. The 55 entries accumulated a purse of over $2,000, which also went to DFD. The one and only Ch. Nornay Saddler, with over 50 such awards to his credit, played the stellar role in this collection of all-stars.

Harry I. Caesar was DFD's founding president. In barely a year's time, he had rallied support from the American Kennel Club, the Professional Handlers Association, obedience training clubs across the country, not to mention Seeing Eye, Inc., which lent them a trainer, and finally the Army and Navy Departments. "We are now," he said in *Popular Dogs,* "the sole and official procurement agency for War Dogs." The agency was now shipping between 400 and 500 dogs per week to the training centers.

1944

Walked Longest to Get There: The Stabers from California. On the trip across it was fifteen cars from their bunks to the baggage car that housed their Pointer.—Popular Dogs, March 1944

War Dogs

This was the third Westminster since America had entered World War II. The proceeds were again donated to Dogs for Defense. The show's theme was War Dogs; the talk was Strong Dogs. "Never," said *Popular Dogs,* "has the emphasis been so placed on soundness, movement, bone."

And no breed, said *Dogs in Canada,* had so impressed itself on the mind of the American public during the war as the Doberman Pinscher. "Because of its intelligence, daring and dauntless courage in the South Pacific, the 'devil dog' of the Marine Corps has made history." Hundreds had gone overseas to the front lines. There were 107 benched, 38 more than last year.

Right: Mrs. Geraldine R. Dodge and former President Herbert Hoover at the show, 1943 —*WKC, Brown photo*

Opposite: Burris Jenkins, Jr., on the War— *WKC, Reprinted special permission King Features Syndicate*

The largest entry was of Dachshunde (still spelled in the German manner), numbering 121.

Once more, the closing session was spectacular. There was a parade of two dozen Coast Guardsmen and Soldiers, who put their war dogs through a roster of obedience, guard, attack and casualty duties. The breeds were Dobermans, German Shepherds, Airedales, Dalmatians and Boxers. William Kendrick in *Popular Dogs* lamented that his own breed, the Bull Terrier, widely used by the British, was not among them.

There was a parade of champions, each paying a minimum entry of $25. There was a puppy lottery in which anyone purchasing a War Bond of any denomination was entered.

Then came what Henry R. Ilsley of the *Times* called "one of the most exciting demonstrations ever witnessed at Westminster." It was an auction in which the top bidders had first choice of puppies of "famous ancestry." The bidding was in war bonds to go to the fund of Dogs for Defense. The highest bid was $130,000, made by Mrs. Emily

Best Brace in Show, 1943. Owner Mrs. Sherman Hoyt and Kennel Manager Mac McBrian, handling Broadrun Cheerio and Broadrun Cheery, with judge Gerald Livingston and Chief Steward Caswell Barrie— *WKC, Brown photo*

Left:
U.S. Coast
Guard exhibi-
tion, 1945—
*WKC, Brown
photo*

**Opposite,
Bottom Left:**
John W. Cross,
Jr.—*WKC*

**Opposite,
Bottom Right:**
Mementos of
John Cross's
Westminster
career—*WKC*

Coster Morris for a Fox Terrier puppy by Ch. Nornay Saddler. The total amount of bonds sold was in excess of $500,000.

1945

The Last Show?

Rumor had it that this would be one of the last dog shows held in the United States "for the duration." Word went the rounds that no shows would be permitted after March 9th until V-Day.

Everyone was caught off guard. People suddenly knew what a great privilege they had been enjoying and what a void would be created if they could no longer show their dogs. The *Gazette* remembered the boost the show had given the K-9 Corps in the early days when many doubted the value of war dogs. They would not hazard a guess as to what type of activity might be worked out to sustain show interest without hampering the war effort or conflicting with the government's restrictions on travel.

The show was given this year for the benefit of the National War Fund. A War Dog Show, conceived and planned by dog trainer Lt. Willie Necker, drew thunderous applause. Henry R. Ilsley in the *Times* called it a "nerve-tingling" exhibition of trained dogs by a detail from the

United States Coast Guard. A parade of champions followed. This led to Best in Show, in which all six finalists were American-bred, and all were handled by their owners.

Popular Dogs later issued a report on the year. They said that despite the war, travel restrictions and rationing, there were 138 all-breed shows and 75 specialties. Of the 29 states that housed at least one all-breed show, California led the country for the first time. With its 20 shows, it was ahead of both New York and Pennsylvania, which tied at 14 each. Best in Show awards were, as the magazine put it, pretty much a matter of "letting every dog have its day." No one dog earned more than five finals.

1946

The One-Day Show

The war was over. The club wanted to ease the crowded conditions at the show. They planned 12 rings instead of 17. They shortened lunch and dinner breaks. Judging would proceed in all rings without interruption. Breed judging would take a day and a half. Three groups would be done on the second afternoon, followed by Children's Handling. The evening would include the remaining groups and Willy Necker's trained dogs.

They would then do Best in Show. They little realized what lay ahead.

The two-day event was to open on Tuesday, but on Monday, the eve of Lincoln's birthday, Mayor William O'Dwyer closed the city down. A tugboat strike was in its ninth day. Tugboats towed coal and oil barges to the islands on which most of the city stood. Fuel supplies were low. He had already closed schools and dimmed streetlights. Then, as of midnight Monday, he shut down every nonessential business, including stores, theaters, restaurants, bars, and most assuredly Madison Square Garden.

Editors at *The New Yorker* would later recall passing the holiday as part of "a smiling, idle crowd" in Central Park. They liked it. It was a different story at the Garden, where several hundred dogs were already benched and preparations were under way to start judging at 10 the next morning. The *Times* said that Westminster had survived World War II but would almost certainly be "torpedoed" by the tugboats.

A Tuesday headline read, DOG SHOW OPENING HANGS IN BALANCE. Finally in the afternoon, it was announced that at 6 PM, business could resume its normal course. The news brought cheers from the hundreds of exhibitors still at the Garden. Chairman Proctor announced that judging would start at 9 AM, instead of 10. Seventeen rings would be used, instead of the 12 that had been so carefully planned for. Exhibitors should arrive early. Loud speakers would tell them when and where their breeds would be judged. The show would probably run until 3 AM.

Instead, by keeping the rings constantly in use, the breeds were completed by 9 PM. The groups followed immediately. Time was found for Willy Necker's dog act. Best in Show was awarded by 12:15 AM, 15 minutes earlier than the year before.

The *Gazette* said it marked "the highest possible point in cooperation among the exhibitors, management, handlers, and the laborers who knocked down and put up rings continually as the judging scene shifted."

And the tugboats? They were back in service within 24 hours.

1948

John W. Cross, Jr.

John Cross, 39, became Westminster's Chairman in 1948 and served (except for 1955) through 1968. He had joined the club in 1935.

Under his chairmanship, WKC maintained the rich tradition that kept it at the forefront of the country's dog events. Cross was identified with pure-bred dogs for more than 30 years. He bred and exhibited Bullmastiffs. He imported some of the first of the breed to come to this county and owned the first Bullmastiff to be registered by AKC. He was one of the organizers of the Bullmastiff Club of America, which was elected to AKC membership in 1936, and was the club's first delegate to AKC. His Bullmastiff, Ch. Jeannette of Brooklands of Felon's Fear, whose sculpture we see here, won BOB at the Garden in 1936.

Cross also owned and showed Labrador Retrievers, Standard Schnauzers, Welsh Terriers and Kerry Blue Terriers. In 1945, he became AKC delegate of the San Mateo Kennel Club, serving them until 1955.

Cross was a member of AKC's New York Trial Board from 1936 to 1939. He was licensed to judge all working breeds and had many assignments in this group until

Jeannette of Brookland's of Felon's Fear, owned by John Cross. Bronze by June Harrah, 1948—WKC

he retired as a judge in 1963. In 1968, Cross resigned as WKC Chairman and was elected as the Senior Vice-President of AKC. He also served on the board of managers of ASPCA.

1950

Rule Creates Rhubarb

The rhubarb, as John Rendel of the *Times* called it, was all about cleaning agents.

A new rule specified that if any substance was used in a dog's coat for cleaning purposes or any other reason, all traces of it were to be removed before the dog entered the ring. White powder, for example, was commonly employed to make white dogs whiter, and exhibitors had come to feel very free about bringing dogs into the ring with powder very much in evidence. Now, however, if a judge found any trace of such substance in a dog's coat, the dog was to be

dismissed from the ring. What would judges do? This was the first show under the new rule. There were doubts about whether it would or could be enforced.

The test came with a white miniature Poodle, Ch. Snow Boy of Fircot, owned by Mrs. Sherman Hoyt, a prominent breeder-exhibitor, who had become famous in 1935 as the first woman to handle a dog—in this case her own dog—to Best in Show at the Garden. The judge was Mrs. Beatrice Godsol, a well-known arbiter from California. Mrs. Godsol judged the Poodle in the normal manner, gaiting him first and then going over him with her hands. The examination finished, she looked at her hands and then rubbed them down the sides of her dress. The dress was of a dark solid color, and the chalk that was now very evident on it left no doubt at ringside as to what she had found on the dog.

When she dismissed the dog, Mrs. Hoyt charged "bias," saying she would protest to AKC. The AKC field representative Alfred M. Dick—who in 1968 would become AKC president—said that the judge had had no choice. He said that he himself had seen that powder had remained in the dog's coat.

1951

Last week's most photogenic performers were the pooches at the Dawg Show. Such hams. —*Walter Winchell, February 20, 1951*

Old Timer

"How many Westminsters have you attended?"

It's a common question, and Arthur Frederick Jones of the *Gazette* complained that there always seemed to be someone who could top your story. However, he reported this year that to the best of his knowledge, there was only one person present who had attended every one of the 75 Westminsters. It was A. Clinton Wilmerding, in his 92nd year.

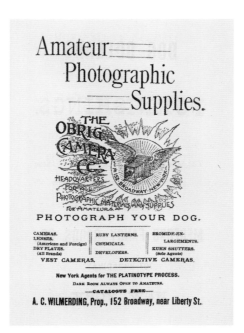

Amateur Photographic Supplies.

THE OBRIG CAMERA CO.

HEADQUARTERS FOR PHOTOGRAPHIC MATERIALS AND SUPPLIES FOR AMATEURS.

PHOTOGRAPH YOUR DOG.

CAMERAS. LENSES. (American and Foreign) DRY PLATES. (All Brands) VEST CAMERAS.	RUBY LANTERNS. CHEMICALS. DEVELOPERS.	BROMIDE-EN-LARGEMENTS. KUHN SHUTTERS. (Sole Agents) DETECTIVE CAMERAS.

New York Agents for THE PLATINOTYPE PROCESS.

Dark Room Always Open to Amateurs.

—CATALOGUE FREE—

A. C. WILMERDING, Prop., 152 Broadway, near Liberty St.

The National Geographic Magazine visited the show in 1953 for publication at show time 1954. Their pictures show off the distinctive red and yellow colors of Foley's benching and ring equipment.

1957

French Bulldogs

Ralph and Amanda West of Detroit were owners of the champion in the Breed-Winning Department this year. Their French Bulldog Ch. Bouquet Nouvelle Ami, as noted by *Times* writer John Rendel, was just under six years old, and this was his fifth straight Best-of-Breed medallion at Westminster.

In time, the dog would take a total of eight consecutive breed wins there, and eventually Amanda West with her French Bulldogs would establish the longest unbroken string of breed wins in Westminster's history, having first won the award in 1953 and taking the breed every year thereafter through 1973 (see page 101).

1958

Country in the City

There had been a demonstration of field dogs at every show since 1951. There would be two more of them in 1962 and 1963. Chairman John Cross, writing about the show of 1953 in the National Geographic Society's publication, *The Book of Dogs,* described the scene of these special features very nicely.

He had been part of the pure-bred scene since his early teens. A breeder, exhibitor and judge of spaniels, he officiated at Westminster several times in the 1880s and 1890s.

"Many things," said Jones, "that to us are just historical statistics in cold type are to him intimate memories, and he tells of them with all the warmth that belonged in that era long ago."

1954

George F. Foley, Superintendent

It was his 27th Westminster. There would be 15 more. According to *People Today* of February 19, 1954, George F. Foley had more to do with dogs than any other man in the country. "Fifty-two weeks a year," said the magazine, "the 5' 7", shiny-bald czar of the canines moves around the East as chief superintendent of major dog shows from Chicago to Boston, from Bar Harbor to Havana."

Foley provided everything from $50,000 worth of benching and ring equipment to a safe avenue of escape for a harassed judge. The Foley Dog Show Organization of Philadelphia handled 140 dog shows a year.

When an event like Westminster was imminent and all entries had been received and catalogued, Foley moved his equipment into five red and yellow

trailer trucks that traveled 35,000 miles a year. For Westminster, he uprooted 25 of his staff for the trip to New York. Once there, he hired 100 itinerants to help set up the 12 judging rings and turn the 201 x 375 foot Garden basement "into a livable place for 2,500 yammering performers."

An ex-breeder himself, Foley had once kenneled 140 Boston Terriers, but he was too busy now to keep even one dog of his own. He liked to remind owners that "just having a dog jump up on you when you come home at night" might be better than winning a blue ribbon.

Among his many honors, Foley was named Man of the Half-Century, in a nation-wide poll conducted in 1950 by the Gaines Dog Research Center—the same poll in which. Mrs. Geraldine R. Dodge was named Dogdom's Woman of the Half-Century.

WESTMINSTER *continued from page 31*

KEEPING TROUBLE OUT OF DOG SHOWS IS HIS BUSINESS

THE FRIGHTENING TASK of bringing together under one roof at the same time 2,500 highly strung and priceless show dogs, plus their owners and handlers, is a job so nearly impossible that only one man in the country has for the past 27 years been allowed to do it. He is 72-year-old George Foley of Philadelphia, the professional superintendent of the Westminster show since 1928.

Normally a quiet-voiced little man with the kindly patience and demeanor of a Sunday School teacher, Foley's lifetime of bossing the nation's top dog shows has left him with the tenacity of a deaf bulldog, and if provoked, the fighting instincts of a great Dane.

DETECTIVES GUARD DOGS

Foley found out a long time ago that there was no such thing as a smoothly run dog show. A show's success can be judged only in how low the number of trouble-making incidents can be kept. His basic principle

GEORGE FOLEY became professional supervisor of Westminster show in 1928.

and officials on the doors. Every unused and locked exit door is fastened with a Foley seal (a paper sticker) to make sure nobody gets in or out except through the proper gates. While

sands of dollars and large chunks of their own vanity and ego invested in the dogs, will stop at nothing short of murder to win—and even that has been tried more than once. A prize Boston terrier owned by. Frank Brumby, of Long Island, was fed ground glass and died before it could get into the ring and a best-in-show contender was once slashed with a razor.

In addition to attempts at murdering the competition, belladonna has been put into a dog's eyes to make them shine more winningly; badly marked dogs have been dyed; others have had spots painted on them with boot black; judges have been accused of favoritism and outright dishonesty, and at least one has been banished from the ring for having the smell of drink on his breath. Hardly a show goes by that Foley doesn't have to referee a quarrel, calm down upset losers and convince at least six people that the judge hasn't been fixed.

Left:
George F. Foley, Czar of the Canines—*WKC*

Above Left:
A. Clinton Wilmerding. as seen in the Keystone Kennel Club catalog, 1893 —*AKC*

Above Right:
Wilmerding's WKC catalog ad 1888—*WKC*

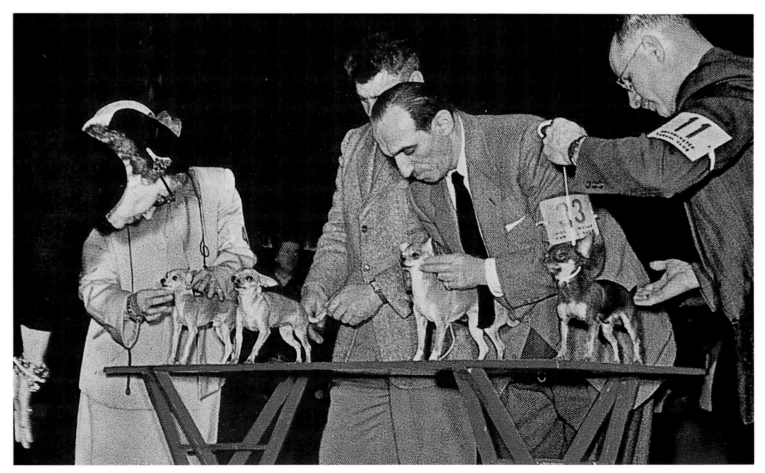

National Geographic at the Show, 1953

Above Left:
Sealyhams under
judgement
—*Robert Sisson/NGS*
Image Collection

Above Right:
Joan Gordon with
her Yorkie Ch.
Star Twightlight
of Clu-Mor
—*Culver, W. R./*
NGS Image
Collection

Bottom: Mrs.
Justin Herold
judging
Chihuahuas
—*Culver, W. R./*
NGS Image
Collection

Above: Field Demo, 1955 —*Gazette*

Right: Willard Mullin, in the *New York World-Telegram* and *The Sun,* February 8, 1954—*WKC, permission granted by the Estate of Willard Mullin and Shirley Mullin Rhodes*

Far Left: Mrs. West's 21 Best of Breed Medallions— WKC, *Gift of Ron Pemberton*

Left: Mrs. Amanda West with Ch. Bouquet Nouvelle Ami, Best of Breed, 1953, and judge Louis Murr— *Shafer photo, courtesy Jim Grebe*

Right: Mrs. Hyslop's silver prizes—*Private Collection*

Far Right: Mrs. Hyslop at the Garden, February 11, 1945 with Cairn Terrier, Ch. Kilmet of Cairndale and Great Dane, Vance of Rosehall—*Dogs in Canada*

"It is 5 o'clock and a sudden change takes place," he wrote. "Corn shocks, small evergreens, and piles of brush are brought into the ring, and Westminster, harking back to its founding days, presents an indoor demonstration of how bird dogs work in the field.... These are true working bird dogs going through their paces in the most alien environment one can imagine – before the eyes of thousands in the heart of a great city. They point.... They demonstrate their retrieving skill.... The shooting is done with blank cartridges."

Full credit for staging most of these events went to Evelyn Monte, dog writer, field trial judge and noted authority on field trial dogs.

See page 41 for an engraving of one of the earliest field dog demonstrations at the Garden.

1959

Cairns

Mrs. Betty Hyslop of Brockton, Ontario, Canada, had the winning Cairn terrier this year, Ch. Redletter Miss Splinters. The win ended what would be Mrs. Hyslop's longest unbroken string of Best of Breed wins at the Garden, a total of 14. She would never take more such awards consecutively.

However, by 1993, she would set the all-time record for total Best of Breeds at Westminster, having taken the award there 40 times in 55 years.

Mrs. Hyslop started in Cairns and Danes in the 1930s—hence her kennel name, Cairndania—but later focused exclusively on Cairns. Her last awards at the Garden were Best of Opposite Sex and

an Award of Merit in the breed in 1995. Mrs. Hyslop died in 1998.

1960

Aussies!

There was a startling entry in the Miscellaneous Class this year of 59 Australian Terriers. The class, in which no championship points were awarded and which was open to breeds not registered in the AKC studbook, usually had an entry of less than half a dozen.

The turnout was the work of Mrs. Nell Fox of Pleasant Pastures Kennels, Point Pleasant, N.J. She was said to have canvassed the entire U.S. to find 59 dogs with willing owners.

Mrs. Fox was a New Zealander who

moved to the U.S. in the early 1900s. In 1945, she imported her first Aussies from England, where they had been registered since 1933. In time, she prevailed on Australian breeders to help her establish the breed here. It made its WKC debut in Miscellaneous in 1957. At that time John Rendel of the *Times* remarked that AKC "does not take new breeds into its cherished stud book haphazardly, and when it does, a tremendous amount of paper work is involved."

This year's record entry marked the end of Mrs. Fox's struggle. AKC opened its studbook to the breed later that year. Aussies were shown for championship points in 1961. Best of Breed at Westminster that year was Mary P. Barth's Seven Oaks Tucker Box.

1961

Profound Regret

TV coverage of the show had begun in 1948, but this newest of the media was still not without its problems. In particular, the judging of Best in Show this year did not provide the event with a satisfactory finale. The final award was unquestioned, but judge Dr. Joseph Redden had taken barely a minute per dog. He was clearly "time conscious" and kept glancing at his watch. He seemed unhappy. Indeed, George Berner, editor of *Dog World,* said he looked "extremely angry." He had not seen Dr. Redden's face himself but had talked with friends

Photo by Brown

Right:
The closing of the "old" Garden, 1968. From left, Chairman Cross, Madison Square Garden President Ned Irish, WKC President W.A. Rockefeller, Percy Roberts and Anne Rogers Clark—*WKC, Shafer photo*

Below:
William Brown, photographer and friend of dogs—*WKC*

who—along with all other viewers—had seen him clearly on television.

When the judging ended, there was a polite round of applause. The crowd also booed. The abruptness of the decision seemed to leave the handler as surprised as anyone.

In a statement the next day, Westminster expressed "profound regret" for what had happened. They said that an on-the-spot decision had been made to try to let the most possible people see the Best-in-Show judging. They had advised the judge to try to finish before 11 PM when most television channels would cut off the show for their regular newscasts.

In trying to meet this deadline, Dr. Redden, who had had nine earlier Westminster assignments – doing a group on three occasions – gave the impression that his judging was not thorough. Further, in judging Best Brace in Show, which took place just before Best in Show, he named the Keeshonden as winners although an eligible brace of Basset Hounds had not yet entered the ring.

A month later, AKC fined Westminster $500 for its part in the hasty judging that spoiled the drama of Best in Show and destroyed the validity of the Best Brace in Show. Regarding Best Brace in Show, the AKC board declared "no contest" and canceled the award.

AKC fined Superintendent George Foley $100. They also suspended Dr. Redden's judging privileges. In 1963, having been reinstated, Dr. Redden returned to

Westminster to judge a number of sporting breeds.

1963

Brownie

"Smile at the birdie... Say cheese... Don't move. These were the familiar instructions of the photographer. Not so with William Brown of New Hyde Park, L. I. He growls or barks like a dog."

Thus began Sam Goldaper's tribute to William Brown in *The Herald Tribune* after this year's show. Brown, or "Brownie" as he was affectionately known, had been Westminster's official photographer since 1939. He came from Cincinnati, where during the depression, badly needing work, he turned a hobby into a livelihood. Now 72, he was traveling 35,000 miles a year, covering 100 shows. He had taken by his own estimate over a million dog photographs.

According to Goldaper, the photographs were catalogued in 100 filing cabinets in Brown's home. A handful of his pictures survive in Westminster's archives, together with a file of dog magazine covers, which frequently carried Brown's photographs.

1968

Fond Farewells

This year's show would close Garden III.

"After the dogs, come the wreckers," said the *Times*.

In a ceremony just before Best in Show, Ned Irish, president of the famous sports site, presented engraved silver trays commemorating the closing to Westminster officers and two charter members of the Garden's new Hall of Fame. Those honored were President William A. Rockefeller, Secretary Dr. Samuel Milbank, Chairman John W. Cross, Jr., and the hall-of-famers, Anne Rogers Clark and Percy Roberts. The last two accounted between them for seven Best in Shows at the Garden, three for Mrs. Clark and four for Mr. Roberts.

In presenting the symbolic silverware, Ned Irish said that Westminster had been a tenant of Madison Square Garden longer than any other group. Mrs. Clark later expressed what must have been the feelings of many. "Westminster will never be the same for me again," she told Sam Goldaper of the *Times*. "The ghosts will live here forever for me, the great dogs, the outstanding handlers, the people who taught me the basics of dog handling. They're all being left behind. Westminster at the new Garden won't be able to replace these memories."

A Souvenir

Westminster's box holders were always listed in the show catalog, and for most of the shows in Madison Square Garden III, the American Kennel Club's box or loge number was 39.

In the highly utilitarian building, the loges, which circled the arena, were divided from each other by railings of heavy iron pipe. Each loge number was displayed on a sign fastened to the railing. Here we see a picture of the sign for Loge 39. About three by ten inches in size, it was found in the American Kennel Club's library in an envelope on which Beatrice Peterson, AKC's librarian from 1937 to 1975, had written "AKC Loge plaque from old Madison Square Garden Westminster Show."

It seems likely that at some point during the final show there, an AKC board member, armed with a screwdriver, helped himself to this souvenir. We will never know just who it was, but Miss Petersen knew a good thing when she saw it and squirreled the sign away for Barbara Kolk, AKC's librarian in the year 2000, to share with Westminster's historian.

1969

A kind of Lincoln Center for the perspiring arts.—The New York Times, 1968

Madison Square Garden IV

As early as 1959, there was talk about a new Madison Square Garden. It would be built on an unspecified site on the

Above: Souvenir from Garden III
—*Courtesy AKC*

Left: Garden IV, a circular complex atop Penn Station—*Courtesy Madison Square Garden*

Above:
Sensation, 1972,
by Iwan Lotton,
oil—*Courtesy Tom
Crowe*

Far Right:
Sensation as
Cover Dog. The
Iwan Lotton
painting has been
flipped over to
meet an editor's
needs—*Courtesy
Tom Crowe*

West Side at a cost reported by *Time* to be $38 million. In 1961, *Time* said the site would be the air space atop Pennsylvania Station and upped the estimated cost to $75 million. In 1963, *Business Week* raised the ante to $105 million—noting among other things that it would be necessary for the builders not to interrupt train service in Penn Station, over which the new complex was to be built and through which 200,000 commuters circulated daily.

Kurth Sprague, in his *History of the National Horse Show,* described the process of bringing it all about in some detail. Charles Luckman Associates were to design the complex, and according to the project architect, Sherman Schneider, a primary goal was to provide an unobstructed view of the main arena from all seats. The seating arrangement around the main arena would be an oval. Overhead would be a circular ceiling with its center portion supported by cables, the first of its kind in Manhattan. The roof as a unit would rest on 48 perimeter columns.

The plans outraged historical preservationists, who argued that Penn Station was an architectural landmark. The American Institute of Architects called the new design "a vulgar tour de force of entertainment." *Time* held that while no one was likely to mourn the passing of the previous Garden, many would regret the leveling of the "grayed, Grecian, granite Penn Station," modeled on the ancient Baths of Caracalla.

The new Garden finally arose above Penn Station on the western half of the two-block area bounded by 31st and 33rd Streets and 7th and 8th Avenues. It occupied 8½ acres, of which over half was taken up by a plaza landscaped with trees and shrubbery. The "Madison Square Garden Sports and Entertainment Center" included "the Garden," seating 20,234, the 5,227-seat Felt Forum, a 501-seat movie theatre, an exposition rotunda, a 48-lane bowling center (later converted to restaurants), a hall of fame and art gallery, and a 29 story office building. A four-lane roadway between the Garden and the office building could handle 2,000 cars an hour. Joining the two buildings was a large glass-enclosed mall.

The main arena was in a large circular structure, and spectators entered and left it by means of four glass-and-steel escalator towers that, as Sprague put it, were "affixed like cereal boxes to the exterior wall." The building's amenities were distributed over three main levels that were split into 13 floors. An inside truck ramp, following the curved outline of the building, extended from the street up to the fifth level, where the main arena was. A freight elevator took dog show exhibitors and their dogs and equipment up to this level, where the benching area was located.

The dog show world's introduction to the new Garden came at Westminster in 1969, in the midst of one of the bitterest snowstorms in many years. Airports were shut and highways clogged. Walter Fletcher wrote in the *Times* about some of the extraordinary difficulties that exhibitors overcame to get their dogs into the ring.

Robert Sharp bogged down on the New England Thruway at 4 PM Sunday. At 5:30 the next morning, he set out with a Lhasa Apso under his arm and trudged more than six miles, reaching the Pelham Bay subway at 9:30.

Mr. and Mrs. Leo Farrell left Boston at 9 AM Sunday and ended up twelve hours later in a snowbank at 182nd Street near Tremont Avenue in the Bronx. When they tried to take their 180-pound Great Dane into the subway, a policeman stopped them, saying it was against the law. A man who saw their plight said he worked with juveniles in conjunction with the 46th Precinct, and went to the station house, where he got them a pass so they could take their Dane on the subway.

Mrs. Gayle Gerber Bontecou left Millbrook, N.Y., at noon on Sunday with a Scottish Deerhound, ran into a snowbank on the Taconic State Parkway near Yorktown Heights and finally arrived at the Garden at 2 PM, Monday. The normally three-hour trip had taken 26 hours.

Mrs. Clayton Thomas and Mrs. Caroline Kierstead, with a Pembroke Welsh Corgi, started from Northampton, Mass., at 9:30 AM on Sunday. They spent most of the night snowbound on Route 95, finally warmed up in an all-night bowling alley in the Bronx and reached the Garden at 9:30, a 24-hour trip.

There were many others, including an army of exhibitors who had shown dogs on Sunday in the terrier specialty shows at an uptown armory in Manhattan. They brought their dogs downtown by subway. Happily, none of the animals had the size or heft of a Great Dane. They encountered reluctance but no outright resistance from transit police.

It was also Superintendent George Foley's 42nd Westminster, and he found himself at the Garden with many, many people who would normally have gone back to their hotels but had chosen not to venture outside. So many stayed the night that the virtually brand new "Sports and Entertainment Center" was affectionately dubbed "Foley's Flophouse."

1972

Sensation Again

In the early 1970s, Iwan Lotton created an oil portrait of Sensation for Superintendent George Foley.

Based on the Wellstood engraving, published in 1879, Lotton's painting is the only color rendition we have of the great lemon and white Pointer.

The portrait appeared on the cover of *Popular Dogs* in February 1972, though in reproducing it for that purpose, it was flipped over. Presumably the editors wanted the dog to point away from the spine of the magazine rather than toward it. The publication offered full-color 16" x 20" prints of the picture at $3.95, plus $.90 shipping. A copy of the magazine has survived in the club's archives, though no copy of the print itself.

The oil painting hangs today at the headquarters of MB-F, Inc., Westminster's current show Superintendent.

1976

Evelyn Shafer

In 1942, shortly after William Brown became the club's official photographer, Percy T. Jones came on as a second photographer with the same title. The show clearly warranted having two to share the workload. However, after six years, because of failing health, Jones closed his studio permanently. At that point, he asked Westminster to consider Evelyn Shafer as a replacement. She had been associated with him for 10 years, he said, and he recommended her highly.

Evelyn M. Shafer was hired, starting with the show of 1948, and covered 29 Westminsters in all. Here we see her at the governors' dinner on Sunday evening before the centennial show, after announcing that this would be her last Westminster. Club president William Rockefeller has just presented her with a gift commemorating her years of service.

Right: The Poodle as King, by Arnold Roth, 1980 — *Sports Illustrated, courtesy Arnold Roth*

Below: Evelyn Shafer with President William Rockefeller, 1976 — *WKC*

Below Left: Shafer's ad — *WKC*

Official Photographer - - - Westminster

Evelyn Shafer

FINE PHOTOGRAPHS   BENCH . . . FIELD

54 West 71st Street   New York 23, N. Y.   Trafalgar 3-2256

1980

Zounds! No Hounds!

Sports Illustrated gave the show lengthy coverage this year—with pictures! It was a long lament by E. M. Swift to the effect that a "hound dog" had never won Best in Show at Westminster and never would. He was sure of it. "Zounds! No hounds!" he said. It was more than he could bear.

Swift didn't say that in 1964 a Whippet had won. He conceded that in 1957 an Afghan had taken the crowning honor, but an Afghan was not what he called a "hound dog." An Afghan was a courser, a sight hound, a glamorous, coated animal that was fast and flashy and raced about

"with its nose in the air." Swift took to scent hounds with short coats and long ears and nose to the ground. All they needed at a dog show was a trim of the whiskers, a bath and a nail-clip, and out they plodded "looking like Huck Finn loose in Tiffany's."

John Cross, when Chairman, once said of the ladies and gentlemen of the press that if they didn't go to many shows, their reporting "tended to lean heavily toward the humorous approach." He was right, though Swift's approach, if untutored, was not unfriendly.

Arnold Roth drew the pictures for Swift's plaint, one of which we see here. It shows the Poodle as King, with a pair of "hound dogs" (a Basset Hound and a Dachshund) carrying the end of his royal train.

This year's Best-in-Show judge, E. Irving Eldredge, didn't accept Swift's views. He said a top dog of any breed could win at the Garden whether glamorous or not. "In fact," he said, "a truly fine Basset Hound looks glamorous to me. A good dog of any breed does."

1982

High Couture

The *Times* was always charmed by the sight of women judging dogs and often went into some detail about the clothes they wore. The paper gave a complete description of Anna Whitney's costume in 1888, for example, and in 1982 when Mrs. Nancy Lindsay judged Best in Show, Walter Fletcher, with his reporter's unerring eye, made a point of saying what a "striking picture" she made in the ring "wearing a long paisley skirt and a sapphire blue jacket."

On the day after the show, the Dog Fanciers Club held its traditional luncheon at which the group and Best in Show judges were asked to comment on the dogs they judged and on the show in general. At this time, Mrs. Lindsay told the story of her costume.

Wanting the right dress for the high honor of judging Best in Show, she visited a well-known couturier and told the clerk just what she wanted. She was looking for a dress with a floor-length skirt that was full enough to move around in easily but not too full. It must be of a material that did not make noise when she moved. The sleeves must be long and narrow, and the neckline, high. She wanted a dark color and no sequins and spangles. The clerk listened carefully and then finally asked: "Are you going to have a religious experience?"

1984

William P. Gilbert

This would be William P. Gilbert's last year as an official photographer at the show. Like Evelyn Shafer, a friendly rival in the dog show world, he was an institution at Westminster. Our photograph shows him at the 1976 governors' dinner at which Shafer announced her retirement. Gilbert was tall and thin and instantly recognizable with his wavy blond hair and a pipe, without which he was seldom seen

Gilbert lived through a professional's nightmare in 1968. It was his third year at the Garden. Color film was just coming into its own at dog shows then, and of the 29 rolls of pictures that he shot that year, 22 were rolls of black and white film mislabeled as color. After processing, the 22 rolls were a total loss. He later said he was cheered "to some extent" by the

Right: William Gilbert, 1976 *—WKC*

Far Right: Gilbert's ad *—WKC*

Below: Bill Cosby and AKC Vice President Terry Stacy, 1987—*Ashbey photo*

unanimously sympathetic reaction from his clients. He was able to settle with the company. In all, he photographed winners at the Garden for 20 years.

1987

Special Edition

W. H. Cosby, better known as Bill Cosby, aka Dr. Huxtable, was co-owner of the Wire Fox Terrier, Ch. Sylair Special Edition, who won this year's terrier group.

Cosby's co-owner was Jean Heath of Pleasanton, Calif. The English import, gaited by Clay Coady, had come to the Garden with what Walter Fletcher in the *Times* called very good credentials, having taken his 29th Best in Show at the Beverly Hills show a week earlier. Glen Somers who judged the group at Westminster, said of him, "He's a beautiful dog, the right size, with a good coat, and he's an outstanding mover."

Having won the group, however, he did not go on to take Best in Show. Cosby is shown here during the group judging with Terry Stacy, a vice-president of AKC.

1990

Ronald H. Menaker

Active in pure-bred dogs for more than 30 years and a member of Westminster since 1985, Ronald H. Menaker became the new Chairman in 1990.

He was a breeder and exhibitor of Giant Schnauzers and also showed Bedlington and Norfolk Terriers. He judges all working breeds, plus two terrier breeds. He is a member of the Bedlington Terrier Club of America, the Giant Schnauzer Club of America and the Norfolk and Norwich Terrier Club of America. As AKC delegate for the Des Moines Obedience Training Club, he served on the AKC board, Class of 1998, and is currently an AKC board member, Class of 2004.

Menaker has brought to the dog world broad experience in both profit and nonprofit businesses. He is the retired Managing Director and head of Corporate Services Worldwide for J. P. Morgan & Co. and retired President and board member of J. P. Morgan Services, Inc. He is Vice-Chairman of the New York Downtown Hospital, a trustee of the New York University/Mt. Sinai Medical Center, a director and past President of the AKC Museum of the Dog, a past trustee of the Morris Animal

Foundation, and a trustee of St. Hubert's Giralda Animal Welfare and Education Center.

1991

Centenary Gift

The Crufts Centenary Dog Show was held in Birmingham, England, this year on January 9-12.

By way of marking this important event, Westminster obtained from the estate of the late James A Farrell, Jr., a past president of Westminster, the trophy that his Lakeland Terrier, Ch. Stingray of Derryabah, had won as Best in Show at Westminster in 1968. Stingray had been Best in Show at Crufts in 1966 and is the only dog ever to have taken the top award at both shows.

The trophy, a silver bowl mounted on a silver-clad ebony base, was taken to England by Westminster member Walter Goodman, who presented it at the show to John MacDougall, Chairman of the Kennel Club. The trophy is on permanent display at the Kennel Club on Clarges Street in London.

Left: Walter Goodman, left, and John MacDougall, Chairman of the Kennel Club, 1991 —*WKC*

1994

MB-F

Moss Bow-Foley became Westminster's show superintendent this year.

The organization, with headquarters in Greensboro, N.C., traced its pedigree back to the early 1900s. Edgar A. Moss of Greensboro, N.C., A. Wilson Bow of Detroit, and George Foley of Philadelphia, were all independent dog show superintendents running dog shows in different regions. In 1967, Tom Crowe, a dog handler for some 15 years and a former associate at Bow Dog Shows, went to Greensboro to join the staff of Moss Dog Shows. Having acquired the stock of Moss, he merged with Bow to form Moss Bow Dog Shows. In 1973, Moss Bow acquired Foley, and by 1976, the firm was superintending some 400 shows a year. Crowe retired as head of MB-F in 1985 and serves as their Chairman of the Board.

Above: Tom Crowe—*Courtesy Tom Crowe*

Left: Ronald H. Menaker, WKC Chairman, 2000 —*Mary Bloom photo*

At Westminster, MB-F functions under the direction of Dorie Crowe-Mick, Tom Crowe's daughter. Her dog show career began as helper to her father when he was a professional handler. She became a licensed superintendent in 1970. She is vice-president and corporate secretary of MB-F.

Take the Lead

Take the Lead is a charitable foundation providing support for members of the dog show family suffering from life-threatening or terminal disease. The organization has helped people from coast to coast who suffered from cancer, heart disease, kidney disease, AIDS, and other illnesses and accidents.

Take the Lead states proudly, "We have made a difference."

In 1994, the group held a benefit at Westminster, a celebration with a light supper and wine after the group judging on Monday. Take the Lead has returned to Westminster each year since then. Chairman of the board of Take the Lead is WKC member Thomas H. Bradley, III.

Take the Lead at Westminster

1995

The Company You Keep

Patricia Craige Trotter set a record this year that has been unequaled. A school teacher from Carmel, Calif., and a breeder and exhibitor of Norwegian Elkhounds, she won the hound group at Westminster for the 10th time. She also competed for Best in Show at the Garden and lost for the 10th time.

Her group winners were:

1970 Ch. Vin-Melca's Vagabond
1971 Ch. Vin-Melca's Vagabond
1974 Ch. Vin-Melca's Homesteader
1977 Ch. Vin-Melca's Nimbus
1979 Ch. Vin-Melca's Nimbus
1986 Ch. Vin-Melca's Call to Arms
1989 Ch. Vin-Melca's Calista
1990 Ch. Vin-Melca's Calista
1994 Ch. Vin-Melca's Marketta
1995 Ch. Vin-Melca's Marketta

In the benching area, 1995 — *WKC, Ashbey photo*

1996

The Super Bowl is the Westminster of football.—Mark Roland, Gazette, 1996

Official Photographers

Of the dozens of photographers at the show, just two are "official." In a photo by Mary Bloom, we see them both, John L. Ashbey, who started taking pictures for Westminster in 1977 and Charles Tatham, who first covered the show officially in 1985.

1999

Changing of the Guard

In November, after 15 years as Westminster's Office Manager, Rita Lynch retired. An inveterate New York Mets fan and collector of baseball memorabilia, Mrs. Lynch came to Westminster from Metromedia, Inc. As the "office voice" of Westminster, she became known to hundreds of fanciers for her patience, her encyclopedic memory and her lovely sense of humor.

Mrs. Florence Foti, seen here with her cell phone, came in as Mrs. Lynch's successor just in time to oversee a move of the Westminster office to new quarters.

Veterinary Scholarships

In 1987, the Westminster Kennel Foundation set up a scholarship program for students at schools of veterinary medicine. Three grants were made, to Cornell, Tufts and the University of Pennsylvania. Since then, with the addition of Michigan State, Tuskegee University and the University of California, Davis, the annual number has grown to six.

The Foundation sends the scholarship money to the school, and the school selects the student. Sixty-seven scholarships have been granted to date.

Each year the Foundation has brought the recipients to New York to attend the dog show. In our picture (see page 112), we see the students of the academic year 1999-2000 at the Garden.

Film and Television

Motion picture cameras made a first appearance at Westminster in 1921. Shortly after 10 o'clock the first evening, a battery of arc lights blazed forth on the main floor, and two motion picture cameras were focused on the fashionably dressed assembly and the dogs. "The dogs did not mind being filmed," said the *Times*, "but society made strenuous efforts to keep out of the picture." The paper said no more.

The dog that began it all was Vagabond, and the rest are his descendents. In her book *Born to Win,* Mrs. Trotter says that her memories of the dogs to which her Elkhounds lost "embrace their breeders, their owners, their handlers, and their personal characters, as well as the contributions they have made to the world of dogs." She was privileged over the years, she says, to have been in the very "best of company."

In our picture, we see Mrs. Trotter and Vagabond in 1981 when they came back to Westminster for a parade of past group and Best in Show winners. Of Vagabond's performance then, Pat Beresford, editor of the *Gazette*, said that he "put on a show at age 14 that could put a dog less than half his age to shame."

Above Top: Mrs. Rita Lynch, 1998 —*Mary Bloom photo*

Above: Mrs Florence Foti, 1999 —*Mary Bloom photo*

Right: Charles Tattham, left, and John L. Ashbey, official photographers—*Mary Bloom photo*

Opposite page: Mrs. Patricia Craige Trotter with Ch. Vin-Melca's Vagabond, 1981 —*Photo courtesy Patricia Craige Trotter*

Left: The veterinary scholarship students at Westminster 2000, from left, Ms. Gabrielle Cohen (University of California, Davis), Ms. Aliya N. Scruggs (Tuskegee University), Mrs. Florence Shaw Rose (Tufts), Ms. Dawn Fitzhugh (University of Pennsylvania), Nicholas Skarich (Michigan State), Ms. Alexa M. Cox (Cornell), with Foundation Trustees, George F. Clements, Jr., Mrs. Robert V. Lindsay and Peter R. Van Brunt—*Ashbey photo*

Motion pictures were introduced as educational features at the shows of 1935 and 1936. Pointers, Setters, Retrievers and Spaniels were seen hunting and retrieving game from field and stream. The films were screened at intervals throughout the show until the start of group judging on the third day. They were projected on a big screen and could be seen from virtually anywhere in the arena.

Newsreel coverage began in the 1930s. Like television news coverage in the year 2000, it consisted of a few short, attention-grabbing moments at the show, the difference being that it was screened at the local movie house and wasn't seen until some days after the fact.

Lengthier films using sustained segments of the show were in wide circulation as early as 1940. Modern Talking Picture Service, Inc., in New York, had operating units from coast to coast. For a fee, they would show films of Westminster to any local kennel club in the country. Correspondence in Westminster's files shows that for the Harrisburg Kennel Club in Harrisburg, Pa., for example, the fee, which included sending the film, the projection equipment and an operator, was $18.

These short subjects were also shown in newsreel theaters. These were small movie houses, generally in or near the railroad station of large cities. There was one in Grand Central Terminal, where a program of short subjects was offered as an alternative to waiting in the waiting room. Newsreel Theatres, Inc., in New York wrote Westminster to report a good response at their various locations to the film of the 1940 dog show, adding that the "soundprint" for 1941 got an even better reaction.

TV coverage of Westminster began in 1948. Less than ten years had passed since August 26, 1939 when the New York Station W2XBS, using only two cameras, had produced the first telecast of a major league baseball game—a doubleheader between the Cincinnati Reds and the Brooklyn Dodgers at Ebbets Field.

A 1948 TV camera was still fairly primitive. Show coverage included an interlude of stunts of the youngsters and dogs of the New England Dog Training club. The aim was to demonstrate the pleasures of owning a trained companion dog. The *Times* noted that the presentation was appreciated by everyone except the television men "whose machines weren't much good when the lights flashed off and on, which they did once in a while to heighten the theatrical effect."

Yet in 1949, Alice Wagner of *Popular Dogs* could say:

Above: State-of-the-art TV camera, 1999 — *Mary Bloom photo*

Left: TV monitor in the arena, 1997 — *Ashbey photo*

Below: WKC ad, 1959 — *WKC*

Opposite Page, Bottom: Poodle watches Poodle, 1951 — *Popular Dogs*

"Television promises to do more for the pure-bred dog in one year than all of the words written in a lifetime!"

Mrs. Sherman Hoyt was then in her second year as TV commentator. Arthur Frederick Jones in the *Gazette* had high praise for her technical explanations of what was happening on screen and for the colorful bits of information she gave about the people involved.

Jones also noted a major technological step forward. "The new coaxial cable," he said, "enabled the telecast of the event to be enjoyed by television set owners as far away as the Middle West. Perhaps by another year the cable will reach all the way to the Pacific Coast."

In 1950, Westminster was the lead story in a "Radio and Television" column in the *Times*. WOR-TV would televise the show on two successive evenings. Edward Everett Horton would be master of ceremonies, interviewing dog owners and handlers in a special "doghouse" set up at the Garden. The actual judging in the show ring would be described by Mel Allen and Mrs. Hoyt. Prior to picking up

the show, said the paper, the station, "normally dark on Mondays," would show a feature film.

After just three years, it was clear that TV had created a sizable new dog show audience, those "privileged to sit at home in an easy chair and watch." Very soon, according to a survey cited in *Popular Dogs,* a majority of American homes would have TV sets.

As the 1900s drew to a close, the world was a very different place. As reported in

the *Times* in 1996, the USA Network televised three hours of the show nationally each night. The Madison Square Garden network showed the same telecast in the Northeast. Between them, the dog show was seen in about 2.8 million homes each evening. Chester Collier, Westminster president, said, "That's more than all the people who have seen every AKC show in person since AKC was founded in 1884."

The Commentators

Mrs. Sherman Hoyt, the first dog expert to take part in guiding TV viewers through the intricacies of the Westminster show, is shown on page 114 with Jimmy Powers and part of a TV camera in 1951.

In the mid-1960s, James E. Clark was invited to be the TV host and commentator. Within a year or so, he persuaded his new wife, Anne Rogers Clark, to be his co-commentator, and they served with great distinction in this capacity for some 20 years. We see them on page 114 talking with handler George Ward after Ward won Best in Show in 1985.

Left:
Commentators Jim and Anne Clark talk with handler George Ward who has just won Best in Show, 1985 — *Ashbey photo*

Below:
Commentators Mrs. Sherman Hoyt and Jimmy Powers at work, 1951 — *Popular Dogs*

Opposite Page, Bottom Left:
Walter Fletcher, left, and President William Rockefeller, 1976 — *WKC*

When the Clarks stepped down, dog judge Joe Tacker was selected for the job. He was very knowledgable in dog matters and took a very low-key approach in his narrative.

In 1990, David Frei did the narration for the first time. He was joined in 1994 by Joe Garagiola, longtime television personality, best known for his television work in baseball and as a co-host and reporter for over 30 years on NBC's Today Show.

Frei, a breeder-owner-exhibitor of Afghan Hounds for over 30 years, is now an active exhibitor of Brittanys, competing in both conformation and field trials. His two dogs are certified therapy dogs, visiting people in health care facilities every week. As a judge of Afghans, he has officiated at shows in the U.S., Europe, Australia and Canada. He is a trustee of Take the Lead.

The Voice of Westminster

For many years, during group judging, Westminster has had an announcer read the history of each breed as the judge examined a dog of that breed in the ring.

Roger Caras took on this job in 1978 at the invitation of Chairman Chet Collier. With his rich melodious voice, Caras came to be known to thousands of spectators at the Garden and in time to millions of television viewers as the Voice of Westminster.

Caras, now President Emeritus of the ASPCA, has been involved with animals since he took his first job at age 10 for 10 cents an hour cleaning the stables of abused horses seized by the Massachusetts SPCA. A prolific author and broadcast correspondent on animals and wildlife, he served for 10 years as the Special Correspondent on Animals and the Environment for ABC Television News and for eight years as the House Naturalist at NBC Television News.

In a lifetime of undaunted dedication to all animals, he has done many things but says that nothing has given him greater pleasure than announcing the dog show.

Walter Fletcher of the Times

The New York Times was a primary source of information about Westminster from the start, but for the first 50 years, the articles were unsigned. The first Westminster report with a byline appeared in 1927. The writer was Bryan Field. He was the first of more than 30 known reporters from the *Times* who would cover the event. Often, several covered the same show in the same year. A few became long-term "regulars."

Henry R. Ilsley got the job in 1928 and stayed with it through 1945, 18 years in all.

John Rendel, a reporter on boating and yachting, who sometimes spoke of a judge as examining a dog "fore and aft

Above Left: Joe Garagiola, right, with Chairman Ronald Menaker, 1999 —*Mary Bloom photo*

Above Right: President and Best in Show judge Chet Collier, left, and David Frei at the Show, 2000 —*Mary Bloom photo*

Far Right: Roger Caras, the Voice of Westminster, and Frank Harra of AKC, 2000 —*Mary Bloom photo*

and amidships," covered Westminster from 1946 through 1970. In 1971, when he retired after 45 years at the *Times*, he was voted dog writer of the year for the third time in a poll conducted by Gaines Dog Research Center. A winner also in 1951 and 1969, he was cited for "maintaining his high standards of professional excellence during 25 years of covering the sport of dogs."

Walter R. Fletcher clearly established the longest record of them all. He started at the *Times* in 1927, the year of that first signed article. In the 1960s he became their regular dog writer, with columns every Thursday and Sunday for over 15 years. He wrote his first signed piece on Westminster in 1969 and his final one in 1996, a period of 28 years. His Westminster debut was at the first show at Madison Square Garden IV, the year

of the big blizzard. Airports were closed and highways clogged. His piece on the opening began: "They came by plane and train. They came by bus, subway, taxi and truck. They walked, trotted and ran. They came by almost every means except dog-sled yesterday." It was a baptism by fire with a difference.

According to the *Times*, Fletcher got more mail than any of his sports-department colleagues. He won frequent awards from the Dog Writers Association, in 1965 sweeping the prizes for reporting, columns and magazine articles. In 1974, the Dog Fanciers Club gave an award for the first time in two decades, honoring him as the ideal dog show reporter: "With an eye for the unusual, his reporting has provided the public with an understanding of the dog fancy in all its aspects."

He officially retired in 1976 but continued as a free-lancer. In 1995 when his retirement from all writing was announced at the Westminster show, he received a standing ovation, which he called "the most touching moment of my life."

In 2000, Fletcher was spotlighted on the air on Monday night in a taped television segment, and his death in Florida at the age of 93 came only hours before Best in Show on Tuesday. "He cared about the sport and knew about it," said Roger Caras. "He had a sense of humor. I called him the Walter Lippmann of the hydrant set, and he loved it."

2000

1927: In the first public demonstration of television, Secretary of Commerce Herbert Hoover spoke in Washington to an audience in New York. Praising the invention, he said: "What its uses may finally be, no one can tell." — The New York Times, December 22, 1999

Chester F. Collier

In 1978, the Board of Governors selected a new Show Chairman, Chester F. Collier. Born in Boston, Collier showed his first dog, a Bouvier des Flandres, in 1966. During his years as an exhibitor, his dogs won more than 50 Best in Shows. His Bouvier, Ch. Taquin du Posty Arlequin, won the Ken-L-Ration award as winner of the most working groups in 1975.

Collier joined Westminster in 1973 and served as announcer in the arena – the Voice of Westminster – for the shows of 1975-77. In 1976-77, he was also Chief Steward. Named Chairman in 1978, he became President in 1989, the position he holds today.

He served for nine years on AKC's Board of Directors. He was president of the American Bouvier des Flandres Club. As a judge of all working and herding breeds, he did Best in Show at Westminster 2000. He is shown here escorting his wife, Mrs. Dorothy N. Collier, into the arena at the Garden in 1997 when she officiated over Best in Show.

Collier, currently Senior Vice-President for Fox News, has been a television executive since the 1950s when television was very new. Prior to joining Fox, he served as Senior Vice President of CNBC Primetime and before that, was executive producer of America's Talking.

Collier served as President of Group W Productions in 1963-77, overseeing the development and production of programs such as "The Regis Philbin Show," "The David Frost Show," "The Mike Douglas Show," "The Steve Allen Show" and "The Merv Griffin Show." He was later president of Westinghouse Broadcasting TV Stations and Chairman of the Board of Group W Productions. After leaving Westinghouse, he was Executive Vice President of Metromedia Producers Corporation. His many awards include seven Emmys, a George Foster Peabody Award and the Robert F. Kennedy Journalism Award.

Collier's 22 years first as Westminster's Chairman and then as President have been unique in the club's history. The show has been followed by an increasingly large segment of the general public. By the year 2000, not only had the TV audience expanded into the millions, Westminster's website was well established, and for the second year, it was possible to follow the breed competition, the results of which were posted in the on-line version of the catalog within minutes after completion.

Looking forward to Westminster 2000, Robin Finn of the *Times* said the upside of it was that after a quarter century behind the scenes, Collier would finally play the "leading man." The downside, she noted, was that he would have to stay out of the Garden for two days, remaining ignorant of the seven finalists, per the club's own rules, "until summoned for the big pick."

When the show was over, Westminster 2000 was declared an overwhelming success. As for television, the dog show walked away with the second highest rating of any show on cable.

Left: Chester F. Collier escorts his wife, Mrs. Dorothy N. Collier, into the arena in 1997 when she judged Best in Show —*Ashbey photo*

Opposite: The arena during the judging of the sporting group, 1998—*Mary Bloom photo*

THE AMERICAN
KENNEL GAZETTE

AN OFFICIAL JOURNAL, PUBLISHED SEMI-MONTHLY BY THE AMERICAN KENNEL CLUB.
(INCORPORATED)

Vol. XIX.—No. 11   JUNE 15, 1907   Price { $2.00 per annum / 20c. single number

SPRATT'S GOLD TROPHY

Was Won by "Champion Warren Remedy"

for the best dog at the Westminster Kennel Club Dog Show, held in the Madison Square Garden, New York City, in February, 1907.

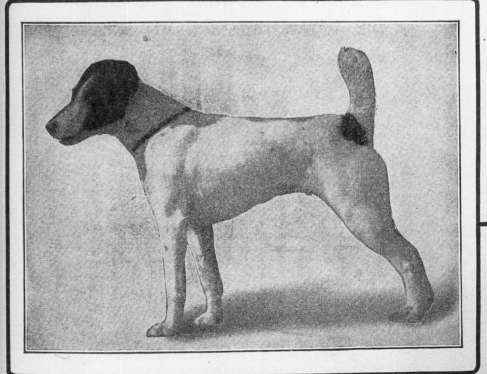

"Spratt's Patent, Newark, N. J.

"Gentlemen:—

" This is my picture.

" I was brought up on SPRATT'S "DOG CAKES and I think there "is nothing like them (Terrier Bis-"cuits for a change). I ate them "at the last Westminster Kennel "Club Show and then I went into "the ring with all the champions "and carried off Spratt's Patent "Gold Trophy for the best dog of "any breed, age or sex in the Show. " How's that for Spratt's?

" Yours truly,
"WARREN REMEDY.
" Per Donald Munro,
" Kennel Manager."

THOUSANDS of the World's Greatest Champions have been reared, fed and conditioned on

SPRATT'S
PATENT
DOG CAKES

We also manufacture specially prepared foods for DOGS, PUPPIES, CATS, RABBITS, POULTRY, PIGEONS, GAME, BIRDS, FISH.

Send for FREE Catalogue "Dog Culture," which contains practical chapters on the feeding, kenneling and general management of dogs, also chapters on cats.

SPRATT'S PATENT
(AM.) LTD.

450 Market St., Newark, N. J.   1324 Valencia St., San Francisco, Cal.
714 S. 4th St., St. Louis, Mo.   1279 Ontario St., Cleveland, Ohio.
11 Union St., Boston, Mass.   988 Notre Dame St., W., Montreal, Can.

Best in Show 1907

Ch. Warren Remedy, 100280

Smooth Fox Terrier, bitch
Whelped June 10, 1905
By Ch. Sabine Resist—Rowton Dainty
Breeder-Owner, **Winthrop Rutherfurd**,
Allamuchy, NJ

February 12–15
Madison Square Garden II
1,999 Dogs
James Mortimer, Superintendent
William Rauch, Chairman

Judges: A panel of 10, names not
recorded

Ch. Warren
Remedy—Ad for
Spratt's Patent
—*Gazette*

Remedy

This was the first year that Best in Show was judged at Westminster. It is not known who did the judging. The *Times* said that "there was a long discussion among the 10 judges selected to decide the weighty issue," but that aside, neither the names of the judges nor the number of them was recorded until 1912.

Priorities were different then. *The American Field* called the award a "most coveted honor," but the win was not part of the official records. The first mention of the win in the *Gazette*, the American Kennel Club's official journal, was an ad on the cover. It was for Spratt's dog food. It included a picture of Remedy and a letter to Spratt's written by Remedy, who said, "Gentlemen, This is my picture." She said she had eaten Spratt's Dog Cakes and then gone into the ring with the champions and carried off the prize.

"How's that for Spratt's?" she asked. A postscript indicated that Donald Munroe, the owner's kennel manager, had carefully checked the letter before it was mailed.

The *Times* called Remedy "a little white, smooth-haired Fox Terrier, perfect of its kind." *The American Field* said she was the greatest Fox Terrier that ever graced the ring, adding, "We may look for a long time for one to beat her."

Seventy-five years later, the late John T. (Jack) Marvin, in his *Fox Terrier Scrapbook*, said she made history that day. "To make the win all the more satisfying," he added, "Remedy was a homebred and was owner-handled to the triumph."

Best in Show
1908

Ch. Warren Remedy, 100280

Smooth Fox Terrier, bitch
Whelped June 10, 1905
By Ch. Sabine Resist — Rowton Dainty
Breeder-Owner, **Winthrop Rutherfurd**,
Allamuchy, N.J.

February 11–14
Madison Square Garden II
2,000 Dogs
James Mortimer, Superintendent
William Rauch, Chairman

Judges: Not recorded

Remedy Wins Again

Remedy's second win as Best in Show at the Garden was very popular.

"Even the casual visitors," said the *New York Daily Tribune*, "could not but admire the sprightly, clean-limbed little miss which took such a proud place and earned such high honors."

Walter S. Glynn, who had come from London to officiate over a number of terriers and who had put Remedy Best of Breed, said, "She is most decidedly the best Fox Terrier living today."

To the *London Field* she was an excellent animal that had simply gotten better. Since they had last seen her, she had "improved immensely." She could withstand "the most severe scrutiny." They said,

Her faults and failings are singularly few, her excellencies, many.

They were pleased that, after winning in the breed, she had gone on to even greater distinction when the jury of judges awarded her, to acclamation, the special prize for best animal in the show.

Ch. Warren
Remedy, by
Muss-Arnolt
(American 1858-
1927), pen-and-
ink — *Gazette*

Best in Show
1909

Ch. Warren Remedy, 100280

Smooth Fox Terrier, bitch
Whelped June 10, 1905
By Ch. Sabine Resist — Rowton Dainty
Breeder-Owner, **Winthrop Rutherfurd**,
Allamuchy, N.J.

February 9–12
Madison Square Garden II
1,936 Dogs
James Mortimer, Superintendent
William Rauch, Chairman

Judges: Not recorded

Remedy's Third Win

Two days before Westminster opened, in a story about dogs that were entered, the *Times* did not even mention Ch. Warren Remedy.

When the show was over, the big news in the paper was not that Remedy had won Best in Show for the third time. Instead, the dog show article opened with a long paragraph, saying that on the final day, William M. Van Norden of Harrison, N.Y., who was president of the Van Norden Trust Company, had bought a French Bulldog there for $2,500. The headline at the top of the column read

Bulldog Gamin II
Sold for Big Price

It was not until the second paragraph of the article that Remedy's triumph was cited, and, at that, she got but one sentence, which said simply that she had established a new record by winning Best in Show for the third year in succession.

The record has never been equaled, but at the time, that third win took a decidedly second place.

Ch. Warren Remedy, by Louis Contoit (American fl. 1908–40), black and white photo of oil (whereabouts unknown) —WKC

Best in Show 1910

Ch. Sabine Rarebit, 118640

Smooth Fox Terrier, dog

Whelped July 6, 1907

By Ch. Sabine Ruler — Ch. Sabine Fad

Breeder-Owner, **Sabine Kennels, F. H. Farwell**, Orange, Tex.

February 9–12

Madison Square Garden II

1,963 Dogs

James Mortimer, Superintendent

William Rauch, Chairman

Judges: Not recorded

Rarebit

Warren Remedy was just over four years old, and there were those who thought she "would again come through the judging" to be Best in Show for the fourth time. But at least two dogs outclassed her.

First, she took second in the Open Bitch class to Sabine Fernie of Sabine Kennels in Orange, Tex.

Then Sabine Fernie was beaten by kennelmate Sabine Rarebit for the Grand Challenge Cup for Best Fox Terrier. Sabine Rarebit also took special prizes for Best Smooth Fox Terrier of the Year and Best American- or Canadian-bred Smooth Fox Terrier in the Open Classes. After this, he took Best in Show.

The final decision was well received. It was said of Rarebit that there was "little question but that he had the better of the argument with Remedy."

Above:
Ch. Sabine
Rarebit, catalog
ad *—WKC*

Right:
Ch. Sabine
Rarebit, by
Mackarness
(American 20th
Century), bronze
sculpture *—AKC
Collection*

Best in Show
1911

Ch. Tickle-Em-Jock, 135459

Scottish Terrier, dog
Whelped June 23, 1907
By Moidart — Lorna Doone
Breeder, M. Whitelaw, England
Owner, *Andrew Albright, Jr.*,
Newark, N.J.

February 13–16
Madison Square Garden II
2,070 Dogs
James Mortimer, Superintendent
William Rauch, Chairman

Judges: Not recorded

Jock

Ch. Tickle-Em-Jock was the first of a number of early Best in Show winners with a "rags-to-riches" story to tell. In the *Times* the day after the show, the following headline appeared:

*Best Dog In Show Once Sold For $15
A. Albright's Scottish Terrier Picked
Up Cheap at London Meat Market*

Two years earlier, Jock had been the property of a butcher in the Leadenhall Meat Market in London. There he attracted the attention of Samuel Wilson of Bradford, Yorkshire, who offered the butcher $15 for the dog. The butcher accepted Wilson's offer.

"Has the dog a pedigree?" asked Wilson. When informed it had, he offered $5 more for the papers.

After some preparation, Tickle-Em-Jock was sent on a round of minor English summer shows, where he was "invariably successful." Then Andrew Albright, on a trip to England, bought the dog for $500 and brought him to the U.S.

At Westminster in 1910, he was Winners Dog. The following year, he repeated that win and went on to be crowned Best in Show "over the heads of more than 2,000 of the most aristocratic bred canines in the United States, England, and Canada."

Ch. Tickle-Em-Jock —*Hedges photo, Gazette*

Best in Show
1912

Ch. Kenmare Sorceress, 144241

Airedale Terrier, bitch
Whelped September 22, 1909
By Resemblance — Queen Oorang
Breeder, W. Thomas
Owner, *W. P. Wolcott*, Readville, Mass.

February 20–23
New Grand Central Palace
1,929 Dogs
James Mortimer, Superintendent
William Rauch, Chairman

Judges: Dr. Henry Jarrett (Philadelphia),
Ralph C. English (Newcastle, Pa.), &
Charles Lyndon (Toronto)

American-Bred vs. Imported

A notable feature this year was the number of victories of American-bred dogs over imports. The success of American breeders had never been so conspicuous. Still, when it came to Best in Show—competition which the *Times* said regularly caused "the greatest gossip in dogdom"—the winner was an import. It was an Airedale bitch, Ch. Kenmare Sorceress, owned and exhibited by W. P. Wolcott.

Wolcott had purchased her from an old bricklayer in Wales—although she was fully bred—and brought her to the U. S. in the fall of 1910. Since her arrival, she had been shown extensively "without having a defeat registered against her."

The American Field complained that when she won Best in Show, she was "entirely out of coat, was right down to the pily soft undercoat." Still, they did not deny that they had held her up as the best of her sex and a fitting candidate for best of her breed "for more than a year."

The owner, William Prescott Wolcott, would later judge at Westminster, 10 times in all, first in 1920 and last in 1946, when he would do Best in Show.

Reserve Best in Show went to Winthrop Rutherfurd's Smooth Fox Terrier Ch. Warren Distinct.

Ch. Kenmare
Sorceress,
Marguerite
Kirmse (American
1885–1954),
etching—*The
Complete Story of
the Airedale, 1913,*
AKC

Best in Show
1913

Ch. Strathtay Prince Albert,
166036

Bulldog, dog
Whelped July 3, 1910
By Chineham Joker — Moston Violet
Breeder, Col. Edelsten
Owner, *Alexander H. Stewart,*
Chicago, Ill.

February 19–22
New Grand Central Palace
1,893 Dogs
James Mortimer, Superintendent
William Rauch, Chairman

Judges: Dr. Henry Jarrett (Chestnut Hill, Pa.) and Gustav Muss-Arnolt (Tuckahoe, N.Y.) with Theodore Offerman (NYC) as Referee

A Non-Terrier?

He had barely gotten rid of his sea legs. He had first set foot in this country only two weeks before. But on the opening day, he defeated all the other Bulldogs, which had an entry of almost 200. Two days later, the judges of Best in Show were faced with a dozen dogs. They looked them over carefully, talked briefly and then announced that Prince Albert was the winner. It came as a surprise, for it was the first time a non-terrier had taken the award.

He had had a hard battle for the honor. His closest competitor was Wire Fox Terrier, Vickery Estelle, from the Vickery Kennels in Evanston, Ill. According to the *Times,* Estelle received the reserve award and growled at Prince Albert as the prize Bulldog was led triumphantly from the ring.

From then on, Prince Albert's handler, George Abbott, was kept busy trying to save him from the hands of the curious. Everybody wanted to pat "his big brindle head."

Prince Albert, white with brindle patches on the sides of the head and ears, was "solemn-faced." He had huge bone and was extremely low to the ground. Three years old, he weighed 41 pounds. His owner had purchased him from Col. Edelsten, a British army officer, who had apparently been unaware of the animal's worth. Edelsten had gone to India, having turned the dog over to a dealer, and it was through the dealer that Stewart made the acquisition.

Ch. Strathtay
Prince Albert
—*Gazette*

Best in Show
1914

Ch. Slumber, 134257

Old English Sheepdog, bitch
Whelped June 1909
By John O'Dreams — Nightmare
Breeder, Mr. Palfrey
Owner, **Mrs. Tyler Morse**, Morse Lodge,
Westbury, N.Y.

February 23–26
New Grand Central Palace
1,921 Dogs
James Mortimer, Superintendent
William Rauch, Chairman

Judge: Midgeley Marsden, Whaley
Bridge, England

Bobtail from England

Note the winner's pedigree. Slumber's sire was John O'Dreams, and her dam was Nightmare.

This year, Mrs. Tyler Morse did what the *American Field* called "her usual winning" in Old English Sheepdogs, then ended up taking the cup for Best in Show. There were upward of 50 winners in the ring contending for the top award, including the Bulldog that had won the year before. Slumber won "hands down."

She had competed at Westminster in 1912 and 1913, taking 1st in the Winners Class for bitches in both years. She had also won a special for Best Non-Sporting Dog or Bitch in 1912.

The decision to name her Best in Show this year was made by Midgley Marsden, a noted English judge, who said she came closer to the accepted model of perfection than any he had ever seen. He declared her "undoubtedly the best dog of this type that ever lived." Said *Our Dogs*, the English paper,

To see her is but to admire.

Vickery Fast Freight, a Wire Fox Terrier from Vickery Kennels, took Reserve.

Ch. Slumber
with owner Mrs.
Tyler Morse
–*Country Life in
America, May
1914, Art &
Architecture
Collection Miriam
and Ira D. Wallach
Division of Art,
Prints and
Photographs New
York Public
Library
Astor, Lenox and
Tilden Foundations*

Best in Show 1915

Ch. Matford Vic, 181693

Wire Fox Terrier, bitch

Whelped March 20, 1912

By Ch. Short Circuit — Brooklyn Girl Scout

Breeder, Mr. Counter

Owner, *George W. Quintard,* Bayshore, N.Y.

February 22–25

Madison Square Garden II

1,711 dogs

James Mortimer, Superintendent

William Rauch, Chairman

Judge: Dr. Henry Jarrett, Chestnut Hill, Pa.

The 10-Dollar Dog — A True Story

Once upon a time, a Cocker Spaniel breeder near Birmingham, England, went on a local buying expedition. He knew little about terriers, but at a farm where he stopped, he saw a puppy, a Wire Fox Terrier bitch that he thought might make a good playmate for his grandchildren. He asked her price and was told it was two pounds—in those days, 10 dollars. He took the puppy home. His sons laughed at him. They said she would not appeal to their children.

The grandfather was unhappy but kept the dog. Then one day he took her to a show where he was exhibiting Cockers. A terrier breeder saw her and called her a fine specimen. Why wasn't he showing her? The man finally put her to the test. She went into the ring—and came out a winner.

Now it was his turn to laugh. He turned down $500 for her and eventually sold her for $1,000. Then George W. Quintard's agent, on a buying trip from the United States, acquired her for his client. He paid $2,500.

In the U. S., Matford Vic, as she was known, immediately won in Boston. She was defeated at Westminster in 1914 but in 1915 took Best in Show. In addition, her kennelmate, Wireboy of Paignton, took Reserve Best in Show. Then those two together won Best Brace in Show and, with two other kennelmates, were Best Team.

In 1916, she was Best at Westminster again. In 1917, the *Times* noted that Mrs. Roy Rainey—who would take Best in Show at the Garden that year with a male Wire—had purchased Matford Vic from Quintard. The price this time was $5,000.

Ch. Matford Vic
—The Complete Fox Terrier by Irving Ackerman, 1939, AKC

Best in Show
1916

Ch. Matford Vic, 181693

Wire Fox Terrier, bitch

Whelped March 20, 1912

By Ch. Short Circuit — Brooklyn Girl Scout

Breeder, Mr. Counter

Owner, *George W. Quintard*, Ridgeway Kennels, Bayshore, N.Y.

February 22–25

Madison Square Garden II

1,704 dogs

George W. Gall, Superintendent

William Rauch, Chairman

Judges: Charles G. Hopton (NYC), Frank F. Dole (NYC), Vinton P. Breese, (NYC), Fred Senn (Bergenfield, N.J.) & W. H. Whittem (Chestnut Hill, Pa.)

One Judge or Five?

In 1915, a single judge officiated over Best in Show and chose Matford Vic for the high honor. A year later, five judges—or as one paper put it, "a panel of five jurors"—were assigned the responsibility, and the end result was exactly the same. Matford Vic was again crowned Best in Show.

On the second occasion, nearly 30 dogs representing as many breeds were led into the ring. The five judges placed the entries according to size at various parts of the enclosure and examined each one individually.

Dogs that did not have a chance "got the gate." By the process of elimination the entrants were finally narrowed down to three. With Matford Vic plus a Scottish Terrier and a Bulldog still present, the five judges took a vote. The Bulldog received only one tally, removing it from the contest. With two dogs left, the officials voted again, unanimously in favor of Matford Vic.

The American Field on this occasion called Vic "one of the best wirehaired bitches that ever stood on four legs."

The Best in Show was not Mr. Quintard's only repeat award this year. In 1915, when Matford Vic first went Best in Show, she and kennelmate Wireboy of Paignton took Best Brace in Show and, with two additional kennelmates, were named Best Team in Show. In 1916, the same dogs took the identical awards.

Ch. Matford Vic
—*WKC*

Best in Show
1917

Ch. Conejo Wycollar Boy, 208284

Wire Fox Terrier, dog

Whelped May 15, 1914

By Ch. Wireboy of Paignton—Queen Collar

Breeder, J. W. Turner

Owner, *Mrs. Roy A. Rainey*, Conejo Kennels, Huntington, N.Y.

February 20–23

Madison Square Garden II

1,886 Dogs

George W. Gall, Superintendent

William Rauch, Chairman

Judge: George Steadman Thomas, Hamilton, Mass.

Wycollar Boy

Mrs. Rainey paid $6,000 for him. Conejo Wycollar Boy was a dog that could inspire exclamations like "There he is!" and "Oh, isn't he a beauty!" But at WKC in 1916, though spectators flocked to ringside to see him, he was defeated in the breed.

However, 1917 was different—another day. George Thomas, a seasoned all-arounder, faced 16 candidates. He discarded one famous dog after another, including Matford Vic, who had been Westminster's top dog for the last two years and was now part of Mrs. Rainey's own kennel. There were finally two dogs left, Ch. Slumber, the Old English who had won in 1914, and Wycollar Boy. The decision was a surprise. Slumber had done well in the breed, which Thomas had judged earlier that day. People thought he would choose her. But the grand victor was Wycollar Boy. Slumber took Reserve.

Said the *Pacific Kennel Gazetteer*, "Mr. Thomas, liking them all, loves a terrier. Ch. Conejo Wycollar Boy is officially the most nearly perfect dog…in the world."

As Mrs. Rainey took the ribbon, there was a burst of applause, a tribute to a popular sportswoman "who has spared neither time nor money to place her kennel at the pinnacle of the dog world."

Best American-Bred in Show was Boston Terrier, Ch. Peter's Captain. Owner Mrs. George E. Dresser nearly missed the award. Her Boston was in the hands of a sleepy attendant who just reached the ring in time. The win pleased Boston breeders because the first "Best American-Bred" at Westminster was a pure American breed.

Ch. Conejo
Wycollar Boy
—*AKC,
Monograph on the
Fox Terrier by
Sidney Castle,
1938, reprinted
courtesy Our Dogs*

Best in Show 1918

Ch. Haymarket Faultless, 236933

Bull Terrier, dog

Whelped August 22, 1916

By Ch. Noross Patrician—
Ch. Glenmere Channel Queen

Breeder-Owner, **R. H. Elliott**,
Ottawa, Canada

February 20–23

Madison Square Garden II

1,644 dogs

George W. Gall, Superintendent

William Rauch, Chairman

Judges: Vinton P. Breese (Newark, N.J.)
and Charles G. Hopton (NYC), with
George S. Thomas (Hamilton, Mass.)
as Referee

Right:
Ch. Haymarket
Faultless, photo-
graph—*Country
Life*

Below:
Ch. Haymarket
Faultless, icon for
Bull Terrier breed
column—*Gazette*,
1928

F. F. H. FLEITMANN, kn[...]
world over as a Dober[...]
pert, is going to Germany and w[...]
goes, yes, a [...]
rier, Nip Ch[...]
name and a [...]
too. This dog[...]
property of M[...]
mons, of Bost[...]
will appear [...]
the leading [...]
shows. You can bet that he will [...]
down to the minute, for Fleitma[...]
owned bullterriers for years. I [...]

Divided Judgment

The *Times* called it "the most remarkable demonstration ever seen" at a show. Judges Charles Hopton and Vinton Breese had eliminated dogs until only two remained, the Bull Terrier, Haymarket Faultless, handled by breeder-owner R. H. Elliott, and a Pekingese, Phantom of Ashcroft, owned by Elbridge Gerry Snow, Jr. Hopton favored the Pekingese, and Breese, the Bull Terrier.

Hundreds of fanciers crowded around. There were boos when Hopton showed prefer-ence for the Peke, while cheers rang out when Breese cast glances at the Bull Terrier.

With the judges deadlocked, referee George Thomas was called. He examined both dogs. "The dainty Phantom," said the paper, "toddled up and down the ring, a tiny bundle of silky fluff." The terrier, full of life, paraded before Thomas, who "beamed" at the terrier. Shortly Thomas, with a parting look at the Peke, pointed to Faultless as winner.

William Kendrick, calling Best in Show at Westminster "the most cherished prize within the gift of American Dogdom," described the incident from a personal point of view. His words appear in David C. Merriam's *The Bull Terrier Club of America: A Centennial History, 1897–1997*. "We Bull Terrier people," he wrote, "had a deep conviction of the greatness of Faultless and an abiding faith in his merit." But he said no one ever dreamed he was "destined to such heights." When the referee was called, he said, "All our hearts beat in unison with a single prayer on our lips." When Thomas gave Faultless the nod, "the crowd went wild."

Best American-Bred in Show was Scottish Terrier Ch. Walescott Whim, of Walescott kennels.

Best in Show
1919

Ch. Briergate Bright Beauty,
224419

Airedale Terrier, bitch
Whelped October 27, 1915
By Squireen—Mistress Roney
Breeder, Mr. Davidson
Owner, **G. L. L. Davis**, St. Louis, Mo.

February 19–22
Madison Square Garden II
1,560 dogs
George W. Gall, Superintendent
William Rauch, Chairman

Judges: Harry T. Peters, Theodore
Offerman and J. Willoughby Mitchell
(all of NYC)

Ch. Briergate
Bright Beauty
—*WKC*

Bright Beauty

The coronation of the Airedale, Briergate Bright Beauty, as queen of all breeds was not unanimously popular. The spectators watching the judging of Best in Show didn't always support the judges.

On this occasion, the previous year's winner, Haymarket Faultless, received the greatest applause right up to the final moment. He was "showing with all the dignity of a statue," said the *Times,* but had to be content with Reserve.

The paper said that the two most likely candidates were Haymarket Faultless and the Pekingese, Phantom of Ashcroft, who had been Reserve to Faultless. There was also talk of other dogs, but Bright Beauty was nowhere mentioned as a possible.

When the field of 28 entered the ring, Faultless was given the loudest reception. Many favored the Pekingese, which the *American Field* singled out as "the only dog shown naturally, that is, allowed to pose without any artificial assistance." One after another, dogs were dismissed until just two remained, the Bull Terrier and the Airedale. The three judges then whispered a few words together and gave the signal to the Airedale.

When it was all over, Bright Beauty did not want for friends. Owned by G. L. L. Davis, she got a warm reception as her handler, Alfred Delmont, one of the top professionals of the day and a familiar figure at Westminster, led her from the ring.

Best American-Bred in Show was Pekingese, Ch. Fan Chee of Yankibourne, owned by Yankibourne Kennels.

Best in Show
1920

Ch. Conejo Wycollar Boy, 208284

Wire Fox Terrier, dog
Whelped May 15, 1914
By Ch. Wireboy of Paignton—
Queen Collar
Breeder, J. W. Turner
Owner, **Mrs. Roy A. Rainey**, Conejo
Kennels, Huntington, Long Island

February 11–14
New Grand Central Palace
1,624 dogs
George W. Gall, Superintendent
William Rauch, Chairman

Judges: Thomas S. Bellin (Albany, N.Y.),
William E. Warner (Grand Rapids,
Mich.), and Norman K. Swire
(Montreal, Canada)

Repeat Performance

After taking Best in Show in 1917, Ch. Conejo Wycollar Boy did not retire. The next year, on the third day of the show, there was a headline in the *Times* about him. It extended all the way across the top of a page in the sport section. It read as follows:

Great Terrier, Conejo Wycollar Boy, Takes Coleman Randolph Cup At Dog Show

The trophy was for best of breed. It brought together all entered Fox Terriers that were so far undefeated at the show. It was a respectable win. Afterwards, he went into the ring for Best in Show—from which competition, however, he was eliminated.

In 1919, he was entered again—but was absent. Then in 1920, nearly six years old and a longtime champion, he returned once more. His 1917 triumph at the Garden was three years behind him. In due course, he entered the ring for the top award with 21 others, all of them winners. None had so far been defeated at the show. The *Times* made note of Wycollar Boy's "lively antics and remarkably fine poses which he struck without the urging of his attendant."

This time, he triumphed. Mrs. Rainey "was almost swamped with congratulations."

His closest contender was Lansdowne Sunflower, a Greyhound bitch owned by Mrs. B. F. Lewis, Broomall, Pa. Sunflower took Reserve. Best American-Bred in Show was Smooth Fox Terrier, Ch. Sabine Fernlike, owned by Thomas Rice Varick.

Ch. Conejo
Wycollar Boy,
1920 — *WKC*

Best in Show
1921

Ch. Midkiff Seductive, 243713

Cocker Spaniel, bitch
Whelped July 16, 1917
By Midkiff Rex—Midkiff Winsome
Breeder-Owner, **William T. Payne**,
Midkiff Kennels, Dallas, Pa.

February 10–12
Madison Square Garden II
1,754 dogs
George W. Gall, Superintendent
William Rauch, Chairman

Judges: Norman K. Swire (Toronto,
Canada) and Charles G. Hopton (NYC),
with Dr. John E. De Mund (Brooklyn,
N.Y.), Referee

Seductive

In 1921, Wycollar Boy, who was Best in Show in 1917 and 1920, did not appear. Haymarket Faultless, the Bull Terrier that had been Best three years earlier, was recognized when he entered the ring and got "a round of applause such as may come to a champion of another day." But he did not make the final cut.

The most talked-about contender was a Pekingese, Phantom of Ashcroft. He had been Reserve to Best in Show three years before. He was now six and was said never to have looked better. Nobody suggested that a Cocker might win.

There were 21 dogs in the finale. After an hour, judges Charles Hopton and Norman Swire had narrowed the field down to two but could go no further. Hopton held out for the Peke, while Swire favored the Cocker. They finally called for referee Dr. John De Mund. He put the dogs through a series of tests for 10 minutes. When he sent them around the ring, the crowd hissed Phantom and cheered for Seductive—who won.

The *Times* reporter called Seductive "a fine specimen in conformation and a beautiful parti-color." Editorially, the paper commented:

The crowning...of this shaggy-haired little miss only adds to the uncertainty which makes the exhibiting of dogs a pleasure and shows also that the condition of the individual dog is the most important factor.

Reserve went to Phantom of Ashcroft. It was his second time in the second spot.

Ch. Midkiff
Seductive—*UPI /
Corbis–Bettmann*

Best in Show
1922

Ch. Boxwood Barkentine, 307147

Airedale Terrier, dog
Whelped July 11, 1920
By Lucknow Comet—Boxwood Bianca
Breeder-Owner, **Frederic C. Hood**,
Brookline, Mass.

February 13–15
Madison Square Garden II
1,796 dogs
George W. Gall, Superintendent
William Rauch, Chairman

Judges: Gustav Muss-Arnolt (Tuckahoe, N.Y.), Vinton P. Breese (Caldwell, N.J.), and Theodore Offerman (Brooklyn, N.Y.)

Barkentine

"First, last, and best of all," said the *Times*, this year's show would be remembered for its victor. Boxwood Barkentine was an Airedale Terrier that "went from the Novice class to Best in Show, from canine obscurity to the throne of American dogdom." They called him

An upstanding dog with an active eye in a square head, a black saddle, chest deep and muscular, hindquarters of power, and tail stiff enough to hang your hat on.

Owned by Frederic C. Hood, Barkentine entered the show almost unnoticed. There were cheers when he took Best of Breed over the winner of the Airedale specialty show of just a few days before. The paper called the other dog, with a touch of irony, one of "the imported wonders of the dog world."

Barkentine, who hailed from Boston, "seemed insatiable in the matter of blue ribbons." After winning Best of Breed and the group, he was designated Best American-Bred in Show, and then went into the ring for Best in Show with 15 competitors. Quickly enough, the field was narrowed to two, Barkentine and a Greyhound bitch, Ch. Lansdowne Sunflower. Sunflower had been Reserve two years earlier. She had 49 Best in Shows to her credit, and her owner was hoping for a fiftieth, after which she would retire.

Alas, it was not to be. Barkentine was Best in Show, and Sunflower, Reserve.

Ch. Boxwood Barkentine —*Airedale Terrier Club of America 1960 Yearbook, AKC, © Airedale Terrier Club of New England, Published with permission*

CH. BOXWOOD BARKENTINE

Airedale Bowl, 1922-23 — Ch. The New King Bowl, 1922-23
From Novice Dog to Best in Show, Westminster Kennel Club, 1922
(Copyright A.T.C. of New England) — Space donated by Mrs. Emmett Warburton —

— 103 —

Best in Show 1924

Ch. Barberryhill Bootlegger

Sealyham Terrier, dog

Whelped December 31, 1920

By Ch. Barberryhill Gin Rickey—
Western Wistful

Breeder-Owner, **Bayard Warren**,
Pride's Crossing, Mass.

February 11–13

Madison Square Garden II

1,782 Dogs

George W. Gall, Superintendent

William Rauch, Chairman

Judges: Walter H. Reeves (Ontario,
Canada) and Norman K. Swire
(Toronto, Canada)

Bootlegger

This year's winner was Ch. Barberryhill Bootlegger. He was named for what some wit surely thought of as "Man's *Other* Best Friend"—which is to say, a discreet source of alcohol. Prohibition had begun in 1920 and would go on for 10 more years. And note Bootlegger's competition, with names like Tom Collins, Home Brew and Egg Nog.

Sealyhams, first shown in England in 1903, were not registered by AKC until 1911. A year later they made their Westminster debut with three entered, of which the *American Field* said, in toto, "they looked enough alike to say that they were one breed." By 1924, there were 30 entered.

This was the first Westminster held under the new rules for group and Best in Show judging. The five group winners competed for Best in Show—a Cocker, a German Shepherd, a Peke, a Chow, and the Sealy. The five were quickly winnowed down to two, Bootlegger and the Shepherd, Dolf Von Dusternbrook, who was Champion of Germany in 1919 and of Austria in 1920.

Paul E. Lockwood in the *Gazette* said the Shepherd was "a master of showmanship and waited coldly, confidently, for the decision." In contrast, the American-bred Bootlegger was "a Massachusetts Yankee of backwoods stock." If the Shepherd gaited with "arrogance," the terrier followed handler Joseph Thompson as though "trotting over a pasture."

Bootlegger "comes very close to perfection," opined Walter H. Reeves, who judged Best together with Norman Swire. He "is beautifully built, teems with type and moves like a piece of machinery."

Far Right:
Ch. Barberryhill
Bootlegger
—*Gazette*

Right:
Ch. Barberryhill
Bootlegger, by
Wm. G. Schnelle
(American 20th
Century), oil
—*AKC Collection*

THE AMERICAN
KENNEL GAZETTE
AND STUD BOOK

Vol. 41, No. 2
Per Year $4

AMERICAN KENNEL CLUB
A·K·C
INCORPORATED

FEBRUARY 29, 1924
Per Copy 50 Cents

CH. BARBERRYHILL BOOTLEGGER
Sealyham Terrier Awarded Best in
Show at Westminster

PUBLISHED OFFICIALLY BY THE AMERICAN KENNEL CLUB

Best in Show
1925

Ch. Governor Moscow, 331420

Pointer, dog

Whelped 1921

By Mallwyd Moscow—Queen Mason

Breeder, Earl Brown

Owner, ***Robert F. Maloney***,
Pittsburgh, Pa.

February 10–12

Madison Square Garden II

2,078 Dogs

George W. Gall, Superintendent

William Rauch, Chairman

Judges: Ralph C. English (Port Matilda, Pa.), Walter S. Glynn (Bletchley, England), Theodore Offerman (NYC), and Robert A. Ross (Montreal, Canada)

Moscow

Ch. Governor Moscow became the first Pointer to take Westminster's top award, though the club's symbol had been a Pointer for nearly 50 years.

Robert F. Maloney, a Pittsburgh coal magnate, had acquired Moscow as a shooting and show dog. Handled by Ben Lewis, Jr., he had taken the breed a year earlier. The *Times* spoke of his great bone and carriage and of "that little dish in front of the eyes, which gives that game expression so desirable in a dog of the type."

In the finale, there were only four competitors—one group winner had been defeated in pursuit of a special prize, making him ineligible for Best. One by one, the contenders mounted the judging block in the center of the ring. Arthur Frederick Jones, a new writer for the *Gazette*, was in top form. He said that, when Moscow's turn came, "The gods of art...combined to bring before the human eye the perfect statue of a living dog." Did Moscow know that he had stopped the show? Jones asked.

To Moscow (wrote Jones) the adoration of the crowd means nothing. But to him, a bit of gray dawn, a hand on his back, a crack of a gun, and a chase o'er the field bring visions of a canine Heaven, ruled by the spirit of Diana of the Hunt.

When Moscow won, "pandemonium broke loose."

The Airedale, Warbride of Davishill, of Davishill Kennels, Fort Thomas, Ky., was Reserve to Best in Show. Best American-Bred in Show was the Borzoi Ch. Ivor O'Valley Farm, of Valley Farm Kennels.

Ch. Governor
Moscow—*WKC*

Best in Show 1926

Ch. Signal Circuit of Halleston,
477684

Wire Fox Terrier, dog
Whelped August 11, 1923
By Ch. Fountain Crusader—Peri
Breeder, A. Kirk, England
Owners, *Mr. and Mrs. Stanley J. Halle*,
Halleston Kennels, Chappaqua, N.Y.

February 11–13
Madison Square Garden III
2,261 Dogs
George W. Gall, Superintendent
William Rauch, Chairman

Judges: J. Robinson Beard (NYC), W. L.
McCandlish (Redditch, Worts,
England), Tyler Morse (NYC), C.
Frederick Neilson (Shrewsbury, N.J.),
and Walter H. Reeves (Ontario, Canada)

Signal Circuit

It was Westminster's Golden Jubilee and their first show in the "new" Garden. The winner was Ch. Signal Circuit of Halleston, owned by Halleston Kennels.

He had won in a field of 200 Fox Terriers, which was nearly a tenth of the total show entry. He was shown by Percy Roberts, who had imported him from England. The breed judge was Winthrop Rutherfurd, whose Fox Terrier had won Best in Show at the Garden in 1907, '08 and '09. Rutherfurd named him best Wire and Best of Breed. The dog was said to have "a beautiful body" with "phenomenal length of head and sound movement." He was all white, with a patch of tan around his eyes and on his ears.

During the final judging, he was the first dog examined. His appearance brought a murmur of admiration from the crowd. Then, in gaiting, he trotted down the ring and made a turn, at which point the crowd burst into applause. The volume was such that Roberts raised his hand for silence as the dog had been distracted and thrown off stride. After a pause, dog and handler came back to the judges, who continued their work.

The victory earned a silver cup offered by the Kennel Club in England for best dog in Westminster's 50th show. When the panel of judges had completed its evaluation, the cup was handed to panel-member W. L. McCandlish, Chairman of the English Kennel Club, who personally made the presentation.

Best American-Bred in Show was St. Bernard Ch. Hercuveen Aurora Borealis, of Hercuveen Kennels.

Ch. Signal
Circuit of
Halleston—*WKC*

The AMERICAN

KENNEL GAZETTE

Vol. 44, No. 2
Per Year $4

February 28, 1927
Per Copy 50 Cents

Photo by Tauskey

FREDERIC C. BROWN'S CH. PINEGRADE PERFECTION
Best in Show at the Westminster Kennel Club Exhibition

PUBLISHED OFFICIALLY by the AMERICAN KENNEL CLUB

Best in Show 1927

Ch. Pinegrade Perfection, 474063

Sealyham Terrier, bitch
Whelped June 21, 1924
By Bowhit Poppett—Molton Dot
Breeder, T. Watts
Owner, *Frederic C. Brown*, NYC

February 10–12
Madison Square Garden III
2,133 Dogs
George W. Gall, Superintendent
William Rauch, Chairman
Samuel Milbank, Chief Steward

Judges: John G. Bates (Morristown, N.J.), Dr. C. Y. Ford (Montreal, Canada), G. V. Glebe (Bryn Athyn, Pa.), Enno Meyer (Milford, Ohio), and C. F. Neilson (Shrewsbury, N.J.)

Perfection

Bryan Field's opening words in the *Times* were as follows:

A Sealyham Terrier out-swanked all the blue-bloods of dogdom and trundled out of the show ring with the Westminster crown tilted —but nonetheless securely fastened—over one eye.

The people, said Field, were "overwhelmingly pro-Perfection." He was impressed that spectators, who didn't know whether Sealyham was the name of a dog, a tapestry or a breakfast food, came to the same conclusion as the experts. He found the breed an amusing oddity. They had very short forelegs and much longer hind legs. He said they didn't walk; they waddled.

Then came the authoritative voice of the *American Field*. They had seen Perfection take Best in Show at the Sesquicentennial Bench Show in Philadelphia the previous fall. They described her as "an unusually sound and typical Sealyham...whose superb condition and splendid ring manners appealed to all."

All agreed that no small share of the glory belonged to her handler, Percy Roberts. He had handled a dog to Best in Show at Westminster just a year earlier. He would eventually take four dogs to that top honor.

Best American-Bred in Show went to the Pointer, Ch. Dapple Joe, owned by Rumson Farm Kennels. Dapple Joe had many field trial victories. He was an out-of-doors bird dog that could hunt to the gun as well as go on parade.

Left: Ch. Pinegrade Perfection —*Tauskey photo, Gazette*

Right: Ch. Pinegrade Perfection (to right) with Ch. Pinegrade Scotia Swell, by Lilian Cheviot (English, 20th century), oil on canvas—*AKC Collection*

Best in Show
1928

Ch. Talavera Margaret, 592242

Wire Fox Terrier, bitch

Whelped September 29, 1925

By Talavera Simon—Talavera Unity

Breeder, Capt. H. R. Phipps

Owner, **Reginald M. Lewis**, Warily
Kennels, Ridgefield, Conn.

February 13–15

Madison Square Garden III

2,133 Dogs

George F. Foley, Superintendent

John G. Bates, Chairman

Samuel Milbank, Chief Steward

Judges: Mrs. Reginald F. Mayhew
(Forest Hills, N.Y.), Alfred Delmont
(Wynnewood, Pa.), Otto H. Gross
(Pittsburgh, Pa.), C. Frederick Neilson
(Shrewsbury, N.J.), and J. Bailey Wilson
(Media, Pa.)

Ch. Talavera
Margaret
—*Tauskey photo,
Gazette*

Margaret

Wires had the largest entry of any breed. Stanley Halle, who had taken Best in Show with
a Wire in 1926, judged them. After winning the breed, Ch. Talavera Margaret went into
the terrier group, where she met the Sealyham that had taken Best in Show the year
before. The Sealyham was a sentimental favorite. When Margaret won that "battle
royal," as the *Times* called it, she received cheers that were "only a little more vociferous"
than those given the Sealy who was second.

In connection with Best in Show, Arthur Frederick Jones of the *Gazette* noted a moment
of old-fashioned gallantry. When Margaret entered the ring for the finale, she was
greeted with hand clapping on all sides. Said Jones:

*Margaret does not seem to pay any attention, but her handler, Alfred Mitchell, looks up and
touches the brim of his hat in recognition.*

Henry Ilsley of the *Times* said that Margaret had never looked better. She was the right
size for the work of a terrier, exceptional in body, remarkably beautiful in head and
expression and with the best of legs and feet.

Her win was immensely popular, and it should be noted that Mrs. Reginald Mayhew of
Forest Hills, N.Y., was a member of the five-judge Best in Show panel. Mrs. Mayhew was
the first woman to have a voice in this important decision at Westminster.

Best American-Bred in Show was taken by the Pomeranian Ch. Bogota Firebug owned
by Miss E. G. Hydon.

Best in Show
1929

Laund Loyalty of Bellhaven, listed

Collie, dog
Whelped May 12, 1928
By Lucas of Ashtead—Jean of Ashtead
Breeder: R. H. Roberts, England
Owner, **Florence B. Ilch**, Bellhaven
Kennels, Red Bank, N.J.

February 10–12
Madison Square Garden III
2,412 Dogs
George F. Foley, Superintendent
John G. Bates, Chairman
Samuel Milbank, Chief Steward

Judge: Dr. Carleton Y. Ford, Montreal,
Canada

Laund Loyalty

There were 121 Collies, of which Mrs. Florence B. Ilch had entered 18.

Among them was a puppy so new to the U.S. that he was not even AKC registered; he was shown as "listed." His last exploit before leaving England was winning a Collie specialty show in which he triumphed over 385 dogs. In taking the breed at Westminster under Dr. Carlton Y. Ford, Loyalty caused a sensation.

Henry R. Ilsley in the *Times* described him as a light sable with white on the feet. He had a magnificent collar and a true Collie expression, enhanced by a splendid carriage of ears.

When he won the working group, he received great acclaim but was not expected to go further. Terriers were still the favorite. Ringsiders expected a Fox Terrier to go to the top. On the final day, when the Collie—who was then nine months old to the day—took Best in Show under Dr. Ford, who had also judged the breed, the result was so unexpected that the crowd was rather taken aback. There was a momentary hush in the arena. It was not a popular win.

There were no feelings against Mrs. Ilch, however. The *Times* said that she had had greater success as a breeder and exhibitor of Collies than anyone else in the country and noted that her other victories at the show were awarded "a full measure of applause."

Best American-Bred in Show was awarded to the Cocker Spaniel Ch. Lucknow Crème de la Crème, owned by Mr. and Mrs. Frederic C. Brown.

Laund Loyalty
of Bellhaven
—*Tauskey photo,*
WKC

Best in Show
1930

Ch. Pendley Calling of Blarney,
717434

Wire Fox Terrier, bitch
Whelped May 2, 1928
By Ch. Chantry Callboy—Sweet
Snowflake
Breeder: J. Smith
Owner: **John G. Bates**, Blarney Kennels,
Morristown, N.J.

February 10–12
Madison Square Garden III
2,673 Dogs
George F. Foley, Superintendent
John G. Bates, Chairman
Samuel Milbank, Chief Steward

Judge: W. L. McCandlish, Foxlydiate,
Redditch, England

"The Way We Were"

The Chairman of Bench Show Committee was scheduled to steward for Best in Show but turned out to be owner-handler of the winning dog. This was John G. Bates.

Walter S. Glynn, a British terrier judge, officiated in the breed. Fanciers were anxious to compare his judgement with that of Stanley Halle who had done the Fox Terrier specialty at the Hotel Pennsylvania on the previous Sunday. Pendley Calling of Blarney had made her U.S. debut there and was named Best of Breed. At Westminster, Glynn made the same choice, which was received with a great burst of applause. Glynn also did the group and gave her first.

Best in Show was judged by W. L. McCandlish, Chairman of the Kennel Club in England. When he handed the rosette to Bates, there was an ovation. Henry R. Ilsley in the *Times* called it "one of the old-time demonstrations."

Ilsley said that the pent-up feelings of the spectators, keyed to the highest tension by competition in the variety groups, were "let loose without restraint." He went on to say that in other years, when the unexpected had happened, there had been ominous hushes when the winner was announced. "No such feeling," he said, "was in evidence in the Garden last night."

Best American-Bred in Show was taken by the Beagle, Ch. Meadow Lark Watchman, owned by Louis Batjer of New Brunswick, N.J.

Ch. Pendley
Calling
of Blarney, by
Frederick
Thomas Daws
(English, b. 1878),
photo of oil on
canvas (where-
abouts of
painting
unknown)
—WKC

Best in Show
1931

Ch. Pendley Calling of Blarney,
717434

Wire Fox Terrier, bitch

Whelped May 2, 1928

By Chantry Callboy—Sweet Snowflake

Breeder: J. Smith

Owner: *John G. Bates*, Blarney Kennels,
Morristown, N.J.

February 10–12

Madison Square Garden III

2,516 Dogs

George F. Foley, Superintendent

John G. Bates, Chairman

Samuel Milbank, Chief Steward

Judge: Tyler Morse, NYC

Pendley Calling Again

In 1931, Pendley Calling of Blarney repeated her 1930 triumph. She defeated 167 other Wires and 48 Smooths to go Best of Breed under F. H. Farwell of Orange, Tex. Henry T. Fleitmann of New York did the group, which she won.

Then came Best in Show. Vernon Van Ness in the *Times* said that she had shown the stuff of which she was made but that her victory was not well received. Mingled with hand-clapping and cheering were "long, loud, and persistent hisses and boos from all parts of the arena."

Van Ness suggested that the cause of this "unusual" reception was the way in which the English Setter, Blue Dan of Happy Valley, had captured the hearts of the crowd. Almost from the start, it was clear that the gallery wanted Blue Dan to win. Every move he made brought forth thunderous applause and cheering.

Arthur Frederick Jones of the *Gazette* was very critical. The fault lay not with the judges or dogs, he said, but with Westminster's "wide open doorway to misunderstanding." He said it was obvious that the person named in the catalog as Westminster's Vice-President and Chairman was owner of the winning dog. There was only one remedy, "for those in charge of staging this great American show to refrain from entering their dogs."

The crowd was somewhat appeased when Best American-Bred in Show was awarded to Blue Dan of Happy Valley, the English Setter, who was owned by Dr. A. A. Mitten of Philadelphia.

Ch. Pendley
Calling of
Blarney—WKC
Catalog ad

Best in Show
1932

Ch. Nancolleth Markable, 817232

Pointer, dog
Whelped July 8, 1929
By Nancolleth Mark—Ella of Crombie
Breeder, Mrs. A. Rowe
Owner: **Mrs. Geraldine Rockefeller**
Dodge, Giralda Farms, Madison, N.J.

February 11–13
Madison Square Garden III
2,350 Dogs
George F. Foley, Superintendent
John G. Bates, Chairman
Samuel Milbank, Chief Steward

Judge: Hon. Townsend Scudder, Glen
Head, Long Island

Pointer

This was the first time that Mrs. Geraldine Rockefeller Dodge scaled the heights at Westminster and the second time in 25 years that the award was taken by a Pointer.

The victory of this lemon and white male was extremely popular. The Pointer that won in 1925 was Governor Moscow, which Arthur Frederick Jones of the *Gazette* said posed like a "carven image." Nancolleth Markable was a different animal. He fixed his gaze on the judge upon entering the ring and from then on hardly looked elsewhere.

The crowd loved him. "He seemed to throw out a magnetic force that drew your eyes to him," said Jones.

During the final examination, there was a great outburst of applause. The dog spun around, giving the crowd a sweeping look, and then turned his attention back to the business at hand. They cheered again when he bounded forward as his handler, McClure Halley, advanced to receive the rosette.

Shooting men considered him one of the greatest Pointers to come across the water in years. He made his debut at Cruft's in London, where he was Reserve to Best in Show among 6,000 dogs. Two weeks later at Manchester, he defeated his conqueror and won Best in Show himself. He had also won his field championship in England, defeating many great field-trial winners there, a rare feat for a bench champion.

Best American-Bred in Show was the Greyhound, Ch. Gamecock Duke of Wales, bred, owned and handled by George S. West.

Ch. Nancolleth Markable, by Ward Binks (English 1880–1950), gouache—*AKC collection*

Best in Show
1933

Warland Protector of Shelterock, listed

Airedale Terrier, dog

Whelped May 15, 1931

By Wrose Anchor—Warland Sprite

Breeder, S. Greenshields, England

Owner, **Sheldon M. Stewart**, Montclair, N.J.

February 13–15

Madison Square Garden III

2,240 Dogs

George F. Foley, Superintendent

John G. Bates, Chairman

Harry I. Caesar, Chief Steward

Judge: Mrs. M. Hartley Dodge, Madison, N.J.

Warland Protector

Never before had the judge of Best in Show at Westminster been a woman. The choice of Mrs. Dodge for the assignment did not meet with the approval of some who considered the office to be "for men only." However, the *American Field* reported that the truly wonderful manner in which she carried out her assignment showed she was thoroughly in touch with type, conformation, sound action and condition. Her awards were received "with unstinted applause."

In her own kennels, Mrs. Dodge's preferences ran to sporting and working breeds. Her Pointer in 1932 had carried off the top award. Yet her final selection of an Airedale was enthusiastically accepted.

Warland Protector of Shelter Rock, handled by Robert Barlow, was one of two Airedales imported from England for Sheldon Stewart, president of the Airedale Terrier Club of America. Neither dog was yet AKC registered, but both were English champions, the other being a bitch, Covert Dazzle, who in breed competition was best of opposite sex to Warland Protector.

Before leaving England, Protector had won the National Airedale Terrier Club show, had gathered seven challenge certificates and was eight times best of all breeds. He was said to be a beautifully proportioned specimen that moved to perfection. Arthur Frederick Jones of the *Gazette* joined in, in praising the dog. "I, too, own an Airedale," he confessed.

Best American-Bred in Show went to the blue-ticked English Setter, Blue Dan of Happy Valley. Blue Dan also won the award in 1931.

Warland Protector of Shelterock with handler Robert Barlow, judge Mrs. Dodge and Chairman John G. Bates—*WKC*

Ch. Spicy Bit of
Halleston, with
handler Percy
Roberts and
President Walton
Ferguson, Jr.
—*Brown photo,
WKC*

Best in Show
1934

Ch. Flornell Spicy Bit of Halleston, 915577

Wire Fox Terrier, bitch

Whelped June 5, 1931

By Ch. Beau Brummel of Wildoaks— Wollescote Colleen

Breeder, A. H. Heathcock

Owner, **Stanley Halle**, Halleston Kennels, Chappaqua, N.Y.

February 12–14

Madison Square Garden III

2,240 Dogs

George F. Foley, Superintendent

John G. Bates, Chairman

Harry I. Caesar, Chief Steward

Judge: Dr. Henry Jarrett, Chestnut Hill, Pa.

Spicy Bit

During the judging of Best in Show, Spicy Bit slipped her lead and headed for the exit, the first recorded instance of a contender trying to desert the grand finale. But she was quickly apprehended and brought back.

There were 146 Wires on the bench. They were judged by Russell H. Johnson, Jr., president of the American Kennel Club. Spicy Bit was a hound-marked bitch with a tan head. Henry Ilsley of the *Times* called her "a superb bit of terrierdom."

Percy Roberts, her handler, had imported her from England. She made her American debut at the Fox Terrier specialty show the Sunday before Westminster. She did not win there but took the breed at the Garden. In the group, she won in a field of 15, which Ilsley said included "the cream of the homebreds and the greatest of the imported specimens."

In the final class, the six contenders were all from other countries: one from Canada, one from Switzerland and the rest from England.

Spicy Bit was the third dog Percy Roberts had guided to the top at the Garden. The earlier occasions were in 1926 and 1927. He would handle a fourth winner in 1937, and in 1967, as an all-breed judge, would come back to judge Best in Show himself.

Best American-Bred in Show was the black Cocker Spaniel, Ch. The Great My Own, owned by Leonard J. Buck.

Ch. Spicy Bit of Halleston, by Mildred Megargee (American, 20th Century) oil —*AKC Collection*

Ch. Nunsoe Duc
de la Terrace of
Blakeen, 1935, by
Maud Earl
(English,
1864–1943), oil
—*AKC Collection*

Best in Show
1935

Ch. Nunsoe Duc de la Terrace of Blakeen, 919471

Poodle, dog

Whelped September 1, 1929

By Prinz Alexander v. Rodelheim—
Leonore v. d. Seestadt

Breeder, Mme. Emile Warnery

Owner Blakeen Kennels, *Mr. and Mrs. Sherman Hoyt*, Katonah, N.Y.

February 11–13

Madison Square Garden III

2,837 Dogs

George F. Foley, Superintendent

Samuel Milbank, Chairman

Harry I. Caesar, Chief Steward

Judge: Alfred B. Maclay, Millbrook, N.Y.

The Duke

There was a playful streak in him.

Nunsoe Duc de la Terrace of Blakeen came from Switzerland and was a champion there as well as in France, England and America. For all that, he was distracted in the final class by a squeaky dog toy in the hand of the Sealyham's handler. The Duke wanted to take possession of it. Mrs. Hoyt, his owner-handler, received permission from the judge to move, and as she led him to a new spot, he made a graceful dive for the Sealyham. The leash stopped him in midair. He took his place obediently then away from trouble.

One observer called the Duke "superbly beautiful...correctly headed, amazingly coated, perfectly conditioned, and close coupled...an eye-catcher." Another said he was "the most striking poodle that has ever been brought to the U. S." A third claimed the only fault to be found with him was that "he was not home-bred."

It was the dog's 12th show in the U.S. and his 12th Best of Breed, his 10th group and his fifth Best in Show. It was also the first time that a woman carried off Westminster's top award. It would not happen again until 1956.

Best American-Bred in Show was Mrs. Cheever Porter's Irish Setter, Milson O'Boy, handled by Harry Hartnett.

Ch. Nunsoe Duc de la Terrace of Blakeen—*Tauskey photo, kennel owner's brochure, WKC*

INT. CH. NUNSOE DUC DE LA TERRACE OF BLAKEEN
3rd BEST IN SHOW—WESTMINSTER 1934
BEST IN SHOW—WESTMINSTER 1935
2nd BEST IN SHOW—WESTMINSTER 1936

BLAKEEN KENNELS
Poodles
MRS. SHERMAN R. HOYT, *Owner*

KATONAH, N.Y.   TELEPHONE 217

Best in Show
1936

Ch. St. Margaret Magnificent of Clairedale, A30935

Sealyham Terrier, dog
Whelped April 12, 1933
By St. Margaret Showman—
Burdon Bliss
Breeder, Mrs. A. Wilkinson, England
Owner, **Mrs. W. O. Penney,** Clairedale
Kennels, Yaphank, Long Island

February 10–12
Madison Square Garden III
2,920 Dogs
George F. Foley, Superintendent
Samuel Milbank, Chairman
Harry I. Caesar, Chief Steward

Judge: C. Frederick Neilson,
Shrewsbury, N.J.

Magnificent

This close-to-the-ground worker, almost all white, had been brought over from England the previous autumn. The importation was made, it was said, not with an eye on Westminster—a common theory about imports—but to bring Mrs. Penney some desirable stock upon which to build a kennel of Sealyhams.

Handled by Leonard Brumby, Sr., St. Margaret Magnificent of Clairedale made a grand showing. In addition to taking Best in Show, he and kennelmate St. Margaret Sweetness of Clairedale were judged Best Terrier Brace.

A close contender for Best was Mrs. Hoyt's white poodle that had won in 1935. His retirement was announced after that victory, but he was brought back by popular demand. He won the breed under Alva Rosenberg and the group under Theodore Offerman, but in the final class was among the favorites that St. Margaret Magnificent "toppled from their pedestals."

The *Literary Digest* spoke of "the not inconsiderable volley of boos" with which the award was greeted. Arthur Frederick Jones in the *Gazette* called it the sort of demonstration that should not be heard. "The general public ought to be taught," he said, "that a judge is in the best position to reach the right decision." He noted that none of the losing owners or handlers expressed resentment. Mrs. Hoyt, for example, simply stepped aside until the photographers had finished shooting the victor and then sincerely congratulated Brumby on his great victory.

Best American-Bred in Show was taken by the Harrier, Mr. Reynal's Monarch, owned by Amory L. Haskell of Red Bank, N.J.

Ch. St. Margaret
Magnificent
—*Brown photo,
Gazette*

Best in Show
1937

*Ch. Flornell Spicypiece of
Halleston, A133147*

Wire Fox Terrier, bitch
Whelped May 9, 1933
By Crackley Starturn—Vane Girl
Breeder, J. Mather, England
Owner, **Stanley J. Halle**, Halleston
Kennels, Chappaqua, N.Y.

February 10–12
Madison Square Garden III
3,140 Dogs
George F. Foley, Superintendent
Samuel Milbank, Chairman
Harry I. Caesar, Chief Steward

Judge: George S. West, Chestnut Hill,
Mass.

Country Girl

Until the fall of 1936, the little pure-white Wire enjoyed life in the Shire country of England. Percy Roberts found her there and brought her from oblivion to the highest pinnacle of fame in American dogdom.

It was the fourth dog Roberts had guided to the top. The others were the winners of 1926, 1927 and 1934.

In 1938, Spicypiece came back as "defending champion." William Kendrick, writing in *Popular Dogs*, remembered her then as "one of the great exhibition terriers of an era." He said that her forte was "perfect balance...with not the slightest trace of exaggeration or deviation in line or detail...Add to this her inimitable character, her will to please, for she puts her whole heart into it when she shows, and you have truly a regal little lady, an orchid of dogdom, if there ever was one." However, while she took both breed and group in 1938, she did not repeat her win as Best in Show.

Best American-Bred in Show was taken by Ch. Torohill Smokey, a Cocker Spaniel owned by Peter Dunne Garvan of Roslyn, Long Island.

Ch. Flornell Spicypiece of Halleston—she came back in 1938 as "defending champion."—*Madison Square Garden Sports Album, WKC*

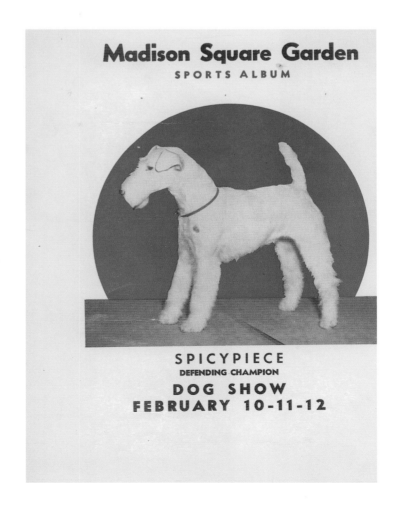

Best in Show
1938

Daro of Maridor, listed

English Setter, dog

Whelped March 18, 1937

By Ch. Sturdy Max— Ch. Lakeland Dawn

Breeder-Owners, **Dwight W. Ellis and Dwight W. Ellis, Jr.**, Maridor Kennels, East Longmeadow, Mass.

February 10–12

Madison Square Garden III

3,093 Dogs

George F. Foley, Superintendent

Harry T. Peters, Jr., Chairman

Harry I. Caesar, Honorary Chief Steward

John W. Cross, Jr., Chief Steward

Judge: John G. Bates, NYC

Daro

Daro of Maridor, not yet 11 months old and unregistered, had never been in the show ring before.

The heavily ticked orange belton English Setter was bred and owned by the Maridor Kennels, which bred for shooting, field trials and bench shows. Charles Palmer handled him.

It was the first time a Setter had ever triumphed at Westminster, and not since 1924 had an American-bred gone Best in Show. Daro automatically took the James Mortimer trophy.

Henry R. Ilsley of the *Times* called him "superb." "Every move he made was indicative of speed and character," he said. "There was beauty in color, in expression and in movement."

The decision of John Bates, who had won Best at Westminster in 1930 and 1931, came at the end of a series of wins unparalleled in Garden history. American-breds dominated in many breeds and prevailed in five of the six groups. Terriers produced the sole foreign-bred representative—last year's Best in Show winner. Some called 1938 a "turning point."

Wrote Kingsley Childs in the *Times*, "American fanciers hereafter may not seek imported dogs so zealously."

Even the judging schedule was changed. Customarily, the James Mortimer Memorial Trophy was decided before the principal honor. However, had this order been followed, there would have been only two dogs in the ring for Best in Show because all defeated contenders for Best American-Bred would have been eliminated.

Far Left:
Daro of Marido,
—*Rotogravure
Section, Herald
Tribune—Acme,
Feb. 20, 1938*

Left:
Daro of Maridor
—*Rotogravure
Section, Times
Wide World
Photos, Boston
Bureau*

THE BEST-IN-SHOW OF AMERICAN DOGDOM POSES
IN HIS HOME SETTING.
Daro of Maridor, the 11-month-old English setter which won the highest award in the Westminster Kennel Club exhibition in Madison Square Garden, photographed in the Maridor Kennels of Dwight W. Ellis at East Longmeadow, Mass., shortly after his return from his first appearance in the country's leading dog show.
(Times Wide World Photos, Boston Bureau.)

Best in Show
1939

Ch. Ferry von Rauhfelsen of Giralda, listed

Doberman Pinscher, dog

Whelped January 9, 1937

By Troll v. d. Engelsburg—Jessy v. d. Sonnenhohe

Breeder, Wilhelm Rothfuss, Germany

Owner, **Mrs. Geraldine R. Dodge**, Giralda Farms, Madison, N.J.

February 10–12

Madison Square Garden III

3,069 Dogs

George F. Foley, Superintendent

Harry T. Peters, Jr., Chairman

J. Gould Remick, Chief Steward

Judge: George S. Thomas, South Hamilton, Mass.

Ferry

It was another foreign-bred, and this one didn't even understand English. He was from Germany and, in the final class, was said to have been taking "pantomime directions" from his handler. Still, he won.

The previous fall Mrs. Dodge had sent McClure Halley abroad in search of a Doberman for her. He saw hundreds of candidates that weren't up to his standards and almost gave up hope. Then in Germany one day, he saw Ferry being exercised in a public park. The dog was an "arresting sight" even from afar. He had "class and quality" written all over him. Halley instantly decided that this was his dog.

He later discovered that Ferry's parents were already in America, both with very respectable show records.

Of imposing size with a brilliantly colored black and tan coat, he was described by William Kendrick in *Popular Dogs* as "a picture of great nobility, accentuated by his lofty head carriage, and generally classical outline."

George S. Thomas, a veteran all-arounder, presided over Best in Show. Except for Ferry, all the contenders were AKC champions. Between them, they had some 65 Best in Shows. But Ferry triumphed, the first Doberman to carry off the supreme honor. In both 1952 and 1953, a great grandson of Ferry would win Best at the Garden.

Best American-Bred in Show was taken by the Cocker Spaniel, Ch. My Own Brucie, handled by his breeder-owner, Herman Mellenthin. In 1940 and 1941, Brucie would take Best in Show and Best American-Bred in Show.

Mrs. Dodge, with Ferry Von Rauhfelsen of Giralda—*Cook & Gormley, Courtesy St. Huberts Giralda*

Best in Show
1940

Ch. My Own Brucie, A84017

Cocker Spaniel, dog
Whelped May 4, 1935
By Red Brucie—My Own Lady
Huntington
Breeder-Owner, **Herman E. Mellenthin**,
Poughkeepsie, N.Y.

February 12–14
Madison Square Garden III
2,738 Dogs
George F. Foley, Superintendent
J. Gould Remick, Chairman
Caswell Barrie, Chief Steward

Judge: Dr. Samuel Milbank, NYC

Brucie

The jet black Cocker Spaniel was bred, owned and shown in the ring by Herman E. Mellenthin, "the squire of Poughkeepsie." It was a triumph for a homebred over an import. It was an overwhelmingly popular win.

All through the show there had been an undercurrent of feeling that Brucie and the Smooth Fox Terrier, Nornay Saddler, would fight it out at the end. Brucie was well remembered from the year before as Best American-Bred in Show. An imported Doberman had nosed him out for the top award.

On the other hand, Saddler, according to Henry R. Ilsley in the *Times*, was "the most famous dog in America." He had so far taken Best in Show a record 51 times, though he had never gone beyond the group at the Garden. This year he swept through his breed and group and came into the final class, undoubtedly a favorite.

After giving Brucie the award, Dr. Samuel Milbank said, "He was in the most beautiful bloom. He showed magnificently every minute and moved more soundly than I ever had seen him move before. He's a real champion."

Asked to name his second choice, Dr. Milbank smiled and said, "You can't have a second king."

Having won Best in Show, Brucie automatically captured the James Mortimer Memorial Trophy for Best American-Bred for the second straight year.

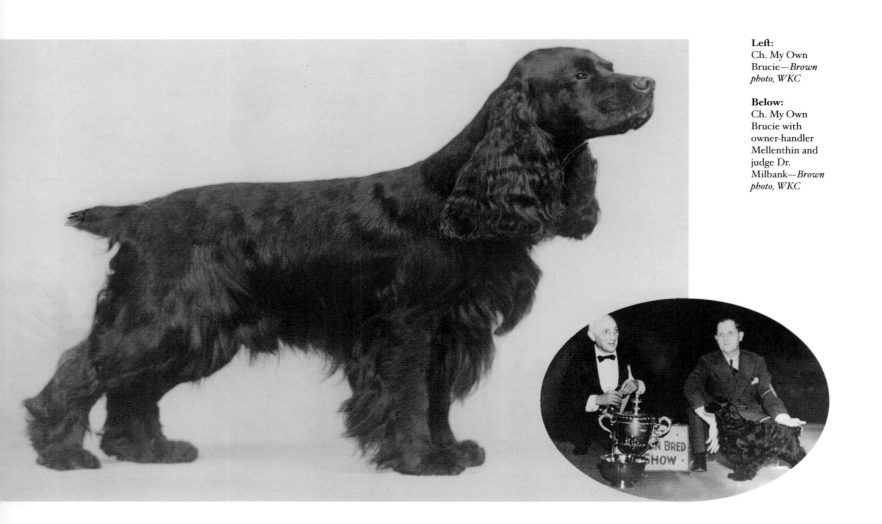

Left:
Ch. My Own
Brucie—*Brown
photo, WKC*

Below:
Ch. My Own
Brucie with
owner-handler
Mellenthin and
judge Dr.
Milbank—*Brown
photo, WKC*

Best in Show
1941

Ch. My Own Brucie, A84017

Cocker Spaniel, dog
Whelped May 4, 1935
By Red Brucie—My Own Lady
Huntington
Breeder-Owner, **Herman E. Mellenthin**,
Poughkeepsie, N.Y.

February 11–12
Madison Square Garden III
2,546 Dogs
George F. Foley, Superintendent
J. Gould Remick, Chairman
Caswell Barrie, Chief Steward

Judge: Joseph P. Sims, Chestnut Hill, Pa.

Encore, Brucie

An "imperturbable little gun dog."

This was how Henry R. Ilsley of the *Times* described Ch. My Own Brucie. He said that when the flashbulbs started popping in Brucie's face and he had no one to appeal to except for his owner, who handled him, scores of people jumped over the low fences and moved in for a closer view. They even tried to touch his coat which "shone like the costliest black satin."

Ever the natural showman, Brucie attended strictly to the business at hand and was attentive to every movement of his master. He was oblivious to applause, seeming to accept it as his due. Though not campaigned extensively, Ilsley said he was a marked dog whenever he entered the show ring. He was probably better known to more dog lovers than any other canine then being shown.

It was Brucie's second year as Best in Show and his third as Westminster's Best American-Bred. And it was not a triumph for Brucie alone. In the judging of Brucie's variety, his progeny took Winners Dog and Reserve Winners Dog, as well as Winners Bitch and Reserve Winners Bitch.

Brucie would not appear at the Garden in 1942. His owner, Herman Mellenthin, would judge Best in Show then.

Ch. My Own
Brucie with
breeder-owner
Mellenthin and,
from left, Vice-
President Dr.
Samuel Milbank,
Chairman Remick,
and judge Sims
—*Brown photo,
WKC*

Best in Show
1942

Ch. Wolvey Pattern of
Edgerstoune, A290740

West Highland White Terrier, bitch
Whelped April 20, 1937
By Wolvey Prefect—Wolvey Privet of
Edgerstoune
Breeder, Mrs. C. Pacey, Wolvey Kennels,
England
Owner, **Mrs. John G. Winant**,
Edgerstoune Kennels, Concord, N.H.

February 11–12
Madison Square Garden III
2,388 Dogs
George F. Foley, Superintendent
J. Gould Remick, Chairman
Caswell Barrie, Chief Steward

Judge: Herman E. Mellenthin,
Poughkeepsie, N.Y.

Pattern

This year's winner was an immaculate white West Highland White Terrier of distinguished ownership and notable ancestry.

It was the bitch Ch. Wolvey Pattern of Edgerstoune, owned by Mrs. John G. Winant of Concord, N.H. She was the wife of the United States Ambassador to the Court of St. James (1941–46). Edgerstoune, one of the largest and most successful kennels of the day, produced more than 40 champions. In 1950, an Edgerstoune Scottie would take Best in Show at Westminster.

The judge was Herman E. Mellenthin, who had taken Best in Show himself at the two previous shows.

Pattern was the only foreign-bred in the final class. Handled by Robert Gorman, she was the first of her breed to take the top award at the Garden. It was Pattern's second Best in Show, her first having been won at the Manchester Kennel Club show in New Hampshire in 1940. AKC records show that Pattern's win there was the first Best in Show taken by a Westie anywhere in America.

Best American-Bred in Show was won a Smooth Fox Terrier, Ch. Desert Deputy, owned by Mr. and Mrs. W. Holden White.

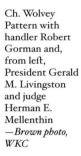

Ch. Wolvey Pattern with handler Robert Gorman and, from left, President Gerald M. Livingston and judge Herman E. Mellenthin
—*Brown photo, WKC*

Best in Show
1943

Ch. Pitter Patter of Piperscroft,
A401250

Miniature Poodle, bitch
Whelped February 1, 1939
By Barty of Piperscroft—Bijou of Rigi
Breeder, Miss D. Homan
Owner, **Mrs. P. H. B. Frelinghuysen**,
Morristown, N.J.

February 11–12
Madison Square Garden III
2,351 Dogs
George F. Foley, Superintendent
John G. Bates, Chairman
Caswell Barrie, Chief Steward

Judge: Gerald M. Livingston, NYC

Pitter Patter

Ch. Pitter Patter of Piperscroft, an imported black miniature Poodle bitch owned by Mrs. P. H. B. Frelinghuysen of Morristown, N.J., and handled by Walter Morris, was judged Best in Show.

The *Gazette* called Pitter Patter a "splendid specimen" and said that anyone close enough to see her had to grant her a place with the 35 other dogs that had scaled the heights.

Gerald M. Livingston was judge of Best in Show. The decision was received with mixed feelings. William Kendrick, in *Popular Dogs*, wrote that it would have been idle to claim otherwise. "The overwhelming sentimental choice," he said, "was the Irish Water Spaniel." He pointed out, however, that dog shows were "very properly...not determined by polling of the assembled spectators, but by the opinions of duly qualified experts." He said that Livingston's qualifications were of the highest order and that, as judge in the ring, he was closer to "the scene of operations" than anyone else. Kendrick was quite content to abide by Livingston's findings. He expressed congratulations to the Poodle's owner, who, with a different Miniature, had won the Non-Sporting Group the year before.

The Irish Water Spaniel was Ch. Mahoney's O'Toole, one of the few that had ever gone Best in Show anywhere in America. He was owned by Mrs. Charles M. Wynns. When he took Best American-Bred in Show, Kendrick said it "somewhat mollified the feelings of the dissenters."

Ch. Pitter Patter of Piperscroft, with handler Walter Morris and, from left, President Dr. Samuel Milbank and judge Gerald Livingston
—*Brown photo, WKC*

Best in Show
1944

Ch. Flornell Rare-Bit of Twin Ponds, A462974

Welsh Terrier, dog

Whelped October 9, 1939

By Ch. Hotpot Harri Boy of Halcyon—Flornell Autograph

Breeder, E. Bland Parkington

Owner, **Mrs. Edward P. Alker**, Great Neck, Long Island

February 11–12

Madison Square Garden III

2,510 Dogs

George F. Foley, Superintendent

John G. Bates, Chairman

Caswell Barrie, Chief Steward

Judge: Theodore Crane, Saugatuck, Conn.

Rare-Bit

Mrs. Alker's Welsh Terrier, Ch. Flornell Rare-Bit of Twin Ponds, gained Westminster's highest honor this year. It was his twenty-second Best in Show victory.

The *Gazette* made two points about the award. One was that the overall quality of the six dogs in the Best in Show line up was "on a par" with most final classes at the Garden. The other was that the judge Theodore Crane knew what he was looking for and was very certain about his decision.

"It is doubtful," said the *Gazette*, "that Best in Show has ever been decided so quickly or more accurately. The Welsh caught his eye from the beginning."

William Kendrick, in *Popular Dogs*, said that Rare-Bit "never stood, moved or turned wrong." He considered this a tribute to the dog's handler, John Goudie. In Kendrick's view, the dog left nothing to be desired in eyes, ears, skull, face, coat, or legs and feet. He was "compact in outline and deep through the middle with a perfect tail-set." Added to all of which, said Kendrick,

He possesses that "look of eagles" that sets him apart from even the good ones of his tribe.

Best American-Bred in Show was taken by the Boxer, Warlord of Mazelaine, owned by Mr. & Mrs. Richard C. Kettles, Jr. and handled by Chief Petty Officer Walter Foster. Warlord would return to the Garden each year until 1947, when he would take Best in Show.

Ch. Flornell Rare-Bit of Twin Ponds with owner Mrs. Edward P. Alker—*Brown photo, WKC*

Best in Show
1945

Shieling's Signature, A690418

Scottish Terrier, dog

Whelped May 19, 1942

By Ch. Shieling's Salute — Ch. Shieling's Symphony

Breeder-Owners, ***Mr. and Mrs. T. H. Snethen***, Allison Park, Pa.

February 12–13

Madison Square Garden III

2,653 Dogs

George F. Foley, Superintendent

W. Ross Proctor, Chairman

Caswell Barrie, Chief Steward

Judge: George S. West, Boston, Mass.

Signature

It was a story the dog's owner would tell many times.

It was about taking Best in Show this year. The winner was a Scottish Terrier named Shieling's Signature. The owner, T. H. Snethen, handled the dog himself. Before a hushed crowd, as he and the dog made one last pass before the judge, George S. West, somebody sitting up near the rafters shouted out,

Look up here, Scottie!

And Shieling's Signature did just that. He cocked his head and stared up where the voice had come from, without missing a step and bringing down the house in applause.

Less than three years old, Signature finished his championship at the show. He was the 13th Scottie champion that the Snethens had bred. He was also the fourth generation of their breeding and was automatically Best American-Bred in Show. He was the first of his breed to go Best since 1911.

Henry Ilsley in the *Times* described Signature as having just about everything that could be asked of a Scottie. He was short-coupled, had a grand front and a most beautiful chiseled head. Moreover, he was a superb showman, without the dourness that was sometimes part of a Scottie's character.

Right:
Shieling's
Signature with
owner Snethen
and President Dr.
Samuel Milbank
—*UPI/Corbis-Bettmann*

Below:
Best in Show,
1945, as seen
from high up
where the voice
came from
—*Brown photo,
WKC*

Best in Show 1946

Ch. Hetherington Model Rhythm, A400432

Wire Fox Terrier, bitch

Whelped August 17, 1939

By Ch. Hetherington Surprise Model— Hetherington Flash

Breeder, Frank L. Trauthwein

Owners, **Mr. and Mrs. Thomas H. Carruthers, III**, Glendale, Ohio

February 13

Madison Square Garden III

2,597 Dogs

George F. Foley, Superintendent

W. Ross Proctor, Chairman

Caswell Barrie, Chief Steward

Judge: William Prescott Wolcott, Milton, Mass.

Mama

This was the one-day show—when New York City was closed down by a tugboat strike, and Westminster miraculously ran through its entire two-day schedule on what would otherwise have been the show's second day.

The winner was Wire Fox Terrier bitch, Ch. Hetherington Model Rhythm, owned by Mr. and Mrs. Thomas H. Carruthers and handled by Jake Terhune. An American-bred, she automatically won the James Mortimer trophy. She and one of her offspring also took Best Brace in Show.

According to Kingsley Childs of the *Times*, the decision irked many spectators who favored the Afghan, Ali Khyber, or the Boxer that had been Best American-Bred in Show in 1944.

Gus Bock of the *Newark Evening News* touched on Model Rhythm's age, noting that one of her sons had won Best of Variety at Westminster in 1944, and that in 1945 one of her daughters had done the same. "It remained," he said, "for 'Mama' to win Best in Show."

William Kendrick, in *Popular Dogs*, also noted the bitch's age. "The fact," he wrote, "that a six-and-one-half year old terrier could be put down in such superb form reflects great credit on her conditioner." He added that her performance in the ring "will not be soon forgotten by those fortunate enough to have witnessed (it)."

William Wolcott, the judge—who had won Best in Show at Westminster in 1912—said, "She showed like a queen and asked for the decision every minute she was in the ring."

Ch. Hetherington Model Rhythm, by C. C. (Tex) Fawcett (American, 20th century) pastel —*AKC Collection*

Best in Show
1947

Ch. Warlord of Mazelaine,
A661773

Boxer, dog

Whelped October 1, 1942

By Ch. Utz v. Dom of Mazelaine—
Symphony of Mazelaine

Breeder, John P. Wagner

Owner **Mr. and Mrs. Richard C.
Kettles, Jr.**, Old Westbury, N.Y.

February 12–13

Madison Square Garden III

2,589 Dogs

George F. Foley, Superintendent

W. Ross Proctor, Chairman

Caswell Barrie, Chief Steward

Judge: David Wagstaff, Tuxedo Park,
N.Y.

Boxer

After trying for three years, the Boxer Ch. Warlord of Mazelaine won Best in Show at the Garden. Owned by Mr. and Mrs. Richard C. Kettles and handled by Nate Levine, he was the first Boxer to attain the honor.

The choice, made by David Wagstaff, met with hearty approval. In 1944, Warlord had been Best American-Bred in Show. In 1946, he took the Working Group but went no further. In the breed this year, he won in the show's biggest class, 154 Boxers. He had done plenty of other winning. It was his 68th breed ribbon. The group win at Westminster would be his 25th, and the Best in Show, his 12th.

The dog, which John Rendel in the *Times* described as a "sturdy statuesque Boxer, fawn, with white chest and a good black mask," won the favor of the spectators, too, as was testified by the strength of applause that burst out whenever Wagstaff stepped before him.

Wagstaff later said he had had "a hard choice" between the Boxer and the Boston Terrier, Ch. Mighty Sweet Regardless. "The Boston impressed me very much," he said, "but the Boxer was best tonight. Perhaps tomorrow the Boston would have the better of it."

All six contenders were American-bred. Five of them had at least one Best in Show, and the Boston, Warlord's closest contender, had 22.

Ch. Warlord of
Mazelaine, with
handler Nate
Levine and, from
left, judge
Wagstaff and
President Harry
Caesar
— *UPI/Corbis-
Bettmann*

the DOG NEWS

The Bedlington Terrier
CHAMPION ROCK RIDGE NIGHT ROCKET
Owned by Rock Ridge Kennels, Greenwich, Conn.

"The National Dog Magazine"

Copyright 1948, Alice ___

Best in Show
1948

Ch. Rock Ridge Night Rocket,
R12241

Bedlington Terrier, dog

Whelped March 6, 1946

By Ch. Canis Laris—Ch. Rock Ridge
Rockette

Breeder-Owners, *Mr. and Mrs. William
A. Rockefeller*, Rock Ridge Kennels,
Greenwich, Conn.

February 11–12

Madison Square Garden III

2,540 Dogs

George F. Foley, Superintendent

John W. Cross, Jr., Chairman

Caswell Barrie, Chief Steward

Judge: Dr. Samuel Milbank, NYC

Newcomer

It was the first time a Bedlington had taken so much as a group first at the Garden, let alone Best in Show.

The winner was Ch. Rock Ridge Night Rocket, owned by Mr. and Mrs. William A. Rockefeller. The dog's half dozen other top awards included Best in Show at Morris and Essex, which he had won the previous May at the age of 14 months.

R. C. Howard, in *Popular Dogs*, called the dog's record a triumph not just for Night Rocket but also for the dog's handler, Anthony Neary. Neary was "the Man from Bedlington." For 35 years, starting long before taking charge of Rock Ridge Kennels, Neary and his wife, Anna, had been working for "these game little dogs."

The *Gazette* said the Nearys lent encouragement to anyone who took the slightest interest in the "deceptively mild-looking Terrier that looked so much like a lamb that it had become the butt of many jokes." The Nearys had long recognized the breed's true worth, carrying, as they knew it did, "the purest terrier spirit." Best in Show at the Garden seemed to justify their endless work.

Dr. Milbank took 15 minutes to make his choice. His comment afterwards: "With the narrowest of skulls, the most perfect of coats, grand expression, a beautiful mover, always alert, he was to me the best dog in the ring." Night Rocket's victory was well accepted by all.

Below:
Night Rocket with handler Anthony Neary and judge Dr. Milbank—
UPI/Corbis–bettman

Left:
Night Rocket
—*Brown photo, Dog News, May 1948, WKC*

Right:
Ch. Rock Ridge Night Rocket embraces Best American-Bred trophy
–*Lisa Larsen/ Life/Timepix*

Best in Show
1949

Ch. Mazelaine's Zazarac Brandy,
W9630

Boxer, dog
Whelped February 5, 1946
By Ch. Merry Monarch — Ch. Warbaby of Mazelaine
Breeder-Owners, **Mr. and Mrs. John P. Wagner**, Milwaukee, Wis.

February 14–15
Madison Square Garden III
2,559 Dogs
George F. Foley, Superintendent
John W. Cross, Jr., Chairman
J. Hartley Mellick, Jr., Chief Steward

Judge: Thomas H. Carruthers, III, Glendale, Ohio

Brandy

Showing superbly, moving with powerful, precise strides and put down in wonderful condition, a Boxer bred and owned by Mr. and Mrs. John P. Wagner, earned the top prize this year. The dog was Ch. Mazelaine's Zazarac Brandy. Judge Tom Carruthers said afterwards,

I've never been a great admirer of the breed and never felt they were great show dogs, but this dog, in shape, general character and showmanship, was to me a better representative of his breed than any of the others were of theirs.

It took Carruthers, who had won Best in Show at the Garden in 1946, just 15 minutes to make his decision. The three-year old, golden-brindle homebred was automatically Best American-Bred in Show. The only other Boxer to have taken Best at Westminster was the 1947 winner, another male bred by the Wagners although they were no longer the owners at the time of the win.

Brandy came to Westminster with 32 Best in Shows to his credit and 43 group firsts.

Earlier in the day, John Wagner had been named "Dog Breeder of the Year" in a national poll, while Phil Marsh, Brandy's handler, had been honored in the same poll as "Handler of the Year."

Arthur Frederick Jones in the *Gazette* said Brandy responded perfectly to Marsh's handling. He also noted that Marsh's "strawberry-blond hair became a torch of victory as the pair posed in the brilliance of the photographers' popping flash bulbs."

Right: Ch. Mazelaine's Zazarac Brandy with handler Phil Marsh and owners Mr. and Mrs. John P. Wagner —UPI/Corbis-Bettmann

Above: Ch. Mazelaine's Zazarac Brandy — Brown photo, Dog News, February 1950, WKC

Best in Show
1950

*Ch. Walsing Winning Trick of
Edgerstoune, R26451*

Scottish Terrier, dog

Whelped September 23, 1946

By Walsing War Parade—Walsing
Whymper

Breeder, W. M. Singleton, England

Owner, **Mrs. John G. Winant**, NYC

February 13–14

Madison Square Garden III

2,532 Dogs

George F. Foley, Superintendent

John W. Cross, Jr., Chairman

J. Hartley Mellick, Jr., Chief Steward

Judge: George H. Hartman, Lampeter,
Pa.

Trick

He nearly missed the Terrier Group. His handler, Phil Prentice, was tied up elsewhere with another dog but finally got Trick into the ring, making something of an "entrance" because of the delay, and took the blue rosette.

The Best in Show was Mrs. Winant's second time at the top at Westminster, her first having been in 1942. The 3½-year-old black-brindle Scottie was officially Ch. Walsing Winning Trick of Edgerstoune. He had gone Best of Breed at the Garden a year earlier and, from opening day this year, was considered a likely top dog.

Among Trick's wins was Best in Show at the prestigious Morris & Essex show. Taking the laurels there and at Westminster was likened by some to the Triple Crown in horseracing, which meant winning the Kentucky Derby, the Preakness and the Belmont all in one year.

It was the Scottie's 23rd Best. In 35 times out, he was undefeated in the breed and had placed first in his group 30 times.

Trick's win was popular, and Hartman had high praise for him. "A truly great dog," he said. "Whenever he stops he stands right. A dog must be made right and be sound when he can do that. He is not only one of the greatest dogs I have judged, but one of the greatest I have ever seen."

Ch. Captain Speck, a Pointer owned by Charles Palmer, took the James Mortimer Memorial Trophy for Best American-Bred in Show.

Below:
Ch. Walsing Winning Trick of Edgerstoune with handler Phil Prentice and, from left, Chairman John Cross, judge Hartman and President W. Ross Proctor —*AP Wide World*

Right:
Ch. Walsing Winning Trick of Edgerstoune after his group win—*AP Wide World*

Best in Show 1951

Ch. Bang Away of Sirrah Crest, W165422

Boxer, dog

Whelped February 17, 1949

By Ch. Ursa Major of Sirrah Crest—
Verily Verily of Sirrah Crest

Breeder-Owners, *Dr. and Mrs. Raphael
C. Harris*, Santa Ana, Calif.

February 11–12, 1951

Madison Square Garden III

2,451 Dogs

George F. Foley, Superintendent

John W. Cross, Jr., Chairman

J. Hartley Mellick, Jr., Chief Steward

Judge: W. Ross Proctor, Pittstown, N.J.

Bang Away

Boxers had now taken Westminster's highest award for the third time in five years. This latest winner was a two-year-old from California, Ch. Bang Away of Sirrah Crest.

He was owned by Dr. and Mrs. Raphael C. Harris of Santa Ana and handled by Nate Levine, who had handled Westminster's first Best-in-Show Boxer in 1947. The Boxer who had won in 1949 was among the dogs Bang Away defeated this year.

William Kendrick reported in *Popular Dogs* that Bang Away seemed playful, always ready for a game with a ball that Levine carried. He was "razor-keen." He "tended to break into a gallop." He was a dog with "superb thrust and propulsion in movement." Kendrick called him "a handful."

But, as John Rendel recorded in the *Times*, there was no playfulness before W. Ross Proctor in the final class. Bang Away was "all business, moving beautifully with his characteristically long-reaching strides."

Proctor said the dog was "put together right everywhere." He called him extremely stylish, magnificent when moving, and "one of the best specimens of his breed I have ever been privileged to judge."

Bang Away was the first dog from the Coast to take the award. Said breeder-owner Dr. Harris: "He's the result of 10 years of constant breeding. I'm extremely proud of winning."

A home-bred, Bang Away was also Best American-Bred in Show. He was young and would eventually set a record for his time by winning over 65 Best in Shows.

Right:
Ch. Bang Away of Sirrah Crest, 1957, by T. Tashiro (Japanese, 20th Century), oil
—*AKC Collection*

Above:
Ch. Bang Away of Sirrah Crest, handler Nate Levine and judge W. Ross Proctor
—*UPI/Corbis-Bettmann*

Best in Show 1952

Ch. Rancho Dobe's Storm, W179626

Doberman Pinscher, dog

Whelped December 12, 1949

By Rancho Dobe's Primo—Ch. Maedel von Randahof

Breeders, Rancho Dobe Kennels, Mr. and Mrs. Brint Edwards

Owners, **Mr. and Mrs. Len Carey**, Greenwich, Conn.

February 11–12

Madison Square Garden III

2,451 dogs

George F. Foley, Superintendent

John W. Cross, Jr., Chairman

M. Oakley Bidwell, Chief Steward

Judge: Joseph P. Sims, Philadelphia, Pa.

Storm

It was the winner's 13th show. His catalog number was 13. And 13 years earlier, his great grandsire had taken Best in Show at the Garden. So much for unlucky numbers.

Ch. Rancho Dobe's Storm, who was also Best American-Bred in Show, was owned by Mr. and Mrs. Len Carey. The breeders had given them pick of the litter when he was two months old. A year later, after his ring debut, he went to the top six out of 12 times out. Said Mrs. Carey:

He loves shows but always is anxious to get home to his own bed—which he generously shares with our son, Jeff.

John Rendel of the *Times* said Storm held one's attention just by standing still. He stared "as though hypnotized, straight at his handler who knelt before him."

Judge Joseph P. Sims called Storm one of the greatest showmen he had ever seen. The dog moved with even, flowing strides, without flaw, hesitation or distraction. "I couldn't get away from him tonight," said Sims. "He is in perfect condition—I might say pluperfect condition."

Dobermans were originally assigned to William Kendrick, who fell ill and was replaced by Henry Stoecker. Many exhibitors protested that Stoecker, who had specialized in Poodles as a professional handler, was not qualified to judge Dobermans. Eighteen withdrew their entries. This was the man who made the choice that started Storm toward the top award—and who later became a distinguished all-arounder who officiated at Westminster on 15 occasions.

Storm with handler A. Peter Knoop and, from left, judge Joseph P. Sims and Chairman John W. Cross, Jr. —*Courtesy of Roger Knoop*

Mrs. Len Carey with her favorite housedog —*Shafer photo, Gazette*

Best in Show
1953

Ch. Rancho Dobe's Storm,
W179626

Doberman Pinscher, dog

Whelped December 12, 1949

By Rancho Dobe's Primo—Ch. Maedel
von Randahof

Breeders, Rancho Dobe Kennels, Mr.
and Mrs. Brint Edwards

Owners, *Mr. and Mrs. Len Carey*, Cos
Cob, Conn.

February 9–10

Madison Square Garden III

2,561 Dogs

George F. Foley, Superintendent

John W. Cross, Jr., Chairman

M. Oakley Bidwell, Chief Steward

Judge: James A. Farrell, Jr., Darien,
Conn.

Storm Prevails

The headline of Dana Mozley's story in the *Daily News* was,

Storm Weathers Storm/To Move Into Dog Final

Storm was last year's winner, and the point of the story was that he was the only one of that year's finalists who had come back to the Garden and was still "alive," as the paper put it. All the others had been defeated and were out of the picture. When Storm repeated his 1952 victory he reaped an extra measure of glory. Only five other dogs had done it.

John Rendel of the *Times* said the performance of dog and handler almost duplicated what they had done the year before. He said Storm gave the impression of utmost calm, yet was spirited "with fire."

"Not a muscle in his ninety-two-pound body twitched," wrote Court Page in the *Herald Tribune*, "which was more than could be said for the nervous Knoop who perspired at a drenching rate."

Owner Len Carey, an advertising executive, watched from a box. A. Peter Knoop, a customer's man on Wall Street, had not handled Storm for several months. Carey was glad to see him get over his rustiness after an extended lay-off from show competition.

James A. Farrell, Jr., after naming Storm Best in Show and Best American-Bred in Show said, "He was as sound as a bell. He won on soundness."

Storm was also a breeder of workers. Macy's had just started using Dobermans to patrol their store at night, and according to the *National Geographic*, their squad of canine detectives included five of Storm's offspring.

Storm with
handler A. Peter
Knoop—*Courtesy
of Roger Knoop*

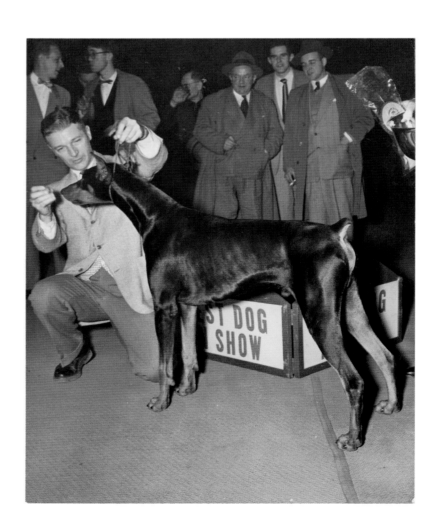

Best in Show
1954

Ch. Carmor's Rise and Shine,
S552108

Cocker Spaniel, dog

Whelped November 10, 1951

By Ch. Carolina Cotton Picker—
Carmor's Honey Dew

Breeder-Owner, **Mrs. Carl E. Morgan**,
High Point, N.C.

February 8–9

Madison Square Garden III

2,572 Dogs

George F. Foley, Superintendent

John W. Cross, Jr., Chairman

Dean Bedford, Vice-Chairman & Chief
Steward

Judge: Virgil D. Johnson, Savannah, Ga.

Rise and Shine!

He was the only contender that had never won a Best in Show before. In six months of showing, Ch. Carmor's Rise and Shine had topped four Cocker specialties and two Sporting Groups. Given the competition, it was a meagre record.

Yet he won. Showmanship turned the tide, according to Arthur Frederick Jones of the *Gazette*. Jones often complained that extensive gaiting was an unnecessary bit of by-play aimed at the gallery. Yet, it was clear, he said, that the Cocker's performance of unbroken gaiting under the guidance of handler Ted Young had been decisive.

John Rendel of the *Times* paid tribute to "a polished show dog in rich, beautiful coat who moved as impassively as though he never had performed before any but large metropolitan crowds." The spectators warmed to him slowly, but the applause at the end indicated that he had earned many supporters.

Mrs. Morgan, his breeder-owner, thought he had quality but entered him with no idea of winning. She would have liked being at ringside, but the cost of the trip to New York had not seemed warranted.

Judge Virgil Johnson, a mail-order-house executive, said that the Cocker "moved excellently and was in beautiful coat. He is one of the best buff Cockers I have ever seen."

American-bred, Rise and Shine also won the James Mortimer Memorial Trophy. Rendel summed it all up, saying, "Rise and Shine rose and shone."

Ch. Rise and Shine, handler Ted Young and, from left, judge Virgil Johnson, Chairman Cross, and President William A. Rockefeller — *UPI/Corbis-Bettmann*

Ch. Rise and Shine and Best American-Bred trophy—*AP Wide World*

Best in Show
1955

Ch. Kippax Fearnought, N192824

Bulldog, dog
Whelped October 25, 1952
By Koper Kernal—Kippax Ann
Breeder, Harold Dooler, England
Owner, **Dr. John A. Saylor**,
Long Beach, Calif.

February 14–15
Madison Square Garden III
2,537 Dogs
George F. Foley, Superintendent
Dean Bedford, Chairman
William Rockefeller, Chief Steward

Judge: Albert E. Van Court,
Los Angeles, Calif.

Jock

As a finalist last year, he was described as moving "with the deliberate rolling gait of a portly old sea captain, as casual as could be." The ringside loved him.

Now he had returned and taken the top honor. Handled by Harry Sangster, he was the Bulldog Ch. Kippax Fearnought.

There were those who would remember him as the best Bulldog ever, bar none. He was clearly the people's choice. There were loud cheers and applause, even the clang of a cowbell as he sauntered along. John Rendel of the *Times* called him "a red and white picture of power when he moved and a stolid, impassive creature when still."

Judge Albert E. Van Court said it was the toughest assignment he could remember. "All the finalists were fine representatives of their breed," he said. "You must have a certain gait and movement to be a true bulldog. This dog had it. He is certainly the best Bulldog I've ever seen."

Owner Dr. John A. Saylor, a young general practitioner, said the dog, called Jock at home, had been in the ring 14 times. This made his ninth Best.

Jock had come to the U.S. in a rather offhand way. Saylor had had no intention of buying a Bulldog but had seen photographs of him sent from England. He had purchased Jock without seeing him in the flesh.

Best American-Bred in Show went to Mr. and Mrs. M. E. Greiner's Boxer, Barrage of Quality Hill.

Left:
Ch. Kippax
Fearnought with
handler Harry
Sangster—*AP
Wide World*

Right:
Ch. Kippax
Fearnought
—*UPI/Corbis
Bettman*

Best in Show
1956

Ch. Wilber White Swan, N133530

Toy Poodle, dog
Whelped December 11, 1951
By Ch. Leicester's Bonbon's Swan
Song—Wilber Victoire
Breeder-Owner, **Bertha Smith**,
Bethpage, N.Y.

February 13–14
Madison Square Garden III
2,560 Dogs
John W. Cross, Jr., Chairman
William Rockefeller, Chief Steward

Judge: Paul Palmer, Pleasantville, N.Y.

Peanut

The Poodle Ch. Wilber White Swan was the first toy of any breed to reach the top.

Coincidentally, White Swan's handler, Anne Hone Rogers, later Mrs. James Edward Clark, was the first female professional handler to scale the heights at the Garden. She was also the second woman to handle a dog to Best in Show there, the first having been Mrs. Sherman Hoyt, an amateur, who handled the winner in 1935.

Of Miss Rogers, William Kendrick in *Popular Dogs* said, "It could not have happened to a worthier person. No more light and knowing hands ever held a dog lead than those of Miss Rogers. We have long admired her ring work in many breeds. It is as versatile as it is skillful."

Regarding the dog, known as Peanut by his friends, Kendrick said he was "maybe not the best Poodle which has ever been seen, but with due allowance for ring demeanor, performance and condition, (he was) certainly one of the all-time greats ever seen anywhere."

Judge Palmer, an executive editor of *Readers Digest*, said the dog "was about perfect in form, amazingly solid, showed great spirit, moved extremely well, and was well handled."

Arthur Frederick Jones in the *Gazette* noted that nothing flustered White Swan. He was held this way and that—tucked under the arm of his handler, plopped into a silver bowl he had won, set up in ring pose, and finally toted down to the basement television studio to go through the whole thing all over again.

He said Peanut had "the spirit of a giant." Peanut was also Best American-Bred in Show.

Ch. Wilber
White Swan and
handler Anne
Hone Rogers
*—UPI/Corbis-
Bettmann*

Best in Show
1957

Ch. Shirkhan of Grandeur,
H482771

Afghan Hound, dog

Whelped August 10, 1954

By Ch. Blue Boy of Grandeur—Mahdi
of Grandeur

Breeder, Sunny Shay

Owners, **Sunny Shay and Dorothy
Chenade**, Hicksville, N.Y.

February 11–12

Madison Square Garden III

2,594 Dogs

John W. Cross, Jr., Chairman

William Rockefeller, Chief Steward

Judge: Mrs. Beatrice H. Godsol,
Woodland Hills, Calif.

Shirkhan

A 2½-year-old Afghan, Ch. Shirkhan of Grandeur, was the first hound to take Westminster's top award. Co-owned by Sunny Shay and Dorothy Chenade, he brought special distinction to Mrs. Shay who was also his breeder and handler.

The decision was well received, though he was a true "dark horse." It was his first Best in Show. He had accomplished less and was probably the least known of all the finalists.

Arthur Frederick Jones in the *Gazette* said there was no question but that "the 65-pound bundle of longhaired animation" outshowed his competitors. When gaiting, Shirkhan seemed to smile. But he did not win on showmanship alone. He was put together right from muzzle to tail, including coat color, said Jones. He was of a striking color that Mrs. Shay described as silver-blue.

Judge Beatrice Godsol said afterwards, "He is a beautifully balanced hound. He has a good oriental Afghan expression, the correct type of lean Afghan head. He was the soundest moving of the six, a very good showman. I think he is a great hound."

A bystander would later recall that the breed standard describes the eyes of the Afghan as "gazing into the distance as if in memory of ages past." The bystander said that in 1957, she had come face to face with Shirkhan just as he was about to enter the ring for Best in Show. "I saw that look," she said.

Shirkhan, the third generation of Mrs. Shay's breeding, was automatically Best American-Bred in Show. He lived with her as house pet and got along famously with her Siamese cat.

Left:
Ch. Shirkhan of Grandeur with trophies
—UPI/Corbis-Bettmann

Above:
Ch. Shirkhan of Grandeur with judge Mrs. Godsol, breeder-owner Sunny Shay and President William A. Rockefeller
—Shafer photo, Gazette

Best in Show
1958

Ch. Puttencove Promise, N261005

Standard Poodle, dog

Whelped January 20, 1955

By Ch. Loabelo Jonny—Astron Lily of Puttencove

Breeder-Owners, **Mr. and Mrs. George Putnam**, Puttencove Kennels, Manchester, Mass.

February 10–11

Madison Square Garden III

2,569 Dogs

George F. Foley, Superintendent

John W. Cross, Jr., Chairman

William Rockefeller, Chief Steward

Judge: William W. Brainard, Jr., Far Hills, N.J.

Promise

A three-year-old white standard Poodle was this year's winner. Ch. Puttencove Promise was owned by Mrs. and Mrs. George Putnam.

John Rendel of the *Times* saw Promise as "a pure white dog with gaiety and substance built into a 65-pound frame covered with a coat in fullest bloom." There was style in the way he moved for handler Robert Gorman. If the dog did not get into his true gait immediately, the problem was exuberance. He was having too good a time. But on the last round, he moved "with flawless and regal strides."

Arthur Frederick Jones in the *Gazette* said Promise had never looked better. He seemed more gorgeously coated than ever and had what Jones said was one of the finest trimming jobs of any Poodle to get into the Westminster finals.

Judge William W. Brainard, Jr., gentleman farmer from New Jersey ("a livestock farmer in a dinner jacket," per *Time* magazine), said afterwards: "It was a very close decision at the end. I found the Poodle immaculate, sound and in beautiful condition."

He was the second Standard Poodle to take Best at the Garden. For many years, there would be white Standards who traced their bloodlines back to him. It was also the second Westminster at which Gorman had taken a dog to Best—he first did it in 1942.

It was Promise's 14th top all-breed award. A home-bred, he was also Best American-Bred in Show.

Below:
Ch. Puttencove Promise with handler Robert Gorman and, from left, judge William W. Brainard and President William A. Rockefeller
—*UPI/Corbis-Bettmann*

Right:
Ch. Puttencove Promise with handler Robert Gorman—*AP Wide World*

Best in Show
1959

Ch. Fontclair Festoon, N253272

Miniature Poodle, bitch

Whelped October 7, 1954

By Rudolph of Pipercroft—Fontclair
Fuchsia

Breeder, Mrs. W. M. Smith

Owner, ***Clarence Dillon***, Dunwalke
Kennels, Far Hills, N.J.

February 9–10

Madison Square Garden III

2,544 Dogs

George F. Foley, Superintendent

John W. Cross, Jr., Chairman

William Rockefeller, Chief Steward

Judge: Thomas H. Carruthers, III,
Glendale, Ohio

Ch. Fontclair
Festoon and
handler Anne
Hone Rogers
*—Courtesy Anne
Rogers Clark*

Tina

Ch. Fontclair Festoon, a 4½-year-old miniature Poodle, was winner. It was her 16th Best
and her swan song.

Owned by Clarence Dillon, she had come from England as a puppy. In 1956, William
Kendrick called her one of the most pleasing sights to catch his eye at the Garden and
said her failure to place in the group was a "stunning upset." In 1958, she was third in the
group. Now, having reached the pinnacle, she would be bred. Some called her one of the
great Miniatures of all time.

She made her exit gracefully. John Rendel of the *Times* said she gaited "primly as a little
lady." He called her

A saucy specimen of compact perfection clad in a rich, smartly-trimmed dark coat in fullest bloom.

Percy Roberts in *Popular Dogs* said he could not remember when a winner had received
"more whole-hearted support from fellow exhibitors and spectators." He added, "How
can one but use superlatives when describing this beautiful specimen!"

Said judge Thomas H. Carruthers: "I judge Best in Show by a process of elimination. I
eliminated down to the Miniature Poodle and the Dane. The Poodle is in beautiful form,
full of quality, and moved perfectly...I couldn't fault the Poodle."

Handling Festoon was Anne Hone Rogers, who had won Best at Westminster in 1956.
Rendel noted that while she was an experienced and usually stolid handler, she obviously
was moved at receiving the honor a second time. "Hard-bitten professionals," he said,
"can be emotional, too."

Best American-Bred in Show was the Bulldog, Ch. Vardona Frosty Snowman, owned by
Dr. Edward M. Vardon of Detroit.

Best in Show
1960

Ch. Chik T'Sun of Caversham, T365043

Pekingese, dog

Whelped September 30, 1954

By Ku-Chik of Caversham—Naxos Ku-Chi Fille of Caversham

Breeders, Mrs. H. Lunham and Miss I. M. De Pledge

Owners, **Mr. and Mrs. C. C. Venable**, Atlanta, Ga.

February 8–9

Madison Square Garden III

2,547 Dogs

George F. Foley, Superintendent

John W. Cross, Jr., Chairman

William Rockefeller, Chief Steward

Judge: George H. Hartman, Lampeter, Pa.

Ch. Chik T'Sun of Caversham and handler Clara Alford—*Shafer photo, Gazette*

Gossie

A brilliant red Pekingese, Ch. Chik T'Sun of Caversham, took Best in Show this year—and ended an extraordinary dog show career.

Gossie, as he was called, had won Best in Show 128 times. The record would not be challenged until the 1970s. But Best at Westminster had eluded him. In 1958, he was defeated in the breed there. He was a finalist in 1957 and 1959, but only now did he receive the judge's final nod.

Imported from England by Nigel Aubrey-Jones, who showed him to Best in Show a number of times, Gossie was later acquired by Mr. & Mrs. C. C. Venable.

According to John Rendel of the *Times*, Gossie moved with flouncing, jogging strides. With his rich reddish hair trailing to the floor, he never missed a step.

Percy Roberts in *Popular Dogs* said the Peke had been shown "fearlessly" from coast to coast "under each judge who came along." He credited Clara Alford—"the dog's devoted slave for two years"—for his invariably superlative coat and condition. Seeing him in the group, he had felt instinctively that the dog would win Best in Show. He likened the Peke to

A little Emperor…wearing his gorgeous coat as if it were royal raiment!

Best in Show judge George H. Hartman said afterward: "The Pekingese was in gorgeous bloom. I make him one of the few great dogs—'great,' I said—that I have ever seen. He could not be denied."

Best American-Bred in Show was taken by Pembroke Welsh Corgi, Ch. Cote de Neige Sundew, owned by Mrs. William H. Long, Jr.

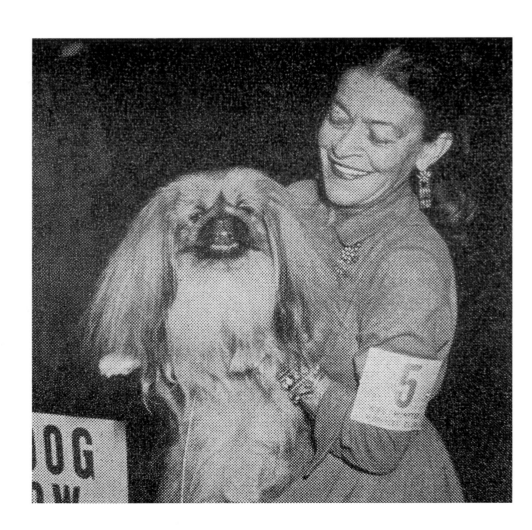

Best in Show 1961

Ch. Cappoquin Little Sister, N405337

Toy Poodle, bitch

Whelped March 6, 1957

By Ch. Ardlussa Gascon—Ardlussa Jou Jou

Breeder, Barbara M. Heying

Owner, ***Miss Florence Michelson***, Ft. Lauderdale, Fla.

February 13–14

Madison Square Garden III

2,548 Dogs

George F. Foley, Superintendent

John W. Cross, Jr., Chairman

William Rockefeller, Chief Steward

Judge: Dr. Joseph E. Redden, East Longmeadow, Mass.

Little Sister

It was a big day for Little Sister, as Alice Wagner, editor of *Popular Dogs*, put it. A black Toy Poodle, officially Ch. Cappoquin Little Sister, owned by Florence Michelson, won Best in Show.

It was her third appearance at Westminster. The first time, she was Best of Winners. A year later, she was best Toy Poodle and fourth in the group. Now she had gone all the way. It was her 14th top award.

Little Sister was handled by Anne Hone Rogers, who was thus the first woman to guide three dogs to Westminster's pinnacle. In 1956, she had won with a white Toy Poodle, and in 1959, with a black Miniature Poodle.

Judge Dr. Joseph Redden took seven minutes to make his decision. He gaited each contender once after preliminary examination and singled out Little Sister and another Poodle, the miniature Ch. Estid Ballet Dancer, for special comparison. He then tapped Miss Rogers on the shoulder, indicating that her dog was winner.

Dr. Redden said afterwards: "It resolved itself into a choice of the two poodles. There was remarkably little difference in their breed characteristics. In my opinion, the toy was better in head and to me that was the deciding factor."

Ch. Cappoquin Little Sister and handler Anne Hone Rogers
—*AP Wide World*

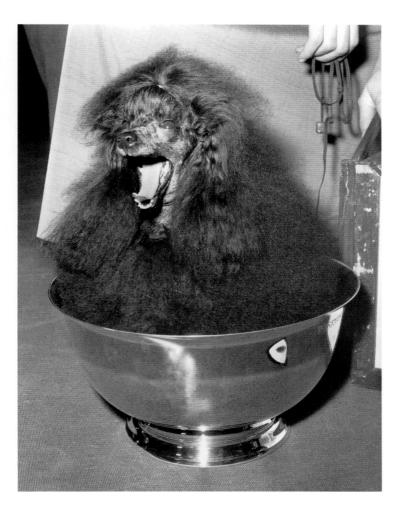

Ch. Cappoquin Little Sister
—*UPI/Corbis-Bettmann*

Best in Show
1962

Ch. Elfinbrook Simon, R240664

West Highland White Terrier, dog

Whelped July 20, 1958

By Calluna the Laird—Ichmell Gay Miss

Breeders, Mrs. and Mrs. H. Mitchell, England

Owners, *Miss Barbara Worcester and Mrs. Florence Worcester*, Wishing Well Kennels, Little Falls, N.J.

February 12–13

Madison Square Garden III

2,569 Dogs

George F. Foley, Superintendent

John Cross, Jr., Chairman

William Rockefeller, Chief Steward

Judge: Heywood Hartley, Richmond, Va.

Simon

A "little white sparkling meteor." Such was the description of the winner by Alice Wagner, editor of *Popular Dogs*.

Before millions of television viewers, Heywood Hartley, a Richmond, Va., printing-firm executive and Scottie breeder, placed him Best in Show just before midnight. He was the West Highland White Terrier Ch. Elfinbrook Simon. The 3½-year-old English importation was owned by Wishing Well Kennels. It was Simon's 17th Best in Show. He also had four Canadian Bests. His handler was George Ward.

Barbara Worcester would later recall that George Ward had not wanted to come to New York for the show. "But rather than let me show Simon," she said, "he came and won the show and was glad he did."

The victory was a popular one. Alice Wagner spoke of the dog's fire and dash. She said his flare for showmanship sparked an electric response from the gallery.

John Rendel in the *Times* said that Simon looked game, hardy and competent and that he gaited with smooth, rhythmic, short-legged strides. He noted that whenever George Ward spoke to Simon, the dog responded with a happy, almost whimsical look upward.

Said Judge Hartley afterward: "The terrier was a stand-out, typey and in superb condition. He showed beautifully and asked for it every minute."

Right:
Ch. Elfinbrook Simon with handler George Ward and, from left, President William A. Rockefeller and Judge Heywood Hartley—*Gazette*

Left:
Ch. Elfinbrook Simon with handler George Ward—*AP Wide World*

Best in Show
1963

Ch. Wakefield's Black Knight, S986689

English Springer Spaniel, dog
Whelped March 17, 1959
By Ch. Kaintuck Christmas Carol—
Ch. Wakefield's Fanny
Breeder-Owner, **Mrs. W. J. S. Borie**,
Gwynedd Valley, Pa.

February 11–12
Madison Square Garden III
2,565 Dogs
George F. Foley, Superintendent
John W. Cross, Jr., Chairman
Robert V. Lindsay, Chief Steward

Judge: Virgil D. Johnson, Savannah, Ga.

Danny

He wore his new crown "at a rakish tilt," said Lincoln A. Werden in the *Times*—because he was a "sporting" dog.

The 3-year-old English Springer, Ch. Wakefield's Black Knight, called Danny (he was born on St. Patrick's Day), was the first English Springer to win Westminster. It was his sixth Best in Show. His breeder-owner was Mrs. W. J. S. Borie of Gwynedd Valley, Pa., who had a kennel of five Springers as a hobby. He was handled by D. L. (Laddie) Carswell, who had successfully shown him since puppy days.

Percy Roberts, reporting in *Popular Dogs*, said Danny was "of ideal size with a most attractive way of going, denoting Springer character."

Fred Hunt, who did the group, said that in his opinion Danny would "go down in history as one of the all-time great sporting dogs."

Best-in-Show judge Virgil Johnson deliberated for 30 minutes. He said: "One seldom sees a Springer with more of the good qualities that are called for in his breed. He was in excellent condition as to body and coat; he was groomed to perfection and in full bloom. And, in my opinion, he was by far the best showman in the ring. The more he was shown and the more he moved, the better he looked!"

Danny was also Best American-Bred in Show. Although his career had been limited to the show ring, supporters of the breed commented he looked like a dog that could go into the field.

Below: Ch. Wakefield's Black Knight with James Mortimer trophy and handler Laddie Carswell —*AP Wide World*

Right: Ch. Wakefield's Black Knight with handler Laddie Carswell —*AP Wide World*

Best in Show
1964

Ch. Courtenay Fleetfoot of Pennyworth, HA327775

Whippet, dog
Whelped October 13, 1960
By Bellavista Barry—Myhorlyns Anita
Breeder, A. E. Halliwell, England
Owner, **Mrs. Margaret P. Newcombe**,
Pennyworth Kennels, Newington, N.H.

February 10–11
Madison Square Garden III
2,547 Dogs
George F. Foley, Superintendent
John W. Cross, Jr., Chairman
Robert V. Lindsay, Chief Steward

Judge: Len Carey, Honolulu, Hawaii

Ricky

"The little longtail," William Kendrick called the winner.

It was the Whippet, Ch. Courtenay Fleetfoot of Pennyworth, owned by Mrs. Margaret P. Newcombe. He arrived in the U. S. in 1962. Robert Forsyth handled him starting then. Though thwarted in the breed at Westminster in 1963, the 22-pound dog—who showed in the ring with all the calm of a quiet summer day—had now taken 23 groups and nine Best in Shows.

John Rendel of the *Times* reported that Ricky, as the dog was called, was something of a mail-order purchase. Mrs. Newcombe had seen him advertised by breeder A. E. Halliwell in a British Christmas catalogue and had sent for him.

There was an echo from the past in the win. Mrs. Newcombe's mother had won Westminster with a Sealyham in 1936.

Kendrick, in his report for *Popular Dogs*, called Ricky "one of the handful of truly great ones." Predominantly white with a light fawn half-blanket, loin patch and ears, he moved as smoothly as a well-oiled machine. He was the first of his breed to take the honor.

Len Carey, a Honolulu advertising executive who had won Westminster's Best in Show in 1952–53, was judge. He said afterwards, "I've never seen a better hound."

John Rendel noted that Forsyth had handled five other group winners at Westminster but that this was his first top win there. Rendel spoke of the dog's "impervious mien." He had "the bearing of an aristocrat—no such mundane activity as racing for him. There was compact fitness in that streamlined body."

Ch. Courtenay Fleetfoot of Pennyworth with handler Robert Forsyth—*AP Wide World*

Best in Show
1965

Ch. Carmichaels Fanfare, R273936

Scottish Terrier, bitch

Whelped May 8, 1960

By Ch. Barberry Knowe Merrymaker—
Ch. Carmichaels Cornelia

Breeder, R. Johnson

Owners, *Mr. and Mrs. Charles C. Stalter*, Woodcliff Lake, N.J.

February 15–16

Madison Square Garden III

2,573 Dogs

George F. Foley, Superintendent

John W. Cross, Jr., Chairman

Robert V. Lindsay, Chief Steward

Judge: Robert A. Kerns,
Philadelphia, Pa.

Mamie

A 4½-year-old silver brindle Scottie, Ch. Carmichaels Fanfare, topped them all. It was her 32nd Best in Show.

Mamie, as she was called at home, was owned by Mr. and Mrs. Charles C. Stalter. They had bought her at the age of two and found themselves with a gem. John Rendel of the *Times* said she was the most successful Scottish Terrier then in competition. She was said to be "honest all the way, with quality built into her sturdy frame, no flashy flourishes needed."

She was the first of the breed to win since 1950 when the prize went to Ch. Walsing Winning Trick of Edgerstoune. Arthur Frederick Jones noted in the *Gazette* that the earlier winner appeared twice in the fourth generation of the present winner's pedigree.

When judge Robert A. Kerns waved the Scottie to the center of the ring, handler John Murphy seemed in a daze. In their box, the owners appeared equally overwhelmed. When they regained some measure of composure, Stalter said it looked as if Mamie might now retire and be bred for the first time.

Judge Kerns said afterwards: "Having been an exhibitor and breeder for more than a few years, I realize the heartaches and difficulties of breeding a top dog in any breed. After careful consideration of all the excellent dogs in a great group of finalists, my selection came down to the Scottish Terrier. I am sure dog fanciers, when they look back, long after this great victory is a matter for the record, will recall with pride this win. This was a great one."

Ch. Carmichaels Fanfare with handler John P. Murphy and, from left, judge Robert A. Kerns and President William A. Rockefeller
—*Shafer photo, Gazette*

Best in Show
1966

Ch. Zeloy Mooremaides Magic, R344400

Wire Fox Terrier, bitch

Whelped May 31, 1961

By Zeloy Emperor—Mooremaides Cha Cha Cha

Breeder, J. Morris, England

Owner, **Marion G. Bunker**, Pebble Beach, Calif.

February 14–15

Madison Square Garden III

2,557 Dogs

George F. Foley, Superintendent

John W. Cross, Jr., Chairman

Robert V. Lindsay, Chief Steward

Judge: James A. Farrell, Jr., Darien, Conn.

Biddy

A Fox Terrier had not won in 20 years.

Ch. Zeloy Mooremaides Magic, a hound-marked Wire Fox Terrier bitch, was imported from England by Barbara Worcester in 1963. Better known as Biddy, she was a polished show dog that now had nine Best in Shows. The present owner was Mrs. Marion Bunker, a terrier devotee for 30 years.

The victory would be the terrier's last. "She's done everything in showing," said Jimmy Butler, a Yorkshireman who was her handler. "Now let's see what she can do in breeding."

Percy Roberts, who judged the breed, called her "beautiful in type, well balanced and very sound." John T. Marvin, who did the group, said she was "an over-all good terrier, not extreme on any point, but well balanced and very well shown."

Best in Show judge James A. Farrell, Jr., took 13 minutes to make his decision. He said, "The bitch is a real sample of the Fox Terrier standard. She is of the right size, had splendid balance, a neat long head and a small pair of ears."

When Farrell pointed to Biddy as winner, Butler, who was kneeling by the dog, paused and then lifted his plaid cap straight up over his head in a salute to the crowd. Then, having put the hat back on his head, he did an about-face and lifted his cap again to the other half of the crowd.

Ch. Zeloy Mooremaides Magic with handler Jimmy Butler—*AP Wide World*

Best in Show
1967

Ch. Bardene Bingo, R401701

Scottish Terrier, dog

Whelped June 28, 1961

By Bardene Blue Starlite—Bardene
Blue Cap

Breeder, G. Young, England

Owner, **E. H. Stuart**, Carnation Farm
Kennels, Carnation, Wash.

February 13–14

Madison Square Garden III

2,548 Dogs

George F. Foley, Superintendent

John W. Cross, Jr., Chairman

Robert V. Lindsay, Chief Steward

Judge: Percy Roberts, Noroton Heights,
Conn.

Bingo

Owner E. H. Stewart twice brought him to Westminster from Carnation, Wash., and got nowhere. In 1965 he was defeated in the breed by Carmichaels Fanfare who went Best in Show. In 1966, Fanfare had retired, and Bingo came back with high hopes, only to be beaten in the breed by Fanfare's kennelmate.

The third time was lucky. Handled by Bob Bartos, the splendid jet-black Scottie from England, Ch. Bardene Bingo, now 5 ½, took his 25th Best in Show.

Judge Percy Roberts was a former professional handler who had taken four dogs to the top at Westminster, the first in 1926. Now judging Best, he followed what Arthur Frederick Jones of the *Gazette* called his typical routine. He was thorough but quick. He knew what he was looking for. If he stressed anything, it was gait. He found his winner in 15 minutes.

John Rendel of the *Times* said the decision was received "with apathy." Jones recorded the same reaction, saying that spectators were often at odds with the judge, but that the judge in the ring was the only person to evaluate a class properly.

Said Roberts afterward: "He is a great dog, a *great* dog. He is the best we've had in years, and that doesn't belittle any of the others. The Scottie is of beautiful type combined with quality. He moved soundly and with confidence and animation. The presentation and handling left nothing to be desired."

"I'm in shock," said Bartos, a handler for 35 years. "It seems as though I have been trying to win Westminster all my life."

Ch. Bardene
Bingo and his
trophy—*AP Wide
World*

Ch. Bardene
Bingo with
handler Bob
Bartos and, from
left, judge Percy
Roberts and
President William
A. Rockefeller
—*Shafer photo,
Gazette*

Best in Show 1968

Ch. Stingray of Derryabah, R524026

Lakeland Terrier, dog

Whelped August 11, 1964

By Hensington Carefree—Trix of Highleadon

Breeders, Mr. and Mrs. W. Postlethwaite, England

Owners, *Mr. and Mrs. James A. Farrell, Jr.*, Darien, Conn.

February 12–13

Madison Square Garden III

2,578 Dogs

George F. Foley, Superintendent

John W. Cross, Jr., Chairman

Robert V. Lindsay, Chief Steward

Judge: Major B. Godsol, La Jolla, Calif.

Skipper

It was headline news. An English dog went Best in Show at Westminster but, before leaving England, had won Best in Show at Cruft's, the Westminster show's London counterpart. No dog had ever won both events before.

Ch. Stingray of Derryabah was "all trim elegance and flawless ring manners," according to John Rendel of the *Times*. Mr. and Mrs. James A. Farrell, Jr., were his owners. Farrell, a shipping executive and racing yachtsman, had given the dog a nautical call-name, Skipper.

Peter Green, a young professional handler from Wales, showed Skipper, who now had 10 Best in Shows. It was the first of four dogs that Green would take to the top at Westminster.

Terence P. Bresnahan who judged the group said, "He was in beautiful condition and was giving out more than any of the others. He was full of the spirit and animation that one wants in a terrier."

Best-in-Show judge Major B. Godsol called him a fine specimen. "He's impressive and has great ring presence," he said. "He made the most of himself in defeating five other excellent dogs. He was in beautiful condition."

Farrell, who judged Best in Show at the Garden in 1953, was composed and beaming when he entered the ring to thank the judge. His voice breaking, he said, "I have wanted this for 40 years."

Skipper's victory ended the last event of any kind to be held in Garden III.

Right:
Ch. Stingray of Derryabah with handler Peter Green and judge Major Godsol
—*AP Wide World*

Below:
Ch. Stingray of Derryabah—*AP Wide World*

Best in Show
1969

Ch. Glamoor Good News,
R434659

Skye Terrier, bitch

Whelped December 27, 1964

By Ch. Glamoor Going Up—
Ch. Jacinthe de Ricelaine

Breeder-Owners, *Walter F. Goodman*
and Mrs. Adele F. Goodman, Oyster
Bay, N.Y.

February 10–11

Madison Square Garden, IV

2,530 Dogs

George F. Foley, Superintendent

Albert E. Van Court, Chairman

Robert V. Lindsay, Chief Steward

Judge: Louis Murr, Spring Valley, N.Y.

Susie the Skye

Their Skyes had won Best of Breed at Westminster for seven years, but not one had taken a group there. Now Ch. Glamoor Good News—aptly named—had won the group and Best in Show. The owners were Walter F. Goodman and his mother, Mrs. Adele F. Goodman.

1969 would long be remembered as the year of the great blizzard.

At one point, before the show opened, with deep snow on the ground and more still falling, Goodman and his mother were seen walking toward the Garden. In his arms, Goodman carried the Skye that would eventually be Best in Show. Suddenly, someone shouted at him, "Hey, Walter, why don't you carry your mother and let the dog walk?" To which Goodman replied, "I'm not showing my mother."

The 4-year-old home-bred was called Susie. She came to the Garden with 12 Best in Shows. She was "done" to "the last shimmering inch," as John Rendel of the *Times* put it. The silver-colored hair was parted down the middle of her back as if by a master barber. Goodman was the only amateur in the finale. He always groomed and handled his own dogs.

Officiating over Best in Show was Louis Murr, real estate broker, owner of Romanoff Kennels and a longtime professional judge. Said Murr afterwards: "In my opinion, she measures up to the breed almost ideally in size and type. She showed almost 100 percent well. She practically knew what she was in there for. They were all nice dogs, but the one that counted was the one that went up."

Right:
Ch. Glamoor
Good News
with Walter F.
Goodman,
Mrs. Adele F.
Goodman and
group judge
E. Pennington
Meyer
—*Shafer photo*
courtesy Walter
Goodman

Far Right:
Ch. Glamoor
Good News with
Walter F.
Goodman and,
from left, judge
Louis Murr and
President
William A.
Rockefeller
—*Photo courtesy*
Walter Goodman

Best in Show
1970

Ch. Arriba's Prima Donna,
WA810016

Boxer, bitch

Whelped August 1, 1966

By Ch. Flintwood's Live Ammo—
Arriba's Alicia

Breeder, Virgil J. Barribeault

Owners, **Dr. and Mrs. P. J. Pagano**,
Pelham Manor, N.Y., and **Dr. Theodore
S. Fickes**, Marblehead, Mass.

February 9–10

Madison Square Garden IV

2,611 Dogs

Alan P. Winks, Superintendent

Albert E. Van Court, Chairman

Robert E. Taylor, Chief Steward

Judge: Anna Katherine Nicholas, White
Plains, N.Y.

Suzie the Boxer

She was Suzie to her friends. To the judge, she was "elegance personified."

She was Ch. Arriba's Prima Donna, a trim red-fawn Boxer with white markings on chest, face and feet. John Rendel in the *Times* called her "finished in movement, slim, slick and well conditioned." Owned by Dr. and Mrs. P. J. Pagano & Dr. Theodore S. Fickes, she had taken Best of Breed in 1969 but now had gone all the way to Best in Show. She was the first Boxer to gain the award since 1951.

Said Anna Katherine Nicholas, who judged the final class:

I have judged most of the great Boxer bitches since the early 1940s and this one is the greatest. She is bringing elegance back to Boxers. I thought (she) was elegance personified, a perfectly beautiful working dog.

The win brought jubilation to the owners but the bitch's future was "uncertain." Perhaps she would be shown again, but motherhood was a strong probability. The owners and the bitch's handler, Mrs. Jane Kamp Forsyth of Southboro, Conn., would hold a roundtable discussion. The only certainty now was that Suzie was a "once-in-a-life-time dog."

Suzie's record included 41 groups and 23 Best in Shows.

Ch. Arriba's
Prima Donna
with handler Jane
Forsyth—*AP
Wide World*

Best in Show
1971

Ch. Chinoe's Adamant James,
SA595936

English Springer Spaniel, dog

Whelped June 30, 1968

By Ch. Salilyn's Aristocrat—
Ch. Canarch Inchidony Brook

Breeder, Ann H. Roberts

Owner, **Milton E. Prickett**,
Lexington, Ky.

February 15–16

Madison Square Garden IV

3,031 Dogs

Alan P. Winks, Superintendent

Lyman R. Fisher, M.D., Chairman

Robert E. Taylor, Chief Steward

Judge: O. Carley Harriman, Pebble
Beach, Calif.

D. J.

Three weeks before the show, Ch. Chinoe's Adamant James, who answered to the name of D. J., served notice that he was going to be very much in the running. The liver and white English Springer Spaniel had gone to Florida where he won seven groups on the citrus belt show circuit, ending up Best in Show three times.

Walter Fletcher of the *Times* called the dog "very flashy, a real crowd-pleaser."

On the final night of Westminster, O. Carley Harriman took 12 minutes to make his decision. He said the English Springer was a nearly perfect dog, adding,

I'd like to take him home with me. He is a wonderful dog in every way.

Clint Harris handled D. J. The strongest opposition came from a Norwegian Elkhound, Ch. Vin-Melca's Vagabond, owned and handled by Patricia Craige. Ironically, it was Mrs. Craige who had showed D. J. to his first Best of Breed award—at Contra Costa, Calif., when D. J. was a puppy.

In addition to D. J., Milton E. Prickett and his wife, who were both veterinarians, owned three other Springers. He was a pathologist at the University of Kentucky, specializing in equine research. His wife had an active practice. D. J. had been a birthday gift to him from his children 2½ years before. For a time, he was a house pet who played with the children and accompanied Prickett to the university lab. Now, having been shown some 40 times, the Springer had captured 26 group firsts and 14 Best in Shows.

Ch. Chinoe's Adamant James with owner Dr. Milton E. Prickett and handler Clint Harris and Mrs. Harris—*AP Wide World*

Best in Show
1972

Ch. Chinoe's Adamant James, SA595936

English Springer Spaniel, dog

Whelped June 30, 1968

By Ch. Salilyn's Aristocrat—
Ch. Canarch Inchidony Brook

Breeder, Ann H. Roberts

Owner, **Milton E. Prickett**,
Lexington, Ky.

February 14–15

Madison Square Garden IV

3,093 Dogs

Alan P. Winks, Superintendent

Lyman R. Fisher, M.D., Chairman

Robert E. Taylor, Chief Steward

Judge: William W. Brainard, Jr.,
Marshall, Va.

Encore for D. J.

In 1971, the year when he first won Best in Show at Westminster, D. J. had made history. Handled by Clint Harris in 97 shows, he took Best of Breed 94 times. His group firsts numbered 86, and his Best in Shows, 48.

According to Walter Fletcher of the *Times*, these numbers set a record for all breeds. The old record of 73 groups and 45 Bests had been made four years earlier by his sire, Ch. Salilyn's Aristocrat.

Now D. J.—who was officially Ch. Chinoe's Adamant James—had taken Westminster's Best in Show for the second time. This had not happened since 1953. William Brainard, who officiated in the final class, said of the liver and white male, "This dog is most nearly perfect in structure and conformation to accomplish the purpose of the breed."

As reported by "Ch. Joe Gergen" in the Long Island *Newsday*, the only solace to other owners and handlers was news that D. J. would not be back. The dog's owner, Milton Prickett, said D. J. would not pursue a third Best. The dog loved to compete, and they felt it wouldn't be fair to keep him away from the ring, but they would spot him in just a few shows. They would also start him in obedience. Prickett added,

D. J. is a great favorite at the university where I teach. He sleeps through all lectures.

D. J., he explained, stands for Diamond Jim, a name they gave him because of a little white diamond-shaped mark on his back.

Far Right:
Ch. Chinoe's Adamant James gaiting with handler Clint Harris—*AP Wide World*

Right:
Handler Clint Harris shows D. J. the rosette they have just won —*AP Wide World*

Best in Show
1973

Ch. Acadia Command Performance, PA77069

Standard Poodle, dog

Whelped February 3, 1971

By Ch. Haus Brau Executive of Acadia—Ch. Chantilly Felice, C.D.

Breeders, Charles F. and Lois Kletsch

Owners, *Edward B. Jenner*, Richmond, Ill., and *Jo Ann Sering*, Portland, Ore.

February 12–13

Madison Square Garden IV

3,029 Dogs

Thomas J. Gillen, Superintendent

Lyman R. Fisher, MD, Chairman

Robert E. Taylor, Chief Steward

Judge: Mrs. Augustus Riggs, Woodbine, Md.

Bart

The 1973 winner was a stunning white Standard Poodle, Ch. Acadia Command Performance.

Bart, as the 67-pounder was called by his owners, Mrs. Jo Ann Sering and Edward B. Jenner, was just over two. Reporting for the *Times*, Walter Fletcher noted that he had become a champion at nine months. He took his first Best in Show on his first time out as a champion, still in puppy trim. He came to the Garden with 18 group firsts and eight Best in Shows.

Frank Sabella, Bart's handler, said he had been handling Poodles for 14 years and had seen some good ones. "But Bart is a really great one," he said.

The final decision was not popular with the spectators. The judge, Mrs. Riggs, said: "The booing didn't bother me at all. The crowd has booed the Best in Show decision plenty of times in the past. I made the final decision on overall quality and the way of moving. The Poodle's mistakes? I don't call exuberance a mistake."

Bart was Mrs. Sering's house pet when not at shows. A registered nurse and operating-room supervisor, she said her husband also worked. "When Bart is with us," she said, "he loves to play ball and delights in having me crawl under the sofa to get the darned thing."

Jenner, who saw the puppy win in Chicago and persuaded Mrs. Sering to let him be a co-owner, was elated with the victory. "I've had dogs at Westminster for 35 years," he said. "I've finally made it."

Ch. Acadia Command Performance with handler Frank Sabella
—*UPI/Corbis-Bettmann*

Best in Show
1974

Ch. Gretchenhof Columbia River, SA688309

German Shorthaired Pointer, dog

Whelped May 29, 1969

By Gretchenhof Moonfrost—Columbia River Della

Breeder: L. V. McGilbry

Owner: ***Dr. Richard P. Smith***, Hayward, Calif.

February 11–12

Madison Square Garden IV

3,146 Dogs

Mario Fernandez, Superintendent

Robert E. Taylor, Chairman

Bernard E. McGivern, Jr., Chief Steward

Judge: Len Carey, Fallbrook, Calif.

Traveler

Because the dog was away every weekend, his owner, Dr. Richard P. Smith, an anesthesiologist, called him Traveler.

It was the first time a German Shorthaired Pointer had taken the top prize. Walter Fletcher in the *Times* called it a "nice comeback." A year earlier at the Garden, Traveler had been beaten in the breed.

He was registered as Ch. Gretchenhof Columbia River. Handled by Jo Shellenbarger, he had gained the top honors 26 times. He had won 99 groups, 60 of them in 1973. This was more than any other sporting dog in America, which made him Ken-L-Ration's Top Sporting Dog of the year.

Group judge Charles Hamilton called him "well-balanced (with) every attribute one looks for in a good show dog. I've judged him before and given him groups, but right now he's at his peak and I think he will hold that peak for some time."

Len Carey took exactly 10 minutes to select him. Carey had also judged him before. He had awarded Traveler his first group three years before. "But I've never seen him better," he said. "He never put a foot down wrong. Wouldn't you like to shoot over him? I would."

He said this although the dog had never run in the field or hunted. "In fact, I've never shot a gun," said the owner. He added that the win was "just a super thrill."

Ch. Gretchenhof Columbia River with handler Jo Shellenbarger and, from left, judge Len Carey and Chairman Robert E. Taylor —*Gilbert photo, WKC*

Best in Show
1975

Ch. Sir Lancelot of Barvan, 894729 (Canada)

Old English Sheepdog, dog

Whelped April 6, 1971

By Ch. Tarawoods Beau Bully D—
Tarawoods Mistee Weather

Breeder-Owners: ***Mr. and Mrs. Ronald Vanword***, Barvan Kennels, Newmarket, Ontario, Canada

February 10–11

Madison Square Garden IV

3,035 Dogs

Mario Fernandez, Superintendent

Robert E. Taylor, Chairman

Bernard E. McGivern, Jr., Chief Steward

Judge: Harry T. Peters, Jr., NYC

Dudley

Ch. Sir Lancelot of Barvan, an Old English Sheepdog, took the honors. He was owned by Mr. and Mrs. Ronald Vanword of Newmarket, Ontario, Canada, and handled by Malcolm Fellows.

Walter Fletcher in the *Times* noted that it was the first time in 61 years that a bobtail had won and that 57 years had passed since a Canadian dog had gone to the top.

The 110-pounder gained his Canadian title in Toronto at the age of 14 months and took his first top award in Montreal at the age of 2. He was also a Bermudian titleholder.

Mrs. Vanword, who had come down to New York on a chartered bus with a party of 22, said that her husband had stayed at home with their three children and three other Old English. She added,

I'll have to find another way to go back. The bus returned on Monday night.

Dudley, as the 3-year old was called, had been Best in Show 20 times north of the border before he was retired from competition there two months before. "He was No. 1 of all breeds in Canada," said Fellows. "We felt there was no more he could do. This is the first time he's been out since. It's his first Best in Show in the U.S., and it's the biggest of all his wins."

"The Old English is a great mover," said Judge Harry T. Peters, Jr. "He is magnificent, the best representative of the breed I've ever seen."

Ch. Sir Lancelot of Barvan and handler Malcolm Fellows—*AP Wide World*

Best in Show 1976

Ch. Jo Ni's Red Baron of Crofton, R890834

Lakeland Terrier, dog

Whelped February 18, 1971

By Ch. Special Edition—Ch. Jori's Jo-Ni Sherwood

Breeders, John E. Mahan and Nicholas Ostopick

Owner, **Mrs. Virginia K. Dickson**, La Habra, Calif.

February 9–10

Madison Square Garden, IV

3,098 Dogs

Mario Fernandez, Superintendent

Robert E. Taylor, Chairman

Chester F. Collier, Chief Steward

Judge: William W. Brainard, Jr., Marshall, Va.

Red Baron

It was Westminster's Centennial Show. The winner was a Lakeland Terrier, Ch. Jo-Ni's Red Baron of Crofton. Owned by Mrs. Virginia Dickson and handled by Ric Chasoudian, the dog was just short of five years old. It was the first Best in Show at Westminster for Chasoudian, who had been coming to the Garden for 27 years.

The Baron was the second Lakeland to win, the first having taken the top award in 1968.

In horse-race parlance, said Walter Fletcher in the *Times*, the Baron would have gone off as a 1-to-4 shot, for he went into the final with by far the most impressive credentials. He had placed second in the Group in 1975 but this year had come to the Garden with a record of 74 top awards, said to be more than four times the combined total of the other five finalists.

"The Baron's a really great showman," said Chasoudian. He then added, "Sometimes, he's a little too spirited for the judges but that's probably because he has a redhead's temperament."

William W. Brainard, Jr., judging Best at Westminster for the third time, took 14 minutes to make his decision. "The Lakeland is in top form," he said later. "I've never seen him as good. He was all confidence and quality. I've judged him before but never sent him to the top. When I had him at Montgomery County, he wasn't in anywhere near the shape he was in tonight. He was just perfection tonight, a truly outstanding dog."

Above: Ch. Red Baron with handler Ric Chasoudian and, from left, President William Rockefeller, judge William W. Brainard, Jr. and Vice-President William H. Chisholm—*WKC*

Right: Ch. Red Baron with handler Ric Chasoudian—*AP Wide World*

Best in Show
1977

Ch. Dersade Bobby's Girl, RA77200

Sealyham Terrier, bitch

Whelped October 10, 1971

By Atusta Curry Sauce—Modern Millie

Breeder, Derrick Thomas

Owner, **Mrs. Dorothy Wimer**, Pool Forge Kennels, Churchtown, Pa.

February 14–15

Madison Square Garden IV

3,065 Dogs

Mario Fernandez, Superintendent

Robert E. Taylor, Chairman

Chester F. Collier, Chief Steward

Judge: Haworth F. Hoch, Villa Ridge, Mo.

Binny

The crowd roared approval at the Sealyham's every turn.

Ch. Dersade Bobby's Girl was owned by Mrs. Dorothy Wimer. When she embraced handler Peter Green, she was jubilant but tearful. She said the win was "by far my biggest thrill in my dog-owning life." She had shown dogs for 35 years.

Green was also emotional, calling the victory more exciting than the first time he had won there, nine years earlier.

Binny, as the bitch was called, was bred in Wales, Green's homeland. Green, who came to the United States in 1958, said she was unusual. "It is very difficult to get a dog of this breed to be good show dog," he said. "Consistently, better dogs of this breed are bred in Europe."

Pat Gleeson, in her *Times* report, noted that the 24-pounder had recently produced a litter of seven. With 51 Best in Show awards, she would now retire as a full-time house pet.

Best-in-show judge Haworth F. Hoch, chairman of a St. Louis investment banking firm and an AKC Board member, said: "This was a very strong field. Any one of the finalists could have won. My selection was not influenced by the crowd's cheering. This is not the first time I have sent a Sealyham to the top, but the last time I gave it to one was so far back I can't remember exactly when."

During the picture taking, Green's daughter Melanie, aged 12, joined her father in the ring and gave the dog a kiss.

Above:
Ch. Dersade Bobby's Girl with handler Peter Green and, from left, Chairman Robert E. Taylor, Judge Haworth Hoch and President William Rockefeller
—*Gilbert photo, WKC*

Left:
Ch. Dersade Bobby's Girl with handler Peter Green and owner Mrs. Wimer—*AP Wide World*

Handler Peter Green's daughter Melanie, aged 12, joins her father in the ring during the picture taking
—*Gilbert photo, WKC*

Best in Show
1978

Ch. Cede Higgins, TB097774

Yorkshire Terrier, dog

Whelped October 8, 1973

By Ch. Clarkwyn Jubilee Eagle—
Cede Bonnie

Breeder, C. D. Lawrence

Owners, **Barbara A. and Charles
W. Switzer**, Seattle, Wash.

February 13–14

Madison Square Garden IV

3,116 Dogs

Mario Fernandez, Superintendent

Chester F. Collier, Chairman

Robert E. Taylor, Chief Steward

Judge: Mrs. James Ednard Clark,
Cecilton, Md.

Higgins

He was the first Yorkie to win. He was everybody's Valentine.

Ch. Cede Higgins, handled by Marlene Lutovsky from Seattle, made a holiday picture. His meticulously brushed steel-blue and gold coat was accented by a red-and-white polka-dot bow in his topknot. The dog was set off nicely by his handler's bright red dress and sandals.

"I always wear red in the ring," said Mrs. Lutovsky—who was a redhead, as noted by Pat Gleeson of the TIMES. *"I'm elated, I'm thrilled. It's a fairy tale come true."*

The 5¾-pounder had also won the Yorkshire Terrier show the day before Westminster. He now had 33 bests, 78 groups and 10 specialties.

It was a family affair. Also on hand were Barbara and Charles Switzer, Mrs. Lutovsky's parents, who owned Higgins. "Every morning I'm up at five," said Mrs. Switzer, "to clean his teeth, brush and oil his coat, change the wrappers and give him clean booties."

Group judge Iris de la Torre Bueno said, "I think the dog is beautiful. He has a lovely texture of coat and color—so very important to this breed. He also has an excellent top line and good rib spring and is a very good showman."

Said Mrs. Clark, Best in Show judge who deliberated for 17 minutes: "He has to be the best Yorkie I've ever seen, and he showed his heart out." She said it was one of the greatest final lineups she had ever seen at the Garden. "And I've been going to this show since I was 12," she added. "The Yorkshire terrier has undeniable star quality."

Ch. Cede Higgins
handled by
Marlene Lutovsky
with, from left,
President William
Rockefeller, judge
Mrs. James E.
Clark and
Chairman Chester
F. Collier
—Ashbey photo

Best in Show
1979

Ch. Oak Tree's Irishtocrat,
SB644600

Irish Water Spaniel, dog

Whelped April 12, 1974

By Ch. Mallyree Mr. Muldoon—
Naptandy's Annie Oaktrees

Breeder-Owner, **Mrs. Anne E. Snelling**,
Ottawa, Ontario, Canada

February 12–13

Madison Square Garden IV

3,154 Dogs

Mario Fernandez, Superintendent

Chester F. Collier, Chairman

Robert E. Taylor, Chief Steward

Judge: Henry H. Stoecker, Holmdel,
N.J.

Dugan

The winner, according to Joan Morden of *Dogs in Canada*, was conceived at a mating in New York during the Westminster weekend five years earlier.

The liver-colored Irish Water Spaniel, Ch. Oak Tree's Irishtocrat, was called Dugan. The first of his breed to take the award, Dugan had been with handler William Trainor from an early age. He was both an American and Canadian champion. This was his 33rd Best.

Breeder-owner Anne Snelling recalled that she had once shown Dugan herself. He was eight months old, and it was the only time he ever was beaten in the breed. She said,

Bill Trainor was so angry...that he charged over and said: "You never will handle Dugan again." I was fired on the spot.

Group judge Elsworth Howell called Dugan, "a living visualization of the standard."

Henry H. Stoecker, judge of Best in Show, called him "a great breed specimen...typey, well balanced and sound. He showed every minute, and he has heart. He's the best of the breed that I've ever seen."

Dugan's future was uncertain. "You can't go any higher than winning Westminster," said Trainor. But Dugan loved showing. "When he hears the van being loaded, he jumps up and down in his stall until they take him out. If we leave without him, he howls and raises hell, tipping over the feed pan, water bowl and anything else in his stall."

Owner Anne Snelling with Dugan and Dragon, who would be Best in Show in 1982 —*Dogs in Canada*

Ch. Oak Tree's Irishtocrat and handler William Trainor after their win—*AP Wide World*

Best in Show
1980

Ch. Innisfree's Sierra Cinnar, WC976104

Siberian Husky, dog

Whelped May 23, 1974

By Ch. Innisfree's Sierra Beau Jack—
Innisfree's Sierra Royal Kate

Breeders, Mike Burnside and
S. Higginbotham

Owner, *Kathleen Kanzler*,
Accokeek, Md.

February 11–12

Madison Square Garden IV

2,769 Dogs

Visser and Visser, Superintendent

Chester F. Collier, Chairman

Robert E. Taylor, Chief Steward

Judge: E. Irving Eldredge,
Middleburg, Va.

Cinnar

When Trish Kanzler piloted her mother's red Siberian, Ch. Innisfree's Sierra Cinnar, to Westminster's top honors, she was 23. She was said to be the youngest person ever to attain the honor.

Best in Show judge E. Irving Eldredge, Irish Setter breeder and an AKC director, took 16 minutes to make his decision. "He is magnificent, was beautifully balanced and presented to perfection," he said later. "I never have seen a Siberian this great. The ear didn't bother me."

"The ear" was a reference to an incident in the Kanzler kennel, which was home to 50 Siberians. In 1978, according to Walter Fletcher of the *Times*, a kennelmate had bitten off the tip of Cinnar's left ear. Until then, Miss Kanzler and Cinnar had had great success, winning 13 Best in Shows and numerous groups.

When the ear healed, Cinnar returned to the ring but was passed over many times. Then in March 1979, all-breed judge Langdon Skarda selected him for the top award at Norfolk, Va. The ice had been broken. The handsome Siberian was back in the picture. He would take 17 more Best in Shows.

Herman Cox, who awarded Cinnar first in the group, said: "The Siberian just flows when he moves. I certainly don't feel he should be penalized for the tip of the ear being missing. It's a scar of honor and doesn't mar his performance."

The Kanzlers had bred Huskies for 20 years, producing 85 champions. Cinnar left his stamp on the breed, siring 25 champions in the United States and 18 in Canada.

Left:
Ch. Innisfree's Sierra Cinnar, with Trish Kanzler and, from left, judge E. Irving Eldredge and President William Rockefeller
—*Gilbert photo, WKC*

Far Left:
Ch. Innisfree's Sierra Cinnar, embraced by Trish Kanzler
—*Gilbert photo, WKC*

Best in Show 1981

Ch. Dhandy's Favorite Woodchuck, TB493820

Pug, dog

Whelped February 21, 1977

By Ch. Chen's A Favorite of the Gods—Ch. Heritage Wicked Witch

Breeders, Mrs. W. J. Braley and Mrs. R. D. Hutchinson

Owner, **Robert A. Hauslohner**, Rosemont, Pa.

February 9–10

Madison Square Garden IV

2,327 Dogs

Visser and Visser, Superintendent

Chester F. Collier, Chairman

Robert E. Taylor, Chief Steward

Judge: Langdon Skarda, Clovis, N.M.

Chucky

The fawn Pug was known as Chucky. The sturdy toy, registered as Ch. Dhandy's Favorite Woodchuck, was the first Pug to be named Best at Westminster.

Chucky's owner was Robert Hauslohner, a Philadelphia lawyer and a trustee of the Philadelphia Museum of Art. Hauslohner said, "I've been in the sport for almost 45 years, and he is the finest animal I've ever owned."

The six finalists were said to have a total of 140 Best in Shows. The triumph was Chucky's 16th top award, and on the way he captured his 64th group. Robert Barlow handled him.

Noting that the dog had been shown some 90 times in 1980, Walter Fletcher of the *Times* asked what "return" there might be, now that the Pug had won Westminster. Hauslohner replied that Chucky's stud fee was $150 and that in 1980, he had been used perhaps a dozen times. Given the breed, which he said was not as popular as Dobes or Cockers, Chucky might be used two dozen times more.

Langdon Skarda, a judge since 1947, took 13 minutes to make his decision. "The Pug has a beautiful head, body and a magnificent top line," he said. "He moved out and covered more ground than any other dog in the class. The last time I sent the Pug around on his side gait, he had that extra little spark of animation and showmanship that put him over the top."

Skarda added, "It was between the Pug and another dog. But no one ever will know who the other dog was."

Below:
Ch. Dhandy's Favorite Woodchuck with handler Robert Barlow and, from left, President William Rockefeller, judge Langdon L. Skarda and Chairman Chester F. Collier—*WKC photo*

Right:
Ch. Dhandy's Favorite Woodchuck and owner Robert A. Hauslohner—*AP Wide World*

Best in Show 1982

Ch. St. Aubrey Dragonora of Elsdon, TB520501

Pekingese, bitch

Whelped September 9, 1976

By Ch. St. Aubrey Laparata Dragon— St. Aubrey Knostro Sandrine

Breeder, R. William Taylor, Quebec, Canada

Owner, **Mrs. Anne E. Snelling**, Ottawa, Ontario, Canada

Feb 8–9

Madison Square Garden IV

2,214 Dogs

Visser & Visser, Superintendent

Chester F. Collier, Chairman

Robert E. Taylor, Chief Steward,

Judge: Mrs. Robert V. Lindsay, NYC

Lee Lee

Big news after the toy group was that the Peke had defeated the Pug that was last year's Best in Show winner.

The Peke was Ch. St. Aubrey Dragonora of Elsdon, a bitch owned by Anne Snelling of Canada. Nicknamed Lee Lee after Mrs. Snelling's husband Lee, she went on to Best in Show—and retirement. "She's coming home to Canada," said her owner, "where she will join her mother and one other Peke we own."

The red 8½-pounder with a black mask was a champion on both sides of the border. She closed her career with a total of 20 American Best in Shows and 50 group wins. She was handled by William Trainor, who piloted Mrs. Snelling's Irish Water Spaniel to Best at Westminster in 1979.

Group judge Dr. Edward McGough said she had won on beauty. "Although the Pug is extremely hard to fault," he said, "I felt he just wasn't giving enough. The Peke was showing all the time."

Mrs. Robert V. Lindsay, Best in Show judge, was unruffled by the applause of the spectators, who clearly favored a German Shepherd Dog. For 24 minutes she sent the finalists through their paces.

Said Mrs. Lindsay afterwards: "The Pekingese standard calls for the animal to resemble a lion...And that's just what she resembled. Despite two hard days, she was putting out all the time. I loved her from the minute she entered the ring. She moved the way she should and displayed great heart."

Ch. St. Aubrey Dragonora of Elsdon with handler William Trainor and judge Mrs. Robert V. Lindsay—*Gilbert photo, WKC*

Best in Show 1983

Ch. Kabiks the Challenger, HC512163

Afghan Hound, dog

Whelped December 16, 1977

By Ch. Kabiks Standing Ovation—Ch. Kabiks Mindy

Breeder-Owners, **Chris and Marguerite Terrell**, Anacortes, Wash.

February 14–15

Madison Square Garden IV

2,621 Dogs

Newport Dog Shows, Superintendent

Chester F. Collier, Chairman

Robert E. Taylor, Chief Steward

Judge: Derek G. Rayne, Carmel-by-the-Sea, Calif.

Pepsi

A wicked snowstorm dumped two feet of snow on the city two days before the show opened. It stopped traffic in the streets and brought an eerie silence to New York, but it kept few exhibitors away.

The winner was Pepsi, a black and tan Afghan from the state of Washington, the first Afghan to win since 1957. Officially Kabiks the Challenger, his breeder-owners were Chris and Marguerite Terrell. Chris Terrell showed him, and it was the dog's 43rd Best in Show. Wins by dogs that were shown by their owners tended to be very popular, and it was Chris Terrell's proud boast that he and Pepsi had made it to the top without advertising in dog magazines.

Pepsi was "an aristocrat, dignified and aloof," said Walter Fletcher of the *Times*, and he was clearly the people's choice.

Derek Rayne took 10 minutes to judge the final. There were seven contenders now because since the previous Westminster, AKC had created the Herding Group, made up of working breeds whose primary function was livestock herding.

Rayne said later: "The dog has the look of an eagle, and I think he could outrun the desert wind. I've been judging for 43 years, and he's the best Afghan I've ever seen. Twice before I've given him the Best-in-Show award, so I tried my best to beat him. But he never let down. He has a magnificent classic head and he's the right size. Too many Afghans today are too big. He's the way I remember the breed in England years ago."

Right:
Ch. Kabiks the Challenger handled by Chris Terrell with, from left, judge Derek G. Rayne and President William Rockefeller.
–*Ashbey photo*

Below:
Ch. Kabiks the Challenger gaiting with Chris Terrell
—*Callea photo, Gazette*

Best in Show 1984

Ch. Seaward's Blackbeard, WE751149

Newfoundland, dog

Whelped July 24, 1979

By Ch. Seaward's Jolly Roger Beaupre— My Lord's Sarah

Breeders, Nancy MacMahan & Katherine Lein

Owner, *Elinor Ayers*, Seaward Kennels, Manchester Center, Vt.

February 13–14

Madison Square Garden IV

2,652 Dogs

Newport Dog Shows, Superintendent

Chester F. Collier, Chairman

Robert E. Taylor, Chief Steward

Judge: Mrs. Maynard K. Drury, Saranac Lake, N.Y.

Adam

He was from Vermont and was said to be the top-winning Newfoundland of all time. Ch. Seaward's Blackbeard was the first of his breed to capture the major honors at Westminster.

The 155-pounder, just short of five years old, was one of 40 Newfoundlands owned by Elinor Ayers, whose mother established the Seaward Kennels in Manchester Center, Vt., in 1932.

"We call him Adam," explained Gerlinde Hockla, his handler, "because he was the first whelped in a litter. I walk him three miles every day. It keeps us both in shape."

Best in Show judge Mrs. Maynard K. Drury had just returned from judging in Australia, New Zealand, Singapore and Malaysia. In 1928, she had shown a Newfoundland at Westminster, and she had bred many good ones over the years. However, she had not bred one in a decade, nor did she own one now.

Unfazed by the crowd's applause, she turned in a 16-minute no-nonsense job of evaluating the seven contenders. Walter Fletcher of the *Times* said the finalists had a total of 221 top awards among them.

"I've judged 1,000 Newfs all over the world in the last year and this one is the finest," Mrs. Drury said later. "This was the greatest group of specials I've ever seen. All seven finalists were gorgeous, but the Newf had it all. He was the best balanced and best mover. He looked at me, smiled and said, 'I'm the best dog yet.'"

Left: Ch. Seaward's Blackbeard embraced by handler Gerlinde Hockla—*Gilbert photo, WKC*

Right: Ch. Seaward's Blackbeard with handler Gerlinde Hockla and, from left, Chairman Chester F. Collier, judge Mrs. Maynard K. Drury and President William Rockefeller—*Gilbert photo, WKC*

Best in Show
1985

Ch. Braeburn's Close Encounter, RA499153

Scottish Terrier, bitch

Whelped October 22, 1978

By Ch. Snadgreg's Headliner—
Ch. Anstamm Happy Moment

Breeders, R. E. and H. M. Girling

Owners, ***Sonnie and Alan Novick***,
Plantation Acres, Fla

February 11–12

Madison Square Garden IV

2,608 Dogs Newport Dog Shows,
Superintendent

Chester F. Collier, Chairman

Robert E. Taylor, Chief Steward,

Judge: Elsworth S. Howell, Darien,
Conn.

Shannon

The victory was the little black Scottie's 184th. Ch. Braeburn's Close Encounter, was owned by Sonnie and Alan Novick. Known as Shannon, she was the first Scottie to win since 1967.

Handled by George Ward, she had taken the Ken-L-Ration award for winning more groups than any other terrier in both 1983 and 1984. The Novicks, in show dogs since 1971, also owned the top group-winning sporting dog for those years.

It was Ward's second Westminster victory. He had taken his first in 1962. A third-generation handler from Michigan who had piloted 750 dogs to their championships, he called Shannon a born "showman." The louder the applause, the more she responded.

Elsworth Howell, president of Howell Book House and a judge since 1938, made the final choice in 14 minutes. "She's the perfect Scottie bitch," he said. "She has fire and spirit and moves like a dream. Then she's spunky like a Scottie should be. I've seen her before but never had the pleasure of judging her, although I've always admired her."

Ch. Braeburn's
Close Encounter
and handler
George Ward, and
from left, judge
Elsworth
S. Howell and
President William
H. Chisham
—*Ashbey photo*

Best in Show 1986

Ch. Marjetta's National Acclaim, SD303592

Pointer, dog

Whelped February 6, 1981

By Ch. Firesign's Smackwater Jack—Ch. Truewithin A Taste of Triumph

Breeder, Marjorie Martorella

Owners, **Mrs. Alan R. Robson**, Glenmoore, Pa., and **Michael Zollo**, Bernardsville, N.J.

February 10–11

Madison Square Garden IV

2,591 Dogs

Newport Dog Shows, Superintendent

Chester F. Collier, Chairman

Robert E. Taylor, Chief Steward

Judge: Mrs. George John Wanner, Largo, Fla.

Deputy

The winner was a liver-and-white Pointer, Ch. Marjetta National Acclaim. His call name was Deputy. Just over five years old, he was co-owned by Mrs. Alan R. Robson and Michael Zollo.

Deputy was the first Pointer to win since 1932. It was a very popular choice. Every time he was gaited, there were cheers from the gallery. "We have 114 acres," said Zollo, "and I run him every day with a half-dozen other Pointers. It keeps them all in good condition."

The five-year-old had sired 20 champions. Shown by Zollo, he had a total of 88 group wins and 16 Best in Shows. Walter Fletcher of the *Times* called Deputy "a polished show dog" and said aplomb was his attention getter. "He was accustomed to the ring and accustomed to its rewards."

Group judge Mrs. Barbara Heller said: "He has the typical classical pointer head, which is the hallmark of the breed. He moves beautifully and has lots of showmanship, which is the name of the game."

Mrs. George John Wanner took 14 minutes to reach her decision on the seven finalists. She said afterwards: "I never judged the Pointer before, but he is magnificent. He was 'there' in every way I wanted him to be. He just never stopped, and on the last go around, he gave more than the others."

Ch. Marjetta's National Acclaim handled by Michael Zollo with Chairman Chester F. Collier, judge Mrs. George John Wanner and President William H. Chisholm.
—*Tatham photo*

Best in Show 1987

Ch. Covy Tucker Hill's Manhattan, WE564915

German Shepherd Dog, dog

Whelped May 4, 1979

By Covy's Flanigan of Tucker Hill—Ch. Covy's Rosemary of Tucker Hill

Breeder, Cappy Pottle and Gloria Birch

Owners, *Shirlee Braunstein*, North Woodmere, N.Y., and *Jane A. Firestone*, Southern Pines, N.C.

February 9–10

Madison Square Garden IV

2674 Dogs

Newport Dog Shows, Superintendent

Chester F. Collier, Chairman

Robert E. Taylor, Chief Steward,

Judge: Louis Auslander, Lake Forest, Ill.

Manhattan

The heavy-coated, black-and-tan seven-year-old was the first German Shepherd Dog ever named Best at Westminster.

Ch. Covy Tucker Hill's Manhattan was the all-time top-winning German Shepherd Dog in America. He had 332 group firsts and 199 Best in Shows.

"Manhattan has quite a fan club," said owner Jane Firestone. "I get many letters."

Handler Jim Moses added that he and the dog had done so much flying that at airports, porters and airline personnel called Manhattan by name. "He's a calm dog," said Moses, "but when he's in the ring and the crowd begins to cheer, it turns him on and he's up on his toes."

William Kendrick had given Manhattan Best in Show at AKC's Centennial show in 1984. With an entry of over 8,000 dogs, it was the largest show ever held in North America. In 1984 and 1985, Manhattan received the Ken-L-Ration award as top group-winner of all breeds in this country. In 1986, he was top group-winner in the Herding division for the third year in a row.

Donald Jones judged the group and said, "He meets the breed standard more correctly than any dog I've seen. The basics are there. Then he has a sterling character."

Louis Auslander, an AKC director, took 15 minutes to make the final decision. Said Auslander: "He's outstanding, just outstanding. Everything I wanted, he showed me. This was the finest class I've ever judged. Quality was everywhere. When a judge gets excited and his heart skips a beat, that's what dog show judging is all about. It doesn't happen too often. The German Shepherd is a great showman, under control at all times."

Ch. Covy Tucker Hill's Manhattan with owner Jane Firestone—*WKC*

Right:
Ch. Covy Tucker Hill's Manhattan facing the cameras—*WKC*

Left:
Ch. Covy Tucker Hill's Manhattan with handler Jim Moses and judge Louis Auslander —*WKC*

Best in Show 1988

Ch. Great Elms Prince Charming II, TC407373

Pomeranian, dog

Whelped December 28, 1984

By Ch. Cedarwoods Image of Diamond —Great Elms Sweet Candy

Breeder, Ruth L. Beam

Owners, *Skip Piazza and Olga Baker*, Avondale, Pa.

February 8–9

Madison Square Garden IV

2,651 Dogs

Newport Dog Shows, Superintendent

Chester F. Collier, Chairman

Robert E. Taylor, Chief Steward,

Judge: Mrs. Michele Billings, Ft. Lauderdale, Fla.

Prince

For the smallest dog in the ring, it was a big victory. The winner was a four-and-a-half pound Pomeranian, Ch. Great Elms Prince Charming II, owned by Skip Piazza and Olga Baker, from Avondale, Pa.

The bright orange toy dog made history, for it was the first time a Pomeranian had triumphed at the Garden. It was his sixth Best in Show.

The group judge Thelma Brown, after choosing the three-year-old for his 36th group win, said: "The Pom has beautiful depth of color, good pigment, a short back and is a lovely breed type. He was pressed by the Brussels Griffon. Both are lovely breed types, but the Pom just showed a trifle better."

It took Michelle Billings, from Fort Lauderdale, exactly 20 minutes to evaluate the merits and demerits of the seven finalists. Said the Floridian: "He makes a positive statement, 'Here I come.' He has a wonderful carriage and was put down in flawless condition. I have judged him once before, and I gave him a group."

The tiny dog, handled by Piazza, was also the choice of the majority of the spectators. Every time he was gaited or Mrs. Billings stopped in front of him, the crowd roared its approval.

Ch. Great Elms Prince Charming II with owner Skip Piazza and judge Mrs. Michelle Billings —*Ashbey photo*

Best in Show
1989

Ch. Royal Tudor's Wild as the Wind, CD, WF640032

Doberman Pinscher, bitch

Whelped October 24, 1984

By Ch. Electra's the Wind Walker— Array Exclusive, CD

Breeders, Beth Wilhite & Judith Bingham

Owners, ***Arthur and Susan Korp***, ***Beth Wilhite***, and ***Richard and Carolyn Vida***, San Jose, Calif.

February 13–14

Madison Square Garden IV

2,628 Dogs

Newport Dog Shows, Superintendent

Chester F. Collier, Chairman

Robert E. Taylor, Chief Steward,

Judge: Mrs. Bernard Freeman, NYC

Indy

She was not just a Champion. The CD after her name indicated she had earned the title of Companion Dog in obedience competition. Her dam also carried the title.

The elegant red Doberman bitch had been a finalist in 1988 and now had come back to take Best in Show, her 45th top award. Handled by Andy Linton, she was the first of her breed to win the Garden since 1953. She had won 19 specialties.

Ch. Royal Tudor's Wild as the Wind, CD, was owned by Sue and Art Korp, Beth Wilhite, and Richard and Carolyn Vida. They called her Indy. On the Friday night before Westminster, as reported by Walter Fletcher of the *Times*, she had received the Science Diet Winners Circle Award of $5,000 as the top dog in 1988, having defeated a total of 68,425 other canines during the year.

Judge Charlotte Clem McGowan, who put the four-year-old first in the group, said: "She's elegant, beautifully balanced, with a superb headpiece."

Best-in-Show judge Mrs. Muriel Freeman, one of the country's foremost breeders of Rottweilers and formerly an eminent golfer, took 19 minutes to make her decision. "She is very elegant, very correct and very balanced," was her terse comment. "She was all the things she's supposed to be."

Ch. Royal Tudor's Wild as the Wind, CD, with handler Andy Linton and judge Mrs. Muriel Freeman
—*Tatham photo*

Best in Show
1990

Ch Wendessa Crown Prince,
TC605792

Pekingese, dog

Whelped May 31, 1986

By Briarcourt's Rule Brittania—
Ch. Wendessa Princess Lyzette

Breeder, Mrs. Ronald S. Bramson

Owner, ***Edward B. Jenner***,
Burlington, Wis.

February 12–13

Madison Square Garden IV

2,932 Dogs

Newport Dog Shows, Superintendent

Ronald H. Menaker, Chairman

Robert E. Taylor, Chief Steward,

Judge: Frank T. Sabella, Santa Fe, N.M.

Prince

A red Peke carried the day. The winner was 3-year-old Ch. Wendessa Crown Prince, owned by Ed Jenner of Burlington, Wis.

Twice before, in 1960 and 1982, a Pekingese—a breed that traced back to the Tang Dynasty of 8th-century China—had prevailed at Westminster. On the Saturday before the show opened, Prince had received the Ken-L Ration Award as top group-winning toy for 1989.

"This will be Prince's last time in a ring," Jenner said. "I now am going to retire him."

The show would also be the last of a sort for Luc Boileau, who had handled Prince to 86 group firsts and 34 Best in Shows. Boileau had announced plans to stop handling and become a judge.

Judge Dr. Jacklyn E. Hungerland, who placed him first in the group, said: "He had a gorgeous head, his eyes were wonderful, he had great legs and body. He could not be in better condition and bloom."

Frank Sabella took 14 minutes to make the final decision. He said:

"The Peke had something, which is sadly lacking in the breed's gait today: a correct roll. He has a beautiful head, a massive chest, is the correct size and was presented in magnificent condition."

Ch Wendessa Crown Prince with handler Luc Boileau and judge Frank T. Sabella. Note at left the Leash Club's Perpetual Challenge Cup for Best in Show if American-Bred. The silver replica in front of the cup is given to commemorate the award.
—*Ashbey photo*

Best in Show 1991

Ch. Whisperwind on a Carousel, PB949147

Standard Poodle, dog

Whelped December 12, 1985

By Ch. Primetime Kristofer— Ch. Pinafore Whisperwind Brooke

Breeder, Linda Blackie and Mrs. Philip Harney

Owners, **Dr. and Mrs. Frederick Hartsock**, Potomac, Md.

February 11–12

Madison Square Garden IV

2,500 dogs

Newport Dog Shows, Superintendent

Ronald H. Menaker, Chairman

Robert E. Taylor, Chief Steward

Peter R. Van Brunt, Assistant Chief Steward

Judge: Mrs. Dorothy Welsh, Neilsville, Wis.

Peter

He was said to be one of the top-winning Poodles in the breed's history. He was Ch. Whisperwind on a Carousel, owned by Joan and Dr. Frederick Hartsock, a surgeon from Potomac, Md.

Handled by Dennis McCoy, the big white standard, known as Peter, had won 229 groups, the last 60 of them consecutively. The Westminster win was his 93rd Best in Show. His Best in Show restored the award to a breed that hadn't triumphed here since 1973.

In 1990, as reported by Walter Fletcher in the *Times*, Peter defeated 62,605 dogs to finish fourth in the Science Diet Winner's Circle competition and also took 110 group firsts, more than any other non-sporting performer, for which he received a Ken-L-Ration award.

Alexander Schwartz, who awarded Peter first in the Non-Sporting group, said: "He's the epitome of the breed for a standard Poodle. He's a graceful, beautiful mover from the side and is absolutely sound. He was a brilliant exhibit."

Dorothy Welsh took 16 minutes to evaluate the finalists. "My job was to find a dog that most exhibited breed type, soundness, the proper attitude and presented itself well," she explained. "I never before have had a Poodle who exhibited all of these qualities."

Elizabeth Bodner, editor of the *Gazette*, said that 1991 would be remembered as "the year five Best-in-Show winners brought down the house." She was referring to Peter, this year's winner, plus the Best-in-Show dogs of 1987, '88, '89 and '90, who appeared in a Parade of Winners. Spectators were deeply moved, she said, by these superb animals. "They were true winners then, and they are winners yet."

Ch. Whisperwind on a Carousel
—*Tatham photo*

Ch. Whisperwind on a Carousel with handler Denis McCoy, judge Dorothy Welsh and, from left Chairman Ronald H. Menaker and President Chester F. Collier
—*Ashbey photo*

Ch. Registry's
Lonesome Dove
with handler
Michael Kemp
and owners
Marion W. and
Samuel B.
Lawrence
  —Ashbey photo

Best in Show
1992

Ch. Registry's Lonesome Dove,
RB262955

Wire Fox Terrier, bitch

Whelped February 2, 1988

By Ch. Galsul Excellence—Tartan's
Heather Pepper

Breeder, Estate of Joan E. and E. Forbes
Gordon

Owners, *Marion W. and Samuel B.
Lawrence*, Orlando, Fla.

February 10–11

Madison Square Garden IV

2,568 Dogs

Newport Dog Shows, Superintendent

Ronald H. Menaker, Chairman

Peter R. Van Brunt, Chief Steward

Judge: Melbourne T. L. Downing,
Timonium, Md.

Lacey

She commanded attention. It was Westminster's first champions-only show. In her Garden debut last year, she was second in the group. Now, at the end of a two-season show career, she had won 147 groups and 93 Best in Shows.

She was a hound-marked Wire Fox Terrier, Ch. Registry's Lonesome Dove, owned by Marion W. and Samuel B. Lawrence. Known as Lacey, she was handled by Michael Kemp.

Adoration for Kemp made her an eager performer. "She knows when she can get away with untying his shoelaces," said Marion Lawrence, "and when to get down to business and charm the judges."

On the Friday before Westminster, she was named the top-winning performer in the Science Diet Winners' Circle competition, having defeated a total of 116,886 dogs in 1991. The awards were based on Science Diet's yearlong tally of dogs' individual performances. She had also taken 120 groups in 1991, more than any other terrier, for which she received a Ken-L-Ration award.

Group judge Michelle Billings said: "This little lady was sort of like a country and western song called 'Close Enough to Perfect for Me.'"

Melbourne Downing, a judge since the 1940s, did Best in Show. He said: "I've judged at Westminster 19 times, and this is the best competition I've ever witnessed for Best in Show...At least five of the finalists would be worthy of going best at any show. The Wire is an outstanding example of the breed. She never let down and was asking for it all the way."

Ch. Registry's
Lonesome Dove
with handler
Michael Kemp
and judge
Melbourne T. L.
Downing
—*Ashbey photo*

Best in Show
1993

Ch. Salilyn's Condor, SF304596

English Springer Spaniel, dog

Whelped October 5, 1987

By Ch. Salilyn's Dynasty—
Ch. Salilyn's Emblem

Breeder, Julia Gasow, Salilyn Kennels

Owners, ***Donna S. and Roger H. Herzig, MD***, Louisville, Ky. and ***Julia Gasow***, Troy, Mich.

February 8–9

Madison Square Garden IV

2,500 Dogs

Newport Dog Shows, Superintendent

Ronald H. Menaker, Chairman

Peter R. Van Brunt, Chief Steward

Judge: Mrs. Barbara F. Heller,
Sarasota, Fla.

Robert

"The jolliest canine to ever commandeer a dog show," said Robin Finn of the *Times*. Walter Fletcher in the same paper called him "joyful." Owner Donna Herzig said: "He makes you laugh."

The English Springer, officially Ch. Salilyn's Condor, belonged to Donna and Roger Herzig and Julia Gasow. He was best of breed for the third year, sporting group winner for the second, and now, as Walter Fletcher put it, "had crafted the ultimate dog-show swan song by going Best in Show."

Handled by Mark Threlfall, he defeated 115,651 dogs to head the Science Diet Winners' Circle, and was Ken-L-Ration's top group-winning sporting dog of 1992.

The Herzigs discovered Robert at Westminster in 1991. They liked his conformation. Happily, Julia Gasow wanted a co-owner.

"Winning Westminster...doesn't make him a better dog," said Herzig. "Just like losing doesn't make him a worse dog. It's been his responsibility to show...what a really good Springer should look like, and he's done that."

Group judge Anne Clark said, "The Springer is the ultimate in a breeder's ability to produce a wonderful dog and place it with people who could bring all the best out of him."

Best in Show judge Barbara Heller said: "He showed his heart out. I had a really hard time deciding. I always think it's easy to judge when you have good dogs, but this time it wasn't that easy because all seven were outstanding."

The cheers that greeted the award were as much for the dog's legendary breeder and co-owner, Julia Gasow, as for the dog. She had been a mainstay in the sport and the breed for half a century.

Left:
Ch. Salilyn's Condor with handler Mark Threlfall
—*Ashbey photo*

Right:
Ch. Salilyn's Condor with handler Mark Threlfall and owner Julia Gasow
—*Ashbey photo*

Best in Show
1994

Ch. Chidley Willum the
Conqueror, RB319475

Norwich Terrier, dog

Whelped April 11, 1989

By Ch. Royal Rock Don of Chidley—
Chidley Chestnuthill's Sprite

Breeder, Karen Anderson

Owners, *Ruth L. Cooper*, Glenview, Ill.,
and *Patricia P. Lussier*, Lake Placid,
N.Y.

February 14–15

Madison Square Garden IV

2,580 Dogs

MB-F, Inc., Superintendent

Ronald H. Menaker, Chairman

Peter R. Van Brunt, Chief Steward

Charles M. Curry, Jr., Assistant Chief
Steward

Judge: Walter F. Goodman, Miami, Fla.

Willum

Ch. Chidley Willum the Conqueror captured Best in Show.

"Willum" was also the name of one of the winner's ancestors, a Norwich who had come from England in 1914 and was America's introduction to the breed. It was called the Jones Terrier then, after Frank "Roughrider" Jones, his English breeder.

Willum the Conqueror's handler, Peter Green, had taken Best in Show at the Garden twice before, in 1968 and 1977, and in 1998 he would win it again.

Willum the Conqueror was the first Norwich to go to the top at Westminster. The four-year-old now had 193 groups and 66 Best in Shows. Among his victories were Montgomery County, the world's largest all-terrier event, in 1991 and 1992. He was second in the Science Diet Winners' Circle, having defeated a total of 87,585 dogs in 1993 and took the Ken-L-Ration award as top group-winning terrier for the year.

The assignment evoked warm memories for Best-in-Show judge Walter Goodman, an AKC director and president of the Montgomery County Kennel Club. Exactly 25 years earlier, he had stood in the very same ring and received the big silver bowl after guiding his homebred Skye, Ch. Glamoor Good News, to Best in Show.

As judge in 1994, he took 15 minutes for his decision. The crowd roared approval when he pointed to the little black-and-tan 12-pounder owned by Ruth L. Cooper and Patricia P. Lussier.

"He's a lot of dog in a little package," said Goodman. "He never looked better and never missed a beat. He did everything that was asked of him."

Ch. Chidley
Willum the
Conqueror with
handler Peter
Green, owner
Ruth L. Cooper
and commen-
tator David Frei
—*WKC*

Best in Show
1995

Ch. Gaelforce Post Script,
RM00411004

Scottish Terrier, bitch

Whelped January 22, 1991

By Ch. Gladmac's Taliesin the Bard—
Ch. Glenlee's Sable Fox

Breeder, Camille R. Partridge

Owners, **Dr. Joe Kinnarney**, Apex,
N.C., and **Dr. Vandra L. Huber**,
Seattle, Wash.

February 13–14

Madison Square Garden IV

2,625 dogs

MB-F, Inc., Superintendent

Ronald H. Menaker, Chairman

Charles M. Curry, Jr., Chief Steward

Peter R. Van Brunt, Assistant Chief
Steward

Judge: Dr. Jacklyn E. Hungerland,
Carmel, Calif.

Peggy Sue

She climbed right into the silver bowl and posed prettily.

It was Ch. Gaelforce Post Script, a perky Scottie, aka Peggy Sue. The 4-year-old was owned by Dr. Joe Kinnarney, a veterinarian from Apex, N.C., and Dr. Vandra L. Huber, professor of business at the University of Washington, Seattle. Handled by Maripi Wooldridge, she was the first Scottie to take the silver bowl in 10 years.

"I guided her to her first Best in Show in Canada, when she was only 18 months old," said Huber proudly, "but Maripi has done all the rest."

Peggy Sue had defeated more than 1,350 Scotties in 1994 and had taken 71 groups. It was her 31st Best. She had won 17 specialties.

Said group judge Stephen Shaw: "She's a little cart-horse of a bitch, what a Scottie should be. She has a nice short, thick neck, a little tail that comes to a point and little ears that never go back. She's a treasure."

Dr. Jacklyn Hungerland, a psychologist and the first woman elected to AKC's board of directors, judged the finale. "Two things had to happen; she had to ask for it and I had to fall in love," she said. "She's a terrier and she looks the part. She looks as though she can challenge the world. She's in excellent condition, and she's just a lovely, lovely bitch."

Peggy Sue, reported Robin Finn in the *Times*, was the result of a "breeding accident" in the Oregon kennel of Camille Partridge. The breeder was about to place the unwanted puppy as a pet when her friend Huber intervened.

Left:
Ch. Gaelforce
Post Script with
handler Maripi
Wooldridge and
judge Jacklyn E.
Hungerland
—*Ashbey photo*

Left:
Ch. Gaelforce
Post Script and
handler Maripi
Wooldridge
—*Ashbey photo*

Best in Show
1996

Ch. Clussexx Country Sunrise,
SM91234807

Clumber Spaniel, dog

Whelped June 5, 1991

By Ch. Smokerise Country Gentleman —Ch. Tanelorn's Bubble and Squeak

Breeders, D. A. Johnson, S. Blakeley, and S. Stockill, England

Owners, *Judith and Richard Zaleski*, Sorrento, Fla.

February 12–13

Madison Square Garden IV

2,571 Dogs

MB-F Inc., Superintendent

Ronald H. Menaker, Chairman

Charles M. Curry, Jr., Chief Steward

Robert E. Taylor, Assistant Chief Steward

Judge: D. Roy Holloway, Reading, Pa.

Brady

His energy seemed boundless. He stayed in condition by chasing tennis balls and could hold three in his mouth at once.

He was Ch. Clussexx Country Sunrise. Friends called him Brady. The 67-pounder was owned by Judith and Richard Zaleski. She was a stockbroker and he, a retired electrician. They also had Brady's brother and a Bloodhound at home.

The Clumber was a sporting breed from England, trained to flush and retrieve game. First registered in America in 1878, AKC registrations in 1995 stood at 150 as against 125,000 Labrador Retrievers in the same period.

Handled by Lisa Jane Alston-Myers, Brady had been attending 100 shows a year, beating more dogs than any other Clumber in history. He now had 76 groups and 13 Best in Shows.

He loved showing, and he was only four years old, but the owners had decided that this show would be his last. He went out in style. Frank Litsky of the *Times* said he won before a crowd that cheered itself hoarse.

Group judge W. Everett Dean, called him a great show dog, saying, "His expression and attitude showed that he enjoyed working for his win."

D. Roy Holloway, who officiated over Best, said he had judged the Clumber many times and had given him the group three weeks before. "If I was going to take a dog home, it would have been the Clumber," he said. "It was the epitome of the breed. My second choice was the Papillon. I would have put it in my back pocket." The Papillon was Loteki Supernatural Being, who would win Best in Show in 1999.

Ch. Clussexx Country Sunrise with handler Lisa Jane Alston-Myers —*Ashbey photo*

Best in Show 1997

Ch. Parsifal Di Casa Netzer,
WP46553801

Standard Schnauzer, dog

Whelped April 14, 1991

By Jan Dum Torre—Nina Del Torre

Breeder, Gabrio Del Torre, Italy

Owners, *Rita Holloway and Gabrio Del Torre*, Newark, Del.

February 10–11

Madison Square Garden IV

2,583 Dogs

MB-F Inc., Superintendent

Ronald H. Menaker, Chairman

Frederick W. Wagner III, Chief Steward

Judge: Mrs. Dorothy N. Collier, Ft. Lee, N.J.

Pa

Pa came from Italy. He was handled by Doug Holloway, and co-owned by Holloway's wife, Rita, and the dog's Italian breeder, Gabrio Del Torre. Del Torre had sent Pa to the U.S. three years earlier, determined to make the dog, already the toast of Europe, an international star.

Officially Ch. Parsifal Di Casa Netzer, the Standard Schnauzer skipped Westminster in 1996 because of a conflict of interest in human connections—his handler and his co-owner were the son and daughter-in-law of the Best-in-Show judge that year. Still, Pa was the country's top working-group winner in 1994, '95 and '96. And in 1996, he had emerged as top dog in terms of the number of dogs defeated: 93,725.

Holloway said Pa would now retire—he had 157 group victories and 66 Best in Shows—and make good on his call name by performing stud duties.

The steely eyebrows of the grizzled veteran, according to Robin Finn of the *Times*, "drifted above his eyes like Spanish moss but interfered not a whit with his movement."

Group judge Charles E. Trotter said: "He never put a foot wrong. He just flowed along and moved like he'd never get tired."

Best-in-Show judge Dorothy Collier had judged Pa before. As a puppy, he finished his championship under her. She also awarded him several Best in Shows. None of this necessarily worked to his advantage. "I think it was probably harder for him to win because I was familiar with him," she said. "I wanted to make sure I gave all the other dogs an equal chance, and he held up. He was everything he's always been."

Ch. Parsifal Di Casa Netzer with handler Doug Holloway and, from left, Chairman Ronald H. Menaker, judge Mrs. Dorothy N. Collier and President Chester F. Collier
—*Ashbey photo*

Best in Show
1998

Ch. Fairewood Frolic,
RM15485701

Norwich Terrier, bitch

Whelped July 23, 1994

By Ch. Royal Rock Don of Chidley—
Ch. Long Valley Fairewood Cheers

Breeder, Lotus Tutton, Canada

Owners, *Mr. and Mrs. Alexander C.*
Schwartz, Jr., Sandina Kennels, Tuxedo
Park, N.Y.

February 16–17

Madison Square Garden IV

2,587 Dogs

MB-F Inc., Superintendent

Ronald H. Menaker, Chairman

Frederick W. Wagner, III, Chief
Steward

Judge: Dr. M. Josephine Deubler,
Philadelphia, Pa.

Rocki

She was handled by Peter Green, who had led her half-brother to Best in Show at the Garden in 1994. She was the fourth dog Green had taken to the top here.

Ch. Fairewood Frolic, a Norwich Terrier called Rocki, was owned by Mr. & Mrs. Alexander C. Schwartz, Jr. According to Schwartz, the 13-pounder had been mated just before the show and her next performance would be producing possible future Westminster winners.

In an odd happenstance, the show entries included two terriers, unrelated but, as Robin Finn reported in the *Times*, owned by two families named Schwartz, families related only by their determination to produce a perfect terrier. One dog was Rocki and the other, a Welsh Terrier, handled by Woody Wornall, Ch. Anasazi Billy the Kid. Billy was owned by Bruce Schwartz.

These archrivals headed a list of Best in Show possibles. Rocki was 1997's top-winning dog in terms of canines defeated; Billy was 10th. Billy had 88 Best in Shows to Rocki's 86. They had each won Montgomery County, the all-terrier show, Billy in 1996, and Rocki in 1997. As things turned out, 1998 was Rocki's year.

Group judge Jon Cole said Rocki was too lovely to overlook. "She's well-balanced, has a beautiful head, and she's in magnificent condition," he said. "Those keen eyes set off her entire head."

Dr. Josephine Deubler, the first female graduate of the University of Pennsylvania Veterinary College in 1938, judged Best in Show. What sealed it for Rocki, she said, was a perfect blend of persistence and self-aggrandizement, two staples of terriers. "She never stopped asking for it," she said.

Left:
Ch. Fairewood
Frolic with owner
Alexander C.
Schwartz, Jr.
—*Mary Bloom photo*

Far Left:
Fairewood Frolic
with judge Dr. M.
Josephine Deubler
—*Tatham photo*

Best in Show
1999

Ch. Loteki Supernatural Being,
TM66531802

Papillon, dog

Whelped December 31, 1990

By Ch. Loteki Supercharger—Ch.
Loteki Devzel Fortuneteller

Breeder, Lou Ann King

Owner, *John Oulton*, Norwalk, Conn.

February 8–9

Madison Square Garden IV

2,574 Dogs

MB-F Inc., Superintendent

Ronald H. Menaker, Chairman

Frederick W. Wagner, III, Chief
Steward

Judge: Edd Embry Bivin, Fort Worth,
Tex.

Kirby

He was an old hand. The eight-year-old Papillon had taken Best of Breed at Westminster in 1993. He was the first of his breed to win the toy group there in 1996, was upended by his nephew in the breed ring in 1997 and took third in the group in 1998. Now, six years after that first Best of Breed win, he triumphed as Best in Show.

Ch. Loteki Supernatural Being, known as Kirby, was a veritable granddaddy among the finalists, all of whom towered over him. As recounted in the *New York Post*, he "bow-wowed the crowd—and judges—as he played up to the cheers, prancing excitedly as the noise mounted."

The six-pounder was so in tune with his handler, said Diane Vasey, editor of the *Gazette*, that "he leapt for joy as soon as John Oulton knew they'd won."

Oulton, his owner-handler from Norwalk, Conn., insisted that the tri-color bundle of energy was not as ethereal as he appeared—or as his registered name might suggest. "At home he's a tough little guy. He tears around the yard with the rest of them."

Edd Embry Biven, a vice-chancellor at Texas Christian University, who judged the finale and awarded Kirby his 31st Best in Show, said the final lineup of seven was "just over-whelming." He found Kirby impossible to resist. "That little dog responded in every way you asked," he said. "He just had this electricity about him. It went on and on."

Ch. Loteki
Supernatural
Being inside the
Best in Show
trophy—*Mary
Bloom photo*

Above:
Ch. Loteki
Supernatural
Being with
owner-handler
John Oulton and,
from left, judge
Edd Embry Bivin
and President
Chester F. Collier
—*Tatham photo*

Best in Show 2000

Ch. Salilyn 'N Erin's Shameless, SN18076703

English Springs Spaniel, bitch

Whelped July 22, 1994

By Ch. Salilyn's Condor – Ch. Salilyn's High Reguard

Breeder, Julia Gasow

Owners, *Carl Blain and Fran Sunseri and Julia Gasow,* Sacramento, Calif.

February 14-15

Madison Square Garden IV

2,595 Dogs

MB-F Inc., Superintendent

Ronald H. Menaker, Chairman

Frederick W. Wagner, III, Chief Steward

Judge: Chester F. Collier, Norwood, N.J.

Samantha

"Sailing along on feathered feet, a lively English Springer Spaniel showed her champion bloodlines and world-class breeding as she took the top honors." So reported the *Journal News*.

She was Ch. Salilyn 'N Erin's Shameless, a 5½-year-old daughter of Westminster's 1993 Best in Show winner, Salilyn's Condor. It was her 50th top award.

"I can't describe the feeling at the end of the lead," said handler Kellie FitzGerald. "She was just working. She was going around the ring, looking at the crowd, getting pumped up by it."

Samantha, as she was called, would now retire. She was bred and co-owned by Julia Gasow, who died in 1999 after devoting 63 years to the breed. The dog's owners were Carl Blain and Fran Sunseri of Sacramento. Blain said that Mrs. Gasow was "totally responsible for what the breed is today, including this wonderful dog."

Group judge, Michelle Billings said, "It was a photo finish with the black Cocker Spaniel. They were both in prime condition. But the Springer, for her breed, had a slightly better head, and when you say that, you've said it all."

"She's perfection for the standard," said Chester Collier, Westminster's president, who judged Best in Show. "She lives up to what the standard says. You saw her line and her energy. That was it. She just kept moving. She wanted. And she got it."

During Samantha's photo-op, she hopped momentarily into the silver champion's bowl. At 42 pounds, she didn't fit as easily as last year's winner, a six-pound Papillon, and quickly hopped out.

Ch. Salilyn 'N Erin's Shameless with handler Kellie FitzGerald and, from left, Chairman Ronald H. Menaker, judge President Chester F. Collier and Vice-President Peter R. Van Brunt
—*Ashbey photo*

Members,
Past and
Present

1943— Trophy
offered by Great
Dane Club of
America for best
9-to-12-month
puppy bitch, won
by Fauna All of
Irwin Dane
("Sunny"), owned
by Mrs. P. W.
Irwin—*WKC, gift
of Helen T. Irwin,
Cerincione photo*

Past and Present Members

The 18 charter members are listed in italics. Dates given are dates of membership.

A

Abbott, Paul, 1939-71
Adee, P. H., 1881-88
Alley, W. S., 1881-83
Appleton, F. R., 1880-84
Appleton, Col. Francis R., Jr., 1947-73
Aspinwall, Lloyd, 1888-93
Auslander, Louis, 1987-

B

Banks, David, 1886-96
Barclay, James L., 1884-93
Barnard, Frederick, 1877-80
Barnes, John S., 1886-1904
Barney, Charles T., 1879-1903
Barnwell, G. G., 1878-85
Barrie, Caswell, 1939-65
Bates, John G, 1925-44
Bates, John Grenville, Jr., 1928-47
Baylis, William, 1880-81
Bedford, Dean, 1934-72
Belknap, Robert Lenox, 1877-80
Belmont, Morgan, 1939-52
Belmont, Oliver Hazard (O. P.), 1885
Belmont, Major Perry, 1880-88
Bement, Edward, 1900-31
Bidwell, M. Oakley, 1950-62
Bishop, Louis F., III, 1966-82
Black, Witherbee, 1948-59
Bliss, Anthony A., 1937-54
Blodget, Alden S., 1953-64
Bloodgood, Hildreth K., 1903-18
Boardman, John L., 1885-89
Bogdanovitch, Philip M., 1990-
Bonner, Douglas G., 1957-60
Bradford, J. H., 1878-85
Bradley, Thomas H., III, 1975-
Brainard, William W., Jr., 1958-90
Brandreth, Col. Franklin, 1894-1928
Brandreth, Ralph, 1890-1902
Breese, William L., 1884-1901
Briggs, Lloyd Cabot, 1939-75
Brown, F. Gordon, 1939-72
Brown, Hobson, Jr., 1989-
Brumby, Leonard, Jr., 1972-90
Bulkley, Edward H., 1894-1903
Bull, Frederic, 1901-36
Bull, Henry W., 1901-57
Bullard, L. H., 1883-1900
Burden, Joseph W., 1881-85
Burden, William P., 1926-33
Burnham, T. Brownell, 1886-1900

Burton, Ernest B., 1953-75
Burton, Howes, 1954-59

C

Cadwalader, Richard M., Jr., 1926-39
Caesar, Harry I., 1929-77
Caesar, Henry A., II, 1939-62
Cannon, Col. Le Grand B., 1877-80
Carey, Len, 1958-79
Caras, Roger A., 1975-
Carruthers, Thomas H., III, 1947-1973
Chapin, Charles Merrill, 1894-1932
Chapin, Charles Merrill, Jr., 1925-72
Chisholm, Hugh J., 1939-59
Chisholm, William H., 1947-
Clark, Cyrus, Jr., 1967-74
Clark, George C., 1881-90
Clark, James Edward, 1972-91
Clark, Louis C., 1881-91
Clements, George F., Jr., 1985-
Coe, Henry E., III, 1962-96
Colburn, George, 1880-85
Collier, Chester F., 1973-
Colt, Charles Craig, 1884-1933
Colt, Caldwell H., 1887-1901
Colt, R. O., Jr., 1881-93
Colt, S. Sloan, 1946-75
Cornell, Robert C., 1877-1902
Coster, Charles, 1901-09
Cowdin, John C., 1882-84
Craig, Robert, 1950-65
Crocker, David, 1893-98
Cromwell, Henry B., 1889-95
Cross, John W., Jr. 1935-69
Curry, Dr. Charles M., Jr., 1979-
Cushing, Harry C., 1950-60
Cutting, W. Bayard, 1883-94

D

Dana, Paul, 1881-90
Davis, Francis B., Jr., 1945-58
Deane, Arthur, 1893-97
DeBary, Adolph, 1883-93
DeForest, George B., II, 1925-63
DeForest, Henry W., 1880-90
DeForest, Shepherd K., 1892-1929
Delafield, Richard, 1941-45
Delmonico, Charles C., 1885-1901
DeLuze, F. O., 1877-1902
DeNeuville, J. J., 1884-88
Denton, Huntington, 1877-80
Dick, Alfred M., 1968-74
Dillon, Milton S., 1933-38
Dodge, A. M., 1884-94
Donner, J. Otto, 1880-95
Donner, O. W., 1899-1915
Douglas, Barclay, 1954-91
Douglas, Barclay, Jr., 1981-
Douglas, William Proctor, 1883-1919
Drayton, J. Coleman, 1880-97

Drury, Maynard K., 1959-66
Duer, J. G. K., 1887-99
Duke, Angier B., 1939-48
Dunham, James H., 1886-91
Duryea, Herman B.,1899-1916
Duryea, William Mairs, 1950-91
Duryea, William Mairs, Jr., 1975-

E

Edley, Frederick, 1893-1906
Elder, George W., 1901-16
Eldredge, E. Irving, 1963-85
Eldridge, Harry, 1927-81
Eldridge, Lewis A., 1890-1930
Eldridge, Roswell , 1903-27
Elliott, Duncan, 1894-99
Ellison, J. B., 1900-03
Ely, Alfred, 1936-59
Engel, Robert G., 1991-93
Everets, John W., 1998-
Ewing, John H., 1948-90
Ewing, William F. C., 1938-60

F

Farrell, James A., Jr., 1944-78
Fell, Philip S. P., 1970-79
Fell, Philip S. P., Jr., 1972-79
Felton, S. U., Jr., 1890-93
Ferguson, Henry L., 1929-58
Ferguson, Walton, Jr., 1897-1936
Field, Marshall, 1933-56
Fisher, Lyman R., MD, 1968-82
Fitzgerald, Gen. Louis, 1889-1908
Fleischmann, Udo M., 1928-52
Fleitman, Henry T., 1926-37
Flint, Edward E., 1887-95
Floyd-Jones, Edward, 1886-96
Floyd-Jones, George Stanton, 1881-93
Floyd-Jones, William Chauncey, 1883-1925
Foley, James E., III, 1994-
Foote, Robert D., 1893-1924
Fowler, Anderson, 1939-97
Frelinghuysen, George G., 1947-79
Fry, Reginald, 1888-91

G

Gambril. Richard V. N., 1926-53
Gans, James H., 1949-69
Gebhard, F., 1892 -96
Gibson, Harvey D., 1936-51
Gildersleeve, Judge H. A., 1895-1901
Godkin, Lawrence, 1897-1901
Goelet, Ogden, 1887-1901
Goodman, Walter, F., 1990-
Goodwin, Wendell, 1880-92
Grant, George DeForest , 1877-1905
Greenleaf, Lewis S., 1959-72
Gregory, D. S., Jr., 1883-85
Griggs, John W., II, 1975-80
Guernsey, Otis L., 1941-68

Index

Index

Page references in italics refer to illustrations.

Endpapers

1934, The Arena—*Stevens & Carrington photo*

1943, Best in Show—*Brown photo*

1975, Ch. Sir Lancelot of Barvan, Best in Show winner, with handler Malcolm Fellows—*AP Wide World*

1994, The Arena—*Ashbey photo*

Colophon

Book written by
William F. Stifel

Book design by
Spagnola & Associates
New York, New York

Tony Spagnola, principal,
Kelly Sorg Evans, senior designer
Rachel Oliver, designer
R. Kyle Shoup, designer

Composed in Hoefler Text,
Hoefler Type Foundry

Still photography by Eric Jacobson/NYC

Printed by Toppan Printing Company America,
Inc. Printed in Hong Kong